# The Career Programmer: Guerilla Tactics for an Imperfect World

CHRISTOPHER DUNCAN

Apress™

The Career Programmer: Guerilla Tactics for an Imperfect World

Copyright ©2002 by Christopher Duncan

ISBN (pbk): 1-59059-008-2

Printed and bound in the United States of America 12345678910

Trademarked names may appear in this book. Rather than use a trademark symbol with every occurrence of a trademarked name, we use the names only in an editorial fashion and to the benefit of the trademark owner, with no intention of infringement of the trademark.

Editorial Directors: Dan Appleman, Peter Blackburn, Gary Cornell, Jason Gilmore, Karen Watterson

Managing Editor: Grace Wong

Copy and Development Editor: Tom Gillen

Production Editor: Sofia Marchant

Compositor: Diana Van Winkle, Van Winkle Design Group

Indexer: Ron Strauss

Cover Designer: Tom Debolski

Marketing Manager: Stephanie Rodriguez

Distributed to the book trade in the United States by Springer-Verlag New York, Inc.,175 Fifth Avenue, New York, NY, 10010

and outside the United States by Springer-Verlag GmbH & Co. KG, Tiergartenstr. 17, 69112 Heidelberg, Germany

In the United States, phone 1-800-SPRINGER, email orders@springer-ny.com, or visit http://www.springer-ny.com.

Outside the United States, fax +49 6221 345229, email orders@springer.de, or visit http://www.springer.de.

For information on translations, please contact Apress directly at 901 Grayson Street, Suite 204, Berkeley, CA 94710.

Phone 510-549-5930, fax: 510-549-5939, email info@apress.com, or visit http://www.apress.com.

*This book is dedicated to the memory of James Michael Graves,*
*my best friend and the brother I never had. I miss you, man.*

# Contents at a Glance

# Contents

# Foreword

When Chris Duncan first asked me to do the foreword to his book, I didn't think it would be that tough to do. How hard could writing a foreword be? Compared to some of the projects I worked on in the past such as BoundsChecker, writing a book, or my current job of debugging others' impossible bugs, writing a foreword should be a piece of cake. However, within reading a couple of pages of *The Career Programmer*, I became extremely nervous because Chris is a far better writer than I can ever hope to be. The last thing I want to do is detract from great writing, and more importantly, an extremely important message for the software business.

You've probably looked at the back cover or flipped through the pages and noticed that this book is not what you would expect to find in the computer books section of the typical bookstore. There are a billion books on how to use the hot technology du jour and maybe a few on project management, but this is the first book to directly address the developer and what it takes to get your real job done. Isn't it amazing that the software engineering field has been around this long and this is the first book written for the real engineer? We'd love to say that we spend our days coding, but we really don't. Instead, we spend much of it doing all the other stuff associated with getting our software released, like sitting in meetings and wondering what planet the marketing people came from. What you hold in your hands is the stuff you really should have learned in school.

Unfortunately, those schools you attended are a major reason we've got many of the problems we have in the software business today. I'm willing to bet most of you have some sort of computer science degree from a four-year university. Having been in the business a little too long, having a computer science degree myself, and hiring many of you with computer science degrees, I can't think of any worse preparation for a job. Few of your courses did much of anything to prepare you to develop software. Don't get me started on the fact that fewer than 1% of schools offer you a class in debugging! With more than 50% of your average project time spent debugging, you were completely cheated by the school and should ask for your money back. Although it's hard to duplicate a real-world environment in school, the schools also failed you in discussing how to prepare and plan for a project. Yes, most of you took some form of software engineering class, but that class was the ivory tower version.

For those of you who were smart enough to get into this field without the time-wasting pit stop in a computer science program, you're slightly better off. However, with many of you coming into software from professions or fields with more common sense you have to wonder what perverse universe software development comes from. A mechanical engineer would never be told that they need to change a load-bearing bracket on the fly without being given the time to do the calculations to see if the change would still support the engine's weight. A software engineer, on the other hand, is told on a Wednesday to change a major part of the internal product architecture and have it done by Friday. Too many people, including software engineers, think of software products as simply a collection of text files you can play with like Play-Doh.

Fortunately, *The Career Programmer* is the School of Hard Knocks in the realities of corporate development. The lessons Chris imparts in this book took years to learn and will truly save your skin on your current and future projects. Pay special attention to Chapter 5 ("Getting Your Requirements Etched in Stone"), Chapter 6 ("Effective Design Under Fire"), and Chapter 7 ("Practical Estimating Techniques"). These are the areas in which you as even the lowliest developer on the team can make an impact. There are years of extremely hard-earned experience in those chapters, and the good news is that Chris will save you years of pain learning those lessons.

One thing I do want to address a little bit in this foreword is attitude. As you read this book, you're going to get quite excited about the real-world techniques that Chris lays out. However, some of you are going to get depressed because you feel that you don't have near enough clout to get these techniques implemented. I can't begin to tell you how many times I have heard this lament. No matter what happens, you are the one in control of your own destiny, not your boss, not the boss's potted plants, and not your coworkers. (The latter two might be one in the same). It's absolutely up to you to make the difference in your job. Start by worrying about getting your own small piece of the pie done and lead the way. Leading by example is the best way to show that the techniques in this book work and make your job fun and interesting. If your company is not interested in doing software the right way, even after you show how it's done, it's time for you to find another job. Yes, plenty of companies out there are doing it right, and they are looking for you.

My big hope for this business is that you all get to feel what it's like to hit a home run and ship on time with high quality. I've been fortunate enough to do it more than most developers, and it's a truly wonderful feeling. The neat thing is that, once you ship on time, you can get away with anything at work. You could burn down the office with a wild party, and, if you shipped on time, the senior management will just say, "Oh, those crazy engineers!" Armed with Chris's book, you'll have a huge head start on the real techniques to hitting your own home runs.

— John Robbins
Cofounder Wintellect (www.Wintellect.com)
Author of *Debugging Applications*

# A Brief Introduction

If you picked this particular book up off the shelves, it's likely that you either make a living as a programmer or plan to do so in the future. Of course, you could just be shopping for something that's precisely the right thickness to prop up your rickety coffee table, but we'll play the odds for the moment and assume that you spend more time in front of a debugger than you do a television.

The first questions we typically have when looking for technical books relate to platform and language. What kind of computer? What flavor of operating system? Which particular set of languages and technologies must we know to benefit from this book? For *The Career Programmer*, it just doesn't matter. Whether we make our living under the flag of Mac or Microsoft, mainframe or mini, our ultimate goals and desires are the same: all we really want to do is make good money, spend our days writing the next killer app, and get our pizza delivered in thirty minutes or less.

However, for those who possess the ability to turn screens full of cryptic statements into state-of-the-art software systems, there's only one slight complication. In order to get paid for doing what we love, we find ourselves working deep in the heart of Corporate America. Nothing we were taught in school prepared us for the illogical, inconsistent, and sometimes downright silly business practices that are the norm in software development shops both large and small.

For instance, deadlines are declared in an almost arbitrary fashion, with no real consideration of what's involved. We're expected to produce specific functionality from vague and ever-changing requirements. We're given little to no time for proper analysis and design, and, when we ask management about hiring professional testers and setting up a QA process—well, I've seen deer in my headlights look less stunned. Internal politics are rampant, threatening everything from our current project to our staplers, which for some bizarre reason seem to be a precious commodity in the cubicle world. In short, from a software developer's point of view, the environment makes no sense. Unfortunately, no matter how unrealistic the deadline, we're expected to work day and night to make it happen, only to have the product shipped with less than fifteen minutes of testing. Care to guess who's going to get yelled at the first time it blows up in the field? I can assure you, the deer have leapt safely out of the glare of the headlights and there's nobody here but us programmers.

Anyone who hasn't worked in our field will by now have labeled me quite the cynic, but I suspect you were shaking your head while reading the last paragraph and remembering the insanities of your own company's releases. As passionately as we want to do good work, it seems that we're checked at every turn by corporate bureaucracy and management that can barely spell the word *computer*, let alone manage a software development process. Of course, we learn all of this the hard way. All of the books on the bookstore shelves teach us how to program, not how to fend off the lunacy of the business world so that we can actually program and deliver excellence.

That's why I wrote this book. I've spent the better part of the past ten years as a mercenary. For the uninitiated, that's a contract programmer, and it means that I've seen a lot of shops. Over the years, I've learned some tricks to help take control of my programming life again, along with how to further my career in general. (I do like to eat well.) For a long time now, I've been working exactly the kinds of jobs that I like, doing the techie stuff that I enjoy, concentrating on the coding, and actually delivering on schedule, not to mention getting paid well in the process.

Much of what I know as a programmer I've learned from other guys who were nice enough to share their experience, and so this is my way of giving a little back. No matter where you fit into your project, you can learn some tricks from this book to help simplify your life and get you back to concentrating on the code. That's the best thing I can think of to give to a programmer.

## Assumptions about the Reader

I assume that you already know how to program and that you either currently make your living programming in the business world or soon will be. The platform or language you work with doesn't matter. This is a book about overcoming the obstacles we encounter as programmers in the real world, and these obstacles are the same regardless of what type of software you write. It probably goes without saying, but I also assume that you rail against any and all limitations that you encounter on the job and that you find anything that interferes with your ability to deliver high-quality software extremely frustrating. That's where I hope to help.

## Who Should Read This

The issues addressed here affect developers at all levels. If you work as a project manager or team lead, you're already a veteran of many battles with management and are always looking for new ways to talk sense into these guys. If you're a front-line programmer, you're the one who ultimately has to pay the price for bad decisions further up the food chain, whether it's from the Suits in the front office or your own project manager. The tactics and techniques work at both levels. If you're not happy with the way things are run and want to change your job so that you can focus more on software development and less on damage control from dubious decisions, this book is for you.

## A Note to Women Who Code

Not everyone who stays up for three straight nights chasing a bug is male. Many women also make a living as professional developers. When the fingers hit the keyboard, it doesn't matter if the nails are polished or not. The compiler doesn't care and neither do I; good code is good code and none of the topics I cover are gender specific. However, the English language simply does not have an easy way to address both genders in a conversational manner. While I applaud the sincere intentions of those who insert a "his/her" or "he/she" into everything they write out of consideration for equality, in practice it can make the text a bit tedious to read.

I'm no Nobel laureate. I'm just a programmer, and I write like I talk. Although the issues we'll cover are serious ones, my priority is to keep this a light, conversational, and easy read. I'm more interested in helping people overcome the many obstacles to good software that Corporate America continually throws our way than I am in being considered a scholarly author. Therefore, to keep it simple, I made a conscious decision to speak to a single gender for the sheer literary convenience of doing so. Because the programming community is overwhelmingly populated by the male of the species, you'll see references to "he" and "him" rather than an attempt to speak to both genders in every sentence. If this is perceived as a lack of political correctness, I hope that the easier flow of words and the matters upon which they touch will compensate. This is a book for programmers. The specifications of your particular body are irrelevant.

## What's Not Addressed

This is not a language or technology book. No matter what programming technique you want to master, plenty of books are available to teach you. This book is about overcoming the obstacles you face on the job that ultimately result in release disasters, stressed-out development experiences, software death marches, and bad software that could have been good. It's not a treatise from the ivory tower of academia. It's a field manual for the software developer grunts who relentlessly toil away in the thick of it, day after day.

## What This Book Brings to the Party

If you worked in a perfect world, you'd have plenty of time for gathering requirements, for analysis and design, and for implementation and testing. You'd also be in charge of what went into the product, the overall design, and which technologies were used, and you'd release it when you were darned well ready. Management would not interfere, and you wouldn't have to contend with any office politics. Everyone would listen and do things exactly as you suggested. Small, furry creatures from Alpha Centauri would be, well, you know.

If you live in such a world, go ahead and use this book for that wobbly coffee table. Oh, yeah, and save me a seat. I'd love to have a job there.

For the rest of us, this book is a collection of very simple and practical observations and techniques for putting us in as much control of the development process as the real world is going to allow. A number of hurdles must be cleared when shipping a good product, and some of these can be handled by modifying the approach we take to design, estimating, and other matters of process.

Other issues result from bureaucracy and politics. No design methodology in the world is going to help you there. The higher-ups tend to ignore the opinions of programmers partly because we've never learned to speak their language or communicate in a way that is meaningful to them. Consequently, our thoughts and suggestions—the very things that could save our projects from disaster—are ignored even though we're the specialists. Before we can show them how we'd like to do things, we must first acquire the skills necessary to make them hear us. In short, we need to learn how to manage our management so that we can get back to doing the job that we love.

You don't need an MBA to figure this stuff out. You just need to pay attention to how things work and modify your approach to one that is realistic and effective in your environment. The bottom line is simple: whether we agree or disagree, more often than not we're simply told to get the job done in the time we're given, or else. Consequently, the approaches that work when we have the luxury of time fail utterly when we have the ability to implement only a quarter of the process. In such moments, we need simple and practical approaches that get the product delivered.

In the chapters that follow, I'll be addressing these issues with the assumption that you don't have time for the perfect solution. That's why I refer to them as *guerilla tactics*. They're direct, effective, and they're not always pretty. These tricks are all taken from real jobs with real pressures. When you have to deliver, or else, neatness just doesn't count. Getting the job done is all that matters.

# A Quick Peek at the Chapters

Here's a look at the rest of the book. Part I explains the problems prevalent in our jobs, and Part II speaks to the issues and their solutions.

## Part I: Software Development in an Imperfect World

### Chapter 1: Welcome to Corporate America

After landing their first job, many programmers are shocked by the reality of life in the corporate world. Your initial dream of sitting undisturbed each day, kicking out clever little apps, is continually disturbed by unrealistic deadlines, unreasonable decisions, bureaucracy, politics, and crisis after crisis. Any of these could reduce your current software project to a pile of smoking rubble reminiscent of the latest Godzilla movie. They don't teach this sort of thing in school, and even seasoned developers have difficulty knowing how to cope with elements that seem beyond their control.

### Chapter 2: Business is War. Meet the Enemy.

To successfully deliver the next killer app, you must fight many battles, the easiest of which is with your debugger. Whether you're a systems architect, project manager, team lead, or full-time coder, your ability to do your job and enjoy your pizza without indigestion is going to be continually assaulted by a host of business-induced problems. The first step in building up your defenses is simply knowing your enemy. Consequently, we'll highlight the problems that most software development teams commonly encounter.

### Chapter 3: Good Coding Skills Are Not Enough

In gazing at the enemy, it's tempting for many programmers to simply shrug off management problems as not being a part of a programmer's job description. However, this will be of little consolation to you when you're plucking the arrows out of your posterior. Software development is a team endeavor. If you don't work at your level to help combat the problems that threaten your project, you'll all go down together. If you don't do anything but code, here's why you still need additional skills to survive.

## Part II: Guerilla Tactics for Front-Line Programmers

### Chapter 4: Preventing Arbitrary Deadlines

It's three o'clock in the morning, your system just crashed again, your debugger shrugs its shoulders and asks for a coffee break, your eyes are so bloodshot that they look like a roadmap of midtown Manhattan, and the product must ship tomorrow if you wish to continue your employment. How did you get into this mess? At this point, there's not much you can do about it beyond persistence, excessive caffeine consumption, and simply hoping for a lucky break. The time to prevent this disaster was much earlier in the game. Where's a good time machine when you need one?

### Chapter 5: Getting Your Requirements Etched in Stone

*Scope creep* is not the title of a bad science fiction movie involving mutant gunsights from outer space; rather, it's one of the foremost reasons that software projects are not delivered on time and within budget. If your features seem to continually evolve as the project progresses, or you find yourself trying to provide well-defined functionality from vague specifications, here's how to nail your requirements down firmly, right at the beginning. If they wiggle, use another nail.

### Chapter 6: Effective Design under Fire

The only problem with many design methodologies is that it takes a significant time investment to work through the entire process. Unfortunately, out here on the front lines, we typically have a hard time convincing management that we need a little time away from the compiler for sleep, let alone for months and months of abstract drawings that they don't understand. Consequently, at such times we must break the rules and roll our own design approach, using the best of all that we've encountered in the time we're given to work with. It ain't pretty, but it works.

### Chapter 7: Practical Estimating Techniques

Arguably the hardest thing to do in our business (beyond finding pizza toppings that everyone agrees upon) is producing an accurate time estimate for any nontrivial amount of code. Furthermore, many unrealistic deadlines arise due to overlooking tasks other than coding that also eat up chunks of time. In the end, if the estimates aren't real, it's the programmers who pay the price at deadline time. Here's a simple approach to help ensure that your next timeline is an achievable one.

## Chapter 8: Fighting for Quality Assurance

No programmer worth his weight in cappuccino ever wants to ship a buggy product. It's bad for the ego, bad for the résumé, and bad on the nerves when your telephone rings in the middle of the night. Amazingly, however, the overwhelming majority of businesses who develop software do not hire quality assurance professionals or otherwise institute any sort of rigorous software testing procedures. This calls for a combination of fighting for change and exercising self-defense wherever possible.

## Chapter 9: Keeping the Project under Control

Keeping a software development team running like a well-oiled machine takes work from people at every level. Code standards, version control, technical documentation, organization, discipline, and good communications are but a few of the skills required to keep a project on track. It matters little that you've prevailed in your political battles if your project simply implodes due to poor structural integrity. From programmer to project manager, here's how to keep things running smoothly.

## Chapter 10: Managing Your Management

If management is to have realistic expectations and a firm foundation upon which they can plan their business strategies, a little retraining is in order. If it were true that those higher up the corporate food chain were immune to the concerns of rank-and-file programmers, the battle would be lost before it began. However, what we're dealing with here is not an abstract concept but is instead real, flesh-and-blood people. Consequently, they can be convinced, directed, inspired, and motivated to do the right things. You simply need to speak a language that they understand. And, of course, let them think that it was their idea all along.

## Chapter 11: Corporate Self-Defense

In companies large and small, internal politics can be the most frustrating and disruptive force that you encounter. People with agendas that are quite different from your own can disrupt, take over, or even completely destroy your project. Many programmers have neither the skill nor the desire to engage in political games; however, just as in the martial arts, many methods of self-defense are available that require little more than attention and redirection—and knowing when to duck. The alternative is to become a professional target.

## Chapter 12: Controlling Your Destiny

No matter how permanent you've been told your position is, software developers have about as much job security as a drummer in Spinal Tap. Whether you move to different projects at the same job, change companies as a contractor, or hang out a shingle and go into business yourself, there are no guarantees. If you want to keep paying the rent by making the compiler dance, it's up to you to look after your career. No one else will. This means keeping yourself marketable, knowing how to negotiate, and always staying prepared by looking to the future.

# Acknowledgments

Many moons ago, Tom Archer, a friend and author who at the time was also running the popular developer Web site CodeGuru, approached me about writing a column for the site. He already had a number of columns by some of the top names in Windows programming who were writing about specific technologies. My task was to instead pen a series of articles about the insanities of Corporate America and the things we programmers grapple with on a daily basis just to get a release out the door. In short, he said, he wanted to add some attitude to the site. It's not often that someone offers to pay you to be a wise guy and a trouble maker. Who could refuse?

In writing that column, *Programming in the Real World*, I received a stream of emails from programmers the world over who told me they felt as though I was looking over their cubicle walls. It seems I'm not the only one who's had to deal with arbitrary deadlines, inept management, corporate politics, and all the other ridiculous situations I've found myself in as a professional developer. This book was directly inspired by all of you who encouraged me to expand upon the things I've learned about navigating the corporate world of software development. I'm grateful for the conversations and for the stories you've told. I hope this helps you avoid some of the disasters I've seen in my own travels.

If it wasn't for Tom and his faith in my writing, however, I never would have taken a swing at either the column or *The Career Programmer*. The bookstore shelves are full of programming books, but they're all about specific technologies and writing code. I've learned from experience that coding is only a very small part of what we have to do to successfully make a living in this business. Still, I never would have taken a shot at writing something as off the wall as this without his encouragement and support. Thanks, man. The next pizza is on me. Yeah, yeah, I know, extra pepperoni. (It's good to have old friends who share your taste in pizza.)

When I mentioned that I was thinking about writing a book, Tom also put me together with Robert Scoble of Thunder Lizard Productions (you just gotta love a name like that), who in turn introduced me to Dan Appleman here at Apress. Robert, if you hadn't done that, heaven only knows how long I would have flailed around trying to figure out how to publish a book. Your kindness made a real difference, and I truly appreciate it.

The truth of the matter is that I was going to chicken out and just ask Dan if he had a language book of some sort that I could write. However, when I was referring to *Programming in the Real World*, I described it to him as "guerilla tactics for an imperfect world." He responded that it sounded like a great title for a book and told me if I had something along those lines in mind he'd rather hear about that first. If you've read many books on programming, you know that there's a pretty consistent format for tech publications. Most publishers do their best to stick with the status quo and color within the lines. I sincerely believe that the programmers of the world would benefit tremendously if there were more people like Dan who were willing to take a chance on something a little different. And believe me, folks, this book is so far from the mainstream it can't even swim. I figured about the time he reviewed the chapter introducing the night watchman's attack Chihuahua I'd get a very polite rejection letter, but not this guy. He's been incredibly supportive throughout the process, and is just a great person in general.

One of the people writing columns for CodeGuru at that time was debugging guru John Robbins, best known for his *Bugslayer* column and recent book *Debugging Applications*. We'd exchanged a couple of emails in the course of things, and I liked his sense of humor. He's also an *extremely* capable techie. When I started work on this book, I asked him if he'd be willing to write the foreword. Given the workload this guy maintains (don't even ask about the frequent-flyer miles), I didn't expect that he'd have time to fool with it, but I figured it couldn't hurt to ask. I'm glad I did, as it's given me a chance to get to know him a little better. He's even more fun on the phone, but I'm certainly not going to tease him too much about it. He was a Green Beret before he started squashing bugs for a living. If that's not the perfect training for life as a professional programmer, I've never seen it. I personally believe that, if we all had that kind of background, management wouldn't try to pull even half of the stunts that I've seen. In any event, thanks for taking the time for this, John. Forget the pizza. Green Berets get beer.

I've heard a lot of people talk about how much work it is to write a book. For the language-oriented books loaded with code, I'm sure they're right. However, I've had an absolute blast doing this, and it's been much more play than work. A long time ago, as I struggled with finding a style of writing that worked for my personal tastes, my old friend Janice Strickland suggested that I simply write like I talk. That was a turning point for my writing, and it's what I've continued to do. It's easy for me. Of course, what that really means is that I get to be as chatty as I please and trust to others to make me look like I actually took English classes in school.

The only thing that I was really nervous about when I started this project was the editing process. My style of writing is loose, conversational, and shows a blatant disregard for many of the conventions of serious literature. Although I didn't want to look like a complete illiterate, neither did I want to get an editor who would delete all of my silliness and try to make this into a formal and conservative piece of work. Thank you, Grace Wong! For those of you who don't know her, Grace is a Managing Editor at Apress and has been in charge of this project.

She apparently knew my concerns before I even voiced them and consequently assigned Tom Gillen as my editor. That was a stroke of luck. As it turns out, he's as much of a wise guy as I am.

Of course, after some of the heavily technical stuff that he's worked on (ask him about economics some time, just don't forget to duck), I suppose this may have done permanent damage to his literary brain cells. I can't imagine how many times his brain must have rebooted from switching back and forth between extremely serious academic works and a programming book that features a maintenance programmer who stockpiles automatic weapons. The magic of it all is that he's saved me from my dubious grasp of the English language and yet somehow managed to leave my casual and irreverent way of speaking completely untouched. (Actually, a few of the one-liners you'll encounter are his own suggestions, but you didn't hear that from me.) In the end, my greatest anxiety has instead become my extreme good fortune. Tom has turned my loose prose into an actual book, and we've had a heckuva lot of fun in the process. Now all I have to do is figure out how to make him a standard part of any future book contracts.

Other folks have also been critical to the success of this book, and their efforts are all the more valued because they never get to see their name in lights. They just make it all happen, quietly and in the background. Sofia Marchant has toiled in the guise of Production Editor, and Diana Van Winkle has attended to the compositing chores. Truth to tell, I'm completely ignorant of the behind-the-scenes stuff that they had to do to turn this into a professional-looking publication. I only know that, if it weren't for them, this would be nothing more than a nicely edited word-processor document.

Gary Cornell, who founded Apress along with Dan Appleman, at least works in a capacity that I can comprehend. Whether it's contracts, expenses, or checks (my favorite part, of course), Gary somehow gets all the business stuff taken care of in between countless road trips and an In basket that would no doubt terrify lesser mortals.

Stephanie Rodriguez also performs a familiar task, all the more appreciated because it's a profession that I love to tease. Stephanie is the head of marketing. In fact, even the cover of the book has her personal touch. However, all joking about marketing aside (and we've all done plenty of it in this business), the bottom line is that nothing happens until a sale is made. If not for her efforts, you simply never would have seen this book in the first place. The fact that she's a joy to work with just makes it that much better.

All in all, I've got it made. I get to sit back, prop up my feet, and ramble on about how I've solved in my own adventures development problems that are common to almost every shop. Behind the curtains, however, a host of talented, professional, and really cool people have all worked their tails off to make this book a success. And yet, I'm the one who gets my name on the cover. What a great gig, eh? I think the most significant thing I've learned while writing this is that, for every book I read, the author is only one small person in a roomful of truly exceptional people. If I had a conscience I'd probably feel a little guilty about that, but when you come right down to it I'd do it all over again. It's been great working with such people.

My sincere thanks to you all. May your ankles never know the wrath of small, hairless canines.

— Christopher Duncan
November, 2001

Part One

# Software Development in an Imperfect World

# CHAPTER 1

# Welcome to Corporate America

You're typing so fast that the keys of your keyboard would threaten to go on strike if only enough of them were visible to form a good union. Aside from the racket of the keys under your fingertips and the continual stream of enhancement requests from management, your office is a fortress of solitude where none dare disturb your rapid-fire coding sessions. Your days are a delight and a blur as you experiment to your heart's content with state-of-the-art technology, rarely taking a break from your creations for even a fresh cup of coffee. Suddenly, you feel an uncomfortable sensation on your forehead and realize, as you peel your head from the keyboard that has been serving as your pillow, that you've been dreaming again. It's two o'clock in the morning, you haven't slept three hours in as many days, the deadline for your release is mere hours away, and your software is about as stable as the maintenance programmer who had to deal with the previous release. A marketing rep drops by after his latest three-martini lunch with your clients and adds yet another do-or-die feature to the stack on your desk. At least he got some extra use out of his cocktail napkins. Now, recovered from your pleasant dream, you shake your head and gaze bleary-eyed over the sea of cubicles to survey your home away from home, deep in the heart of Corporate America. Welcome to reality. We hope you enjoy your stay.

## So You Thought You'd Just Be Coding All Day, Eh?

It matters little if you spent years in college training for a career in software development or simply stayed up night after night with a PC, a compiler, and a language tutorial until you could write a complete piece of software that output more than just "Hello, World". You studied, you coded, and you made the grade. You're a programmer now. Very few people in life are fortunate enough to pursue their passion for a living. Right up there with professional athletes and rock stars, you've devoted your life to a hobby that became a source of income, and a pretty decent source at that.

For most of us, the early days of programming were heady days indeed. Regardless of the hardware, operating system, or language, all software developers share a common joy: that thrill of transforming lines of incomprehensible text into high-powered databases, sizzling graphics, and earth-shaking audio. In our world, we get a special kind of delight in the instant gratification of turning our thoughts into code that then magically instructs a machine to do exactly as we please with just the quick rumblings of a compiler pass. Unlike architects who dream but must wait years to see the resulting building, programming is the closest thing to magic to be found in a day and age when Merlin the Wizard would probably be sent home for violating the company dress code.

In fact, a life of getting paid to play was the siren song to which we all succumbed, lured by the promise of a life of creativity and intellectual challenge into a world where excellence was the common goal and faster ponies always won the race. Although I'm sure many went to school and learned to become programmers because they reasoned that it was a good way to make a living, I have personally never met them. I understand that they're prone to jumping out the nearest window after about the third release. The pressures of our industry are extreme. Without a love of the art to carry you through, it can be a harrying experience for even the stoutest heart. Fortunately, the only windows that actually open in most development shops are located on the first floor, for probably just this reason. No, rather than a cold and calculated career path based on salaries, promotions and longevity, we got into this business for a very understandable motive. People do all sorts of unreasonable things in the midst of a love affair, and we simply love coding.

 If the early days of learning to program were intoxicating, they were balanced by the experience of finding the first job. The software business is no different than any other when it comes to hiring. It's a classic catch-22: you can't get a job without experience, and you can't get experience without a job. Nonetheless, we scratched, clawed, and wrote résumés that would be the envy of any best-selling novelist, but we managed to obtain that holy grail of techies everywhere, a full-time job writing software. However, no college course could ever adequately prepare a new programmer for what comes next.

Just as a teenager with a new electric guitar has visions of becoming an overnight success, selling millions of records and playing to packed houses full of screaming fans, most beginning developers anticipate arriving at their new job Monday morning and being given an office, a computer, and a list of programs to write. What could be better? Well, perhaps a cup of Jamaican coffee, but any form of caffeine will do in a pinch. However, as every veteran of our business knows by now, if you're spending even 75% of your day actually coding, you're way ahead of the game. Much of the day is consumed in meetings of one form or another. When that fails to be a sufficient deterrent to productivity, the corporate world has plenty of other weapons in its arsenal to rely upon: bureaucracy, politics, marketing, clueless management, general confusion, and a host of other little distractions. One notable engineer has actually left the field to make his fortune drawing cartoons that illustrate some extremely fanciful and imaginative scenarios in the business world. No one who has ever lived in the cubicle maze of the software development industry believes it to be fiction.

So, just as quickly as our new hire was sucked into the endless hours of typing and compiling for the sheer pleasure of it, he now more closely resembles the shell-shocked inhabitants of a recently invaded city. Gone are the distraction-free days of coding, the dreams of state-of-the-art software, or even a decent night's sleep for that matter, although few programmers get much of that sort of thing even on a good day. Instead, it's a life that more closely resembles a small domestic rodent running in circles on a treadmill inside his cage. The end result of all the bureaucracy, mission statements, and crisis-driven management is a development cycle awash in vague definition of requirements, last-minute feature requests, buggy releases, and mandatory overtime. Unpaid, of course.

Okay, a quick show of hands here. How many in the audience have already branded me a jaded cynic who has a dismal and unrealistic view of the software development industry? Do I see a few hands in the back? Good. It's always nice to know where the new hires are sitting. The seasoned developers are either grinding their teeth or nodding with a grim acceptance of the nature of the beast. Perhaps both. The reality of the matter, whether we like it or not, is that, to pay the bills doing what we love, we must step into the business world, for that's where the money is. No money, no new toys. For that matter, no house to put them in. Landlords are funny that way.

Actually, it tends to take a few years for all of this to sink in. In the beginning, it's just so cool to have a job where we effectively get paid to play with our favorite toys that we tend to overlook a lot of this stuff. It's also not until you change jobs a few times that you begin to realize that it wasn't just one screwy company that was like this, it's an entire industry. It's long about then that frustration really starts to develop, and such feelings always manage to find an outlet in one form or another. That can be a dangerous time to be in a design meeting with a lot of whiteboard erasers lying about. Those suckers can really sting when you put a little velocity behind them.

## What's a Nice Programmer Like Me…

Of course, the only reason that frustration arises in the first place is due to the nature of the typical techie. We truly care about the quality and content of our work. We are artists, idealists, and inspired creators. We are also quite logical. None of this really meshes very well with the typical corporate environment in which more time is spent on political maneuvering and career enhancement than in actually producing something valuable. Nonetheless, such is our reality. So how did we get here, unwilling partners in an unlikely marriage between artist and businessman? How is it that our environment not only tolerates both types but seems to require them?

Well, it's easy enough to understand how we got here. We like to program and we like to get paid, if for no other reason than to afford the next complier upgrade. Given our preferences, we would live in a world where technical excellence was the only thing that mattered. We certainly have little patience for stuffed suits or anyone else with limited technical understanding. If we get paid for writing software, though, there must be a reason. Furthermore, although it may boggle the imagination, the Suits find us just as incomprehensible as we find them. From their perspective, we are a class of creature that doesn't seem to understand the way the world really works. Besides, we talk funny. And yet, they pay us reasonably well to come in to work each week, no matter how peculiar our mannerisms. Why?

## Why People Run Businesses and Pay Programmers

To grasp how Corporate America came to be populated by such different classes of creatures, we must first understand why people run businesses in the first place. If we take it as a given that the prevailing population of the typical software development shop didn't come about by a freak accident between Noah's ark and an oversized pocket calculator, then there must be an overriding purpose at play. Actually, it's not even that difficult to understand: it's all about the money, the fundamental reason that people start businesses in the first place. No matter what other motivations people may have in terms of their products or services and the impact they might make on our society, unless it's a nonprofit organization you can bet that the very first consideration will be making money. What they actually sell is a secondary matter. In fact, many businesses start out in the planning stages with a financial model and explore a number of products until they find one that matches their market and fiscal expectations.

This is where the typical programmer gets into strange and treacherous waters. In the business world, software is simply a product. It is not high art. It is not a religion. It is just something to give to customers so that they'll part with their money. Keep chanting that until you can at least wipe that incredulous look from your face. You're starting to make the new hires nervous.

Yes, folks, hard as it may be to believe, what we create is simply an inventory item, an excuse to generate an invoice. But what's that you say? Who wrote the invoicing program? Well, that brings up the other type of software that they pay us to create. We either produce a product to sell, or we give them tools to help them sell their products. Either way, the same inescapable logic applies: our software is simply a means to an end, and that end is to bring in money. Now I've hung out with enough musicians in my life to know what the next batch of responses will be, for musicians and programmers are kindred spirits. All of these responses center on how business is destroying art, how commercialism rips the very soul out of software development, how money is evil and is the cause of all the grief that assaults us in our day-to-day life on the job.

Okay, everyone, take a deep breath, and let's take a good look at this. You do like to get paid every week or two, don't you? If not, I have a few projects I'd like to discuss with you. No scope creep. Honest. In fact, all of the professional programmers I know get paid, and furthermore depend on that money a great deal. If you're a musician and don't make much on your gigs, then you get a day job. So what do you do if you're a programmer and don't get paid on your day job? Take up playing music at nights? Sure hope you like macaroni and cheese. The simple fact of the matter is that our lives revolve around money just as much as a businessman's does. Businesses hire us to develop software that's either sold to make money or supports the effort of making money. Profit is not a bad thing. Without it, your company—and your job—ceases to exist.

So, this is why business people hire computer programmers. It's all about money. Another important point to keep in mind is that, regardless of the chaos that they seem to inject into the software development process, the business people are in charge here, not the programmers. Why is that? The Golden Rule, of course, and I don't mean the one about doing unto others; I mean the one that states "The people with the gold get to make the rules." It was a businessperson who conceived of the company, put together a plan to market a product, and got the financing to rent the building, bring in the components to build your spacious cubicle, and provide you with a paycheck. Why shouldn't they be in charge? Programmers are usually busy finding neat new toys to spend money on. We're not real big on bringing more of it back into the corporate bank accounts. If it were up to us to run the companies, we'd die out. Abruptly.

So, we easily recognize that two completely different perspectives are at play in a software development shop: programmers work from a technical and artistic point of view, and those with a business perspective sustain and drive the company. Consequently, the two camps speak completely different languages, which brings up a very important point for those of us who would like to regain control of the software development process. If you wish to succeed in your technical endeavors, you must be able to interact with business people and address their perspective in a language that is meaningful to them. Why can't they just learn our language instead? They don't have to. They have the money, remember?

Actually, we have much more in common with our brethren in the three-piece suits  than we'd like to admit. Both of us are driven by some of the same fundamental goals and desires. It may not sound pretty, but a core motivation for us both is the simple phrase, "What's in it for me?"  For business people, making money is in fact the gig that they signed up for. Those of us who watch the compiler spin for a living also need money, but that's not our passion. Instead, although we may acknowledge the need for financial compensation, our hearts belong to technology. Much of what we want lies in the realm of technical and artistic gratification.

This is the point where we should all take a step back and give a little nod of respect to the Suits. We may not approve of weasel-like marketing tactics or corporate doublespeak, but, without a doubt, they are people who know how to get what they want. Far more than we do. To be able to enjoy more of our day and get what we truly want out of our career, we need to develop the same degree of skill in achieving our own objectives. Very simply put, if you ignore the business realities, you just won't be able to do what you really want to do. A large part of accomplishing this has to do with two fundamental tasks. One is recognizing the realities of the business world for what they are rather than wishing it were otherwise. Having accomplished this, the next logical step is to improve both our communication and navigation skills so that we can not only speak to the Suits in their own language, but manage the conversation skillfully enough to get what we want out of it.

## The Corporate World Is Not Logical

Corporate America is an exercise in the unreasonable, inept, and frequently just plain unfair. I suppose that the same could be said of life in general from time to time, but the business world just seems to excel at it. As a case in point, consider the following.

Early in my career, I worked for a company writing software that was used at remote sites. People in the field needed the ability to update their systems with information in the primary company database as it changed. I was tasked with writing the communications module. This was long before the general public was aware of the Internet's existence. Consequently, you might assume that I would set myself to the task of writing a serial communications subsystem using a dial-up modem. I know that's certainly what I had in mind. However, my manager instead informed me that I needed to design and implement a data transfer module that would allow our program to write the information to a floppy disk and then read it back at the remote site when the reps set up their system. After the reps carried the floppies though the scanners at airport security, of course. Floppies love that sort of thing. If the people in the field needed subsequent updates, we would simply send an overnight letter with new floppies. This happened many times a day.

Sure, these were the pre-Internet days when the term *high bandwidth* usually referred to someone in marketing who had consumed one cup of coffee too many, but I can assure you that the modems of the day were more than equal to the task. In fact, I made those same assurances to my manager, with some degree of enthusiasm. Well, the enthusiasm, to put it politely, was also mixed with a fairly incredulous posture as he was a programmer himself and someone who knew better. I simply couldn't believe that he'd make such a preposterous decree. (It wasn't a suggestion.) Nonetheless, he was a patient guy, and, because he had hired me as the token extrovert for this outfit, he just let me get it all out of my system before offering what he saw as a perfectly understandable explanation. Mind you, he was much more experienced in these matters than I.

This being a somewhat small outfit with employees numbering fewer than fifty, the president of the company was a fairly active participant in all aspects of the operation. Worse still, he'd been tested with genius-level IQ, had many impressive degrees, and consequently approached things with a friendly but inflexible nature. And he was, after all, in charge. When my manager had attempted to explain how the dial-up communications system he'd envisioned would work (I told you he knew better), the president had immediately insisted on the aforementioned floppy disk system instead. (We're talking multiple floppies here by the way, folks.) No matter what argument my boss used, the president had a comeback. When the vulnerability of floppy disks was pointed out, he proposed taking two copies of the disk on the plane instead of one. Many other such topics were covered, of course, but my favorite was the obvious: why not just use modems and be done with it? The president of the company was adamant and explained the reason for his intransigence patiently, as if to a very young child. It was a matter of dependability: what if the modem breaks? And, with that, the conversation he had with the head of our team was declared over and the matter closed. He was, after all, in charge.

In addition to being a rather high-strung young man by nature, I was also new to the software development industry and the corporate world in general. Naturally, I was full of idealism and ideas on how to pursue excellence wherever possible, and I was typically quite vocal about it. I remember this little episode, though, because it was my first encounter with the realities of the business world with which I've become so familiar. I realized in that moment that logic had absolutely no bearing on the matter, that my manager felt exactly the same way about it as I did, and that in the end there just wasn't a darned thing that either of us could do about it. There was one and only one path available: shut up and code. So I did. To detail the adventures encountered by the field reps due to the expected instances of bad things happening to good floppies would be an exercise in the obvious. Although ten years later I now view this as a fairly tame example of corporate ineptitude, it was a real eye-opener at the time. It was at that moment that I realized I wasn't in Kansas anymore.

The first mistake that most new programmers make is assuming that the logical, practical, and most sensible arguments always prevail. I'm certainly not the first to observe this, but there seems to be an almost mathematical formula that dictates a diminishing capacity for common sense as one moves up the corporate ladder. This gets even more exciting when you couple it with technology, for the

Suits often consider themselves an authority on software matters after having read an article on the latest technology trend in an outdated business magazine while visiting the restroom. Having added "chief architect and software engineer" to their list of perceived skills, they are then known to join in the next available software meeting and insist on design and implementation details with all the authority that they possess. Many sets of lungs have been exhausted as programmers frantically try to explain why writing a wireless transmission system to control a toy dune buggy isn't necessarily the most efficient way to deliver interoffice mail. Their arguments are based on the invalid pretext that the businessperson in question would know a network protocol if it bit him on the fanny. They will lose. For what it's worth, however, they will end up having a lot of fun testing the system by having dune buggy races at two o'clock in the morning. Our business is ever an exercise in tradeoffs.

Another area where the nonsensical ways of the business world cause us grief in a very personal way is the matter of deadlines. In a world controlled by programmers, or perhaps Vulcans, a new software project would start out in a controlled and organized manner: gathering requirements, estimating the effort, performing adequate design, and ultimately following a well thought out and achievable schedule of implementation. In the real world, this almost never happens.

The ultimate delivery date—that magical moment on the calendar that signals the end of four straight weeks without sleep—is typically arrived at in an almost unbelievably arbitrary fashion. Sometimes it's due to a management staff that has convinced themselves that they know enough about software development to say how long an effort should take. Other times the marketing department publicizes a release date arrived at without the slightest consideration for the time it takes to write the system. Rather, they do this as a preemptive strike against the competition, to keep the customer from buying Brand X because your new version is coming out "real soon now." Dates are sometimes even given to development teams because that's just the date that management wants the results, with no more logic or reasoning behind it than that.

One might be inclined to simply explain to the decision makers, either patiently or angrily (I've done both), that they can make all the decrees that they like, but the software will be done when it's done. Why, yes, I have changed jobs a few times, now that you mention it. Above and beyond the political peril caused by telling the person who controls your department's budget that you've seen burritos with less potential for hot air than they possess, there's a very simple reality to consider: regardless of whether the deadlines are realistic, if you don't meet them, either you'll be replaced by someone who will or your project will be killed. Sometimes both.

Often, even with unrealistic dates, it is possible to prevail and deliver the goods on time. In order to do this, it's important to possess the ability to manage each stage of the development process effectively in the time that you have to work with. Many of the books and courses on requirements gathering, analysis, design, project management, quality control and the software development process in general are written for a perfect world in which there's plenty of time, and management is never resistant to the development team's way of doing things. In the real world, however, we're rarely given the time that these approaches require. The end result is either a chaotic sequence of events or no sequence at all, with the developers shooting from the hip and making it up as they go along. Either way, you have about as much chance for success as you do landing the space shuttle in the driveway next to your kid's new turbocharged skateboard.

The business world simply doesn't operate in a logical or rational fashion. If you don't recognize this and learn practical methods of coping with it, you'll encounter failure after failure no matter how good your technical skills. Left to their own devices, the Suits will not only shoot themselves in the foot, they'll miss on the first attempt and get yours as well. What does this really mean to you, the working-class programmer, on a day-to-day basis? After all, you didn't sign up to be a project manager; you just wanted to write cool programs. Well, above and beyond the obvious shoe repair bills, you're going to find yourself continually angry and frustrated as you spend your days designing and implementing programs that were doomed before you even fired up your editor.

If you can't win critical battles in all phases of the development process, poor decisions will continually transform your potentially excellent software into a series of well-publicized disasters. If management doesn't trip you up by mandating some form of arbitrary and inappropriate technical approach, you'll find yourself having to perform hack after hack of your own accord just to meet the ridiculous deadlines. Long before the obligatory release crunch, you'll be throwing monitors out of fifth-floor windows to try to vent the stress. All you wanted to do when you got into this business was code. Now, in addition to the meetings, company procedures, paperwork, dress codes, and other trappings of bureaucracy, the very thing that allowed you to put up with it all in the first place, the joy of writing good quality software, is being interfered with on a daily basis. This is when it gets personal.

## You Can't Win If You Don't Play

You most likely didn't start out wanting to be an entrepreneur, project manager, CEO, or anything else with a spiffy title. You prefer the artistry of commanding little silicone chips to do your bidding. In fact, if you're like most of the programmers that I've known over the years, you have an active animosity for any of these positions. The best place for most developers is in a room with a door that has a large enough gap at the bottom to slide raw meat in once a day. If we wanted to be the dashing owner of a Fortune 500 company, we'd have bought pin-striped suits instead of the latest version of that hot rod programmer's editor.

Nonetheless, it's time to wake up and smell the espresso. The single most prevalent reason that programmers don't prevail in internal company maneuvering is the fatal misconception that it's not a part of their job. Most programmers excel in the technical areas but rarely know how to navigate the business environment in which they exist. This isn't for a lack of ability, however; they simply never chose to develop these skills and, as such, become corporate roadkill, along with their favorite development projects. Mind you, they would be quick to make fun of any developer who didn't have solid coding abilities, as these are obviously required to do the job and deliver the software. And, yet, they don't realize that the very same set of rules applies to understanding and effectively dealing with the corporate world. Without the capacity to cope with all that the business world throws at you, it is an inescapable fact that you will not deliver high-quality software on time and within budget. By the way, you might be wondering why you care about the budget. What do you figure your chances are of getting another project to work on if the one you just finished was a financial disaster? It goes without saying what fate befalls the employment status of programmers who have no project.

Remember, too, that if your project dies no one will ever see how cool your code was. That's the artist's reason for caring about the ins and outs of the corporate world, distasteful though it may be. Pouring heart and soul into a project for months only to have management pull the plug on it can be a real stress inducer. It's better to learn how to avoid such things. It's either that or listening to an angry night watchman explain to you why the near miss of a monitor from a fifth-story window is going to cause many more sessions of expensive therapy for his already jumpy attack Chihuahua. And you thought you had problems.

Many an otherwise brilliant developer shrugs these things off as nothing more than politics, as if it's something that pops up only occasionally and is of little importance. In reality, the numbers are actually much more distressing in this area. Whenever three or more people occupy the same room, you have politics. It's human nature. If you choose to ignore this, you will eventually lose a battle that you care about. Actually, you'll probably lose them all. The night watchman's dog will doubtless get some smug satisfaction from this. The very first step towards a better workday is simply recognizing the fact that you must learn to control the scenarios you encounter on the job, or they will control you. From that point on, it's just a matter of getting good at it.

Of course, one of the first steps in learning how to deal with your environment is simply recognizing its key components. If you've had your head buried in a compiler (or the sand), you might not have taken the time to catalog the various aspects of your domain. Let's start by taking a look at one of the most fundamental and critical structures you'll encounter. We're not talking about data structures here, but rather the food chain.

## The Food Chain

As we all know, animals in the wild have their survival threatened on a regular basis according to their position in the food chain. The rules are actually quite easy to understand: it's either get dinner or be dinner. For most of us, the former is much more appealing, particularly when microwaves are involved. However, for the hungry lion that doesn't have a choice between chasing down a zebra on the open Serengeti or just ordering a pizza, the food chain is a critical consideration. Of course, you might hear similar sentiments from the zebra.

You should know that the corporate world has a very similar structure. Just as a salmon isn't going to be much of a threat to a grizzly bear's survival, so too does the president or CEO of your company sleep soundly at night, immune to the attitudes and desires of the rank-and-file programmer. In the business world, there's an oft-used plumbing metaphor about—well, let's say *stuff*—rolling downhill that is actually quite accurate. If the head of the company decides that Software Project X is no longer desirable, due either to fiscal considerations or that three-martini lunch he just had with the manager of Software Project Y, then Project X is history. Just like that. Game over, and if you have another quarter, you'd better save it to call a recruiter. The CEO is the most dangerous beast in the corporate animal kingdom. Not only does he have the power to lay waste to entire departments (it's very rarely a she, for a completely different set of inane reasons), he's also almost always out of touch with the day-to-day realities of your business. The head of your company gets his view from 30,000 feet, not from down on the ground where real people deal with real problems on a daily basis. The fact that he has to depend almost entirely on summaries, reports, upper or maybe middle managers, and the obligatory pie charts guarantees that, from his lofty view, all the details that are critical from your front-line position are lost. However, if he gets good advice from informed and properly motivated managers beneath him, he can still make solid, practical, and informed decisions. So, let's take a look at the next rung in the ladder: upper management.

These short-haired creatures are easily identified by their customary pin-striped suit and the exclusivity of their dwellings, typically posh offices located very high up in the building. This location helps them avoid chance encounters with the packs of programmers known to roam the lower-level halls in search of a Suit who has been separated from the herd. Upper management is actually the same breed as that of the president/CEO; the latter has simply established himself as the dominant male. These managers in turn establish their own territories, such as accounting, marketing, manufacturing, and of course, software development. Although it may seem that the only one of these we care about is the one in charge of the programming department, that's a bit misleading. These critters are known for their aggressive behavior and are always positioning themselves to take over the turf of any other managers who are unwary or who let their guard down. This is how bean counters can end up in charge of an incredibly complex and critical software development project.

Although highly competitive, they are also greatly influenced by each other, reading similar trade publications and frequenting the same watering holes. This also poses a threat to those lower on the food chain, for advice from one manager is taken more seriously than are recommendations from someone at a lower level who actually produces something. Consequently, we find many disastrous decisions that have their genesis in one of these guys taking bad advice from a peer who, while clueless about software development, was considered a good source of information because he was, after all, a manager. If you knew how often this happened, it would only interfere with your ability to sleep nights.

Our next species doesn't worry much about sleeping nights because they're usually spending them at the local watering holes (the very same watering holes, by some strange coincidence, as the ones frequented by upper management). This, combined with the fact that they are directly responsible for bringing money into the company (remember the reason people form companies?), accounts for the high position that those in marketing occupy in the food chain. Their credo—*nothing happens until a sale is made*—is oft ignored by the rest of the kingdoms in the corporate world.

Because I'm a practical person who likes to eat on a regular basis, it's worth noting at this point that I'll be the very first one to buy the drinks when in the company of my publisher's marketing folks. Programmers do love to tease those in marketing, probably because this group is so often responsible for unreasonable deadlines. It also happens to be the group, though, that filled the payroll bank accounts. That's typically overlooked. In fact, of the groups we've reviewed in the food chain thus far, those in marketing are the first to actually produce tangible results. This brings up an interesting survival skill that we'll be touching on later. Although they exist higher up on the food chain and are without a doubt born predators, those in marketing are not always the natural enemy of programmers. It just seems that way. It's not often documented in the wild, but these two species have been known to form powerful unions, elevating the power and status of both within the corporate structure. Just don't ask who usually ends up paying for the drinks. They're in marketing for a reason.

As is so often the case in nature, the greatest threat to survival often comes from those just above you in the natural order of things. Middle management is that class of creatures who are in direct, day-to-day contact with the people who develop software. This group is the most feared by those who actually produce tangible results on a daily basis. Well, feared by everyone but marketing; those guys are fearless by nature. Middle management has a fairly well-ordered social structure. Most of their behavior is dictated, in fact, by the established norm of the pack in which they live. Middle management is the weathervane of the corporate environment, as they're always the first to sniff out new trends. This doesn't guarantee an accurate weather forecast, mind you; it simply means that they're highly driven by which way the wind is blowing. In these parts, it blows a lot. Above and beyond the fact that they have, by position, the ability to control and therefore wreak havoc on the software development community, the additional danger comes from proximity. Being close to developers each day, even sharing the same dwellings in many companies, this group eventually hears enough buzzwords to believe that they actually understand technology. Worse still, they come to the inescapable conclusion that they're more qualified to make decisions in this area than programmers are because they understand technology and are, after all, managers. Of all the dangers in the wild, these harmless looking creatures, attired as they are in their natural "business casual" camouflage, pose the greatest threat to the unwary developer.

At the lowest level of the food chain, at least as far as the programming world is concerned, the software development group is a species that comprises several subgroups. The highest ranking of these is project management. Note that I didn't say "the most dominant." Software developers are always vying for control of some corner of the pack, and the power doesn't always match the position. A veteran coder who is the only one on this planet or any other who understands the cryptic and arcane workings of a critical piece of software is often given deference by the project manager, being appeased with trinkets such as high-resolution monitors, extra computers, and even (in rare cases) an office with a door on it. Nonetheless, when you look at the org chart, the project manager is perched at the top of this group. The greatest threat that a project manager generally poses to the surrounding programmers is not one of direct aggression, but rather that of the entire project being decimated by the project manager's inability to defend the pack from outside predators.

Next in rank (at least as far as structure is concerned), team leads are typically little more than programmers with a full coding load who somehow got suckered into doing some of the project manager's job in addition to their own. This makes the team lead a more dangerous individual than the project manager because, due to the stress induced by the dual workload, the former is much more likely to hand you your head for a stupid interruption. Programmers in general don't care much for distractions, but this subgroup is distinguished by a marked lack of patience and general harried look that sets them apart from those who only code all day. It is a subtle distinction, but one which the expert can learn to recognize.

Tucked away in corners of the building where the sun shines the least (particularly on higher floors where windows overlooking the night watchman are discouraged), programmers are at the very bottom of the food chain. Depending in part on project managers for protection and survival, they exist primarily as nature's way of balancing out marketing. Neither would exist without the other, although you won't hear much of that sort of talk at the local watering holes. Important by implication is the position occupied at the bottom of the heap. Remembering the adage that things tend to roll downhill, programmers are, in fact, at the bottom of the hill. Regardless of the reason, be it a project manager who has no idea how to estimate and create milestones, a middle manager who decides to try the latest management fad, the marketing rep who's just made yet another unsubstantiated promise to customers, or the sweeping decisions of those in upper management, it all falls squarely on the shoulders of the rank-and-file programmer. In short, no matter who screws up in the food chain, you can rest assured that you can kiss your weekend plans goodbye. All the more reason for you to periodically stick your head above the cubical walls and see what's going on in the rest of the world.

Over the years, I've found myself occupying a cubicle in huge international companies as well as small mom-and-pop shops. If you work in the latter, you may think that the preceding descriptions of the corporate world don't apply to your situation. In fact, these categories exist in every company large and small. It's more obvious in the large firm, but, no matter where you work, there is without question a food chain. Learn to recognize it. Remember, it's either get dinner or be dinner.

## The Various Species of Programmers

Having seen a glimpse of the wider world of which you are a part, it's also useful to have an understanding of the different styles of the critters in your own pack. Although they are much less likely to be a threat than those above you in the food chain, making the wrong move with some of these guys will result in your limping back to your cube. Others will make you want to gnaw your arm off just to escape. So, in the spirit of obtaining a better grasp of the programmer's world, let's take a look at some of the more common varieties of coders that you'll meet in your travels.

One of the all-time classics, the crusty and cranky coder is a timeless symbol found in trade magazine advertisements everywhere. Far from fiction, these are very real people. With a diminished patience for others sculpted from many years of corporate ineptitude, these folks tend to be irritable, frustrated, and they just basically want to be left alone. Or else. They may or may not appear to have any teeth, but it's wise not to antagonize them. This is particularly good advice for the young. They may seem powerless to affect your life, but tick them off and you're liable to find out exactly how they've managed to survive in the business world for so long. Not everyone displays their weapons. In general, although there are times when you must press an issue regardless of who you disagree with, choose your battles wisely and avoid confrontations with these guys whenever possible. The best way to get along with them is to simply leave them alone and to make sure that any of your code that they're dependent upon is stable and on time. It also never hurts to pay attention to what they're doing and how they're going about it. You might learn something, no matter how long you've been at it.

The technology evangelist can be a real pain in design meetings. His particular preferences for a brand or product will be promoted without regard to any pragmatic reason. If he thinks that Brand X is the hottest new technology going, then he will most assuredly try to incorporate Brand X into every coding assignment he has a crack at. Attempting to get into philosophical arguments is pointless. So is arguing for your own technology on the same emotional basis, if you happen to be a technology evangelist yourself. The best way to counter any ill-advised recommendations from this sort is to be well prepared with accurate, detailed information about the strengths of your approach and the weaknesses of his. You must also make sure that your appeals are to the rest of the group or to those above him on the food chain. Any presentation you make to him will fall on deaf ears. And no, whiteboard erasers don't help. I've tried.

For some, shucks for most of us, it's easy to adopt the perspective that technology is life. Twenty-four hours a day (because I'm sure they dream about it, too), seven days a week, the only thing that matters to such people is the latest development in computer programming. Social events, family, friends, politics, the weather, you name it, are all completely irrelevant topics and not worthy of discussion. You may find this frustrating if you're trying to make casual conversation at the office. However, bear in mind that it's not for you to determine the life that others should live. It's been said that no one on their deathbed ever wished they had spent more time at the office. Nonetheless, it's their choice. With these folks, talk tech or just leave them alone. When you're at the office, however, these are frequently great guys to hang with. You're there to work as a techie, and these guys are some of the best. You'll not only learn many things that you wouldn't have taken the time to research for yourself, you'll also find a highly enthusiastic ally in your development efforts. Such developers are the epitome of the passionate programmer.

On the complete opposite end of the spectrum, the company man is a strange genetic hybrid between a Suit and a programmer. Technology will not be nearly as important to him as toeing the company line, no matter how insane that may be. Curiously, these are often excellent programmers who fall into this category for the purest of reasons: they want the company to succeed and are under the impression that goose-stepping along with the others is the clear path to this goal. They succumb to the corporate rhetoric that the employees should sacrifice their own lives for the better of the common good. It's useful to note that they're typically young as well. A few years in Corporate America is generally all the treatment that this particular malady requires.

However, this represents another nuisance and even potential danger in the wild. To the company man, good employees work eighty hours a week, every week, because they're dedicated and hard workers. Anyone who doesn't put in this ridiculous level of effort is considered to be a slacker, a malcontent, or some other form of deadwood that should be fired or at the very least relegated to the most tedious and dreary task that can be found. Watch these guys closely and never let your guard down around them, for they will stab you in the back without even a moment's hesitation. Yes, I know that sounds a bit dramatic, but I've seen it too many times. In reality, they've been played for suckers by middle and upper management, but they're not yet sharp enough to realize it. Don't bother trying to convince them; it will only make you an enemy. Just give them a wide berth and always sleep with one eye open.

Even though the company man thinks that most of us aren't really dedicated workers, most of us are actually quite conscientious. There are, however, those in companies here and there who truly are slugs. I've seen hourly workers bill excessive overtime and yet actively dodge assignments and spend their days brazenly reading the newspaper or playing video games at their desk when there was no shortage of coding to be done. Really. My personal inclination with such people involves an open fifth-floor window but, out of consideration for the health and well being of small, hairless canines everywhere, I've learned to just let it go and let them reap their own rewards without my help. In addition to the fact that I have no shortage of flaws myself, trying to get rid of one of these slugs is usually more stress inducing than it's worth. Just concentrate on your own work. Eventually, the wheel will come around for these guys.

The burnout is closely related to the slug, but is a little easier to understand and tolerate. Spend enough time working bad jobs in this business and it could be you. The best thing to do is just be nice to them, and try your hardest to make sure you don't have to depend on them.

Possessing no social skills that I've ever been able to discern, the arrogant bit head is almost always an absolute killer programmer, the best of the best. The problem with this guy is not just his cocky, condescending, and demeaning attitude, but the fact that 9.990872 times out of 10 he can back it up. He's just that good. It's a pity that he holds others in such low regard because, although not everyone achieves god-like status as a software developer, the world is full of really, really good ones. It's worth noting that not all bit heads are terminally arrogant (hence the prefix). Most of us who have any skills at all are a bit on the cocky side. The really good bit heads are almost impossible to convince that they're wrong because they usually aren't. However, once you prove your point with no margin for error, they will quickly and graciously come over to your camp and help you fight the next battle. It's only the arrogant bit heads who cross the line and whose abusive and offensive behavior makes them a personality type that you need to watch out for. Don't bother arguing with these guys unless you *really* know your stuff. Even then, be prepared for a fight that includes innuendo that you have less mental processing facilities than a refried bean factory. If you win the day, they'll usually be sullen about it, but, in general, these aren't particularly political creatures and so the threat is minimal. Fighting with them over technical issues can actually help make you a better programmer if you can avoid killing them before the discussion is done. You just have to learn to detach the emotions and let their poor attitude roll right off you.

One of the more frustrating types to deal with when you're under pressure to meet a deadline is the terminally educated. These folks will spend hours and hours of time that you just don't have to spare pontificating on the "proper process" to follow. Strong on academia, weak on hitting deadlines—that's the hallmark of these guys. Don't get me wrong: I think a little education is a fine thing every now and then. However, out here on the streets, no one has time nor really cares about obtuse studies, ivory tower design philosophies, or anything else that can't bring a tangible result to the party really soon. In a perfect world, I'd love to have the benefit of all that they've studied. Unfortunately, in the incredibly unproductive corporate environment, these guys just chew up bandwidth and create clutter that gets in the way of getting the product out the door in the three-and-a-half days that middle management gave us to do it in. Do your best to avoid meetings with this sort. If you do have to work with them, try to get support from those further up the food chain who realize that there's actual work to be done.

Ever a mix of styles and personalities, the wild man probably just exists for our own personal entertainment. Typically as enthusiastic about coding as he is about rock climbing, loud music, mosh pits, or anything else extreme, he does tend to break up the monotony of the corporate world. He may be a distraction in meetings, but is usually amiable to saving the stories until later if approached in a friendly manner. His animated mannerisms are a great thing to have around when the going gets tough and morale begins to falter. This kind of programmer can usually be counted on when there's a crunch but don't expect him to live at the office otherwise, as he has a life to live. He'll be the very first target of the company man and often doesn't even realize his peril. Keep an eye out and watch his back for him. He might even teach you how to surf, if you're not afraid of getting your pocket protector wet.

While I personally have only seen pocket protectors in bad black-and-white science fiction movies, there was a time on Earth when computer programmers were geeks. Even if they weren't serious dweebs, they were at the very least clean cut, properly attired, and professional in demeanor. The old-school programmer still exists in the world today, although they're typically older than the rank and file. They never caught on to the Wild West attitude that has been so pervasive in our industry since the dawn of the personal computer. You won't catch them hang gliding, nor are you likely to have animated and passionate technical discussions about the latest trends in software development with them. However, it would be a serious mistake to write them off as an irrelevant group with nothing to offer. It is the very fact that they don't have the typical shoot-from-the-hip mentality that brings such value to a team. They are organized, well prepared, and tend to think things though thoroughly before implementing a plan of action. Yes, I know that's kind of an alien concept these days, but heaven only knows how many bugs we could avoid if there were a little more of that mentality. Personally, I'm a Wild West kind of guy who has had to learn discipline for matters of pure survival, and I hope to never lose my passion for coding. However, somewhere between the Wild West and the old-school programmer lies a land where software is stable and pocket protectors are still badges of honor.

Given the explosion of opportunities in the computer business these days, it's not hard to snag a couple of side projects in addition to your day gig. There's certainly nothing wrong with that, as it's just an aspect of reaching for the brass ring. The entrepreneur, however, always seems to be doing this stuff on company time. Mind you, most companies aren't really that anal about whether or not you take a couple of minutes for a personal call, send an email to a friend, or hit the Web to look something up. People need breaks to be productive. However, if you're sitting there on the clock coding an order entry system for a client that you have on the side, you have some serious ethical problems. I tend to deal with these guys the same as I do the slugs.

We're all a pretty opinionated lot, and that's not necessarily a bad thing. The authority, however, knows all things on all subjects, regardless of actual experience. If he doesn't know the answer, he will simply ramble on trying to look knowledgeable. It's even worse when those up the food chain assume that he's a credible source of information, as that tends to lead to some fairly interesting technical directions and hinders those who really are informed in their efforts to steer a sensible course. Probably the most frustrating thing is this person's inability to utter the simple phrase, "I don't know" (which is something I consider to be the very cornerstone of wisdom). Nonetheless, if they have good communication skills or any degree of charisma, they can be quite difficult to deal with. Again, the best way to counter such a problem is to gain enough allies to give the dissenting opinion a fighting chance. Those who are impressed by the authority rarely look too deeply into the detail of things, so your political skills will almost always come into play in countering such a programmer.

So, having explored a wide variety of programmers, each with their own set of nuances and shortcomings, what shall we do? Throw them all out and keep only the good ones? Hope you don't mind coding the entire system yourself. The well-adjusted programmer is an urban myth. I have heard tales of a creature that balances work and play equally, and that has unsurpassed technical skills but the social graces of a saint. If you find one, stick him in the Smithsonian Institute and give me a call. Maybe then I'll believe. From my experience, we're all a pretty strange lot. As with anything else in life, the key to success is not insisting upon a perfect world, but rather in having a firm grasp of reality and operating accordingly. You'll doubtless find programmers that display many of these attributes, just as you'll find some classic examples. In the end, it's not about trying to change someone else. It's only important to learn how to effectively interact with those with whom you spend your days. Remember, you've got a few quirks of your own, and not all buildings lock the windows on the fifth floor.

Having taken the nickel tour of Corporate America, we now have a foundation upon which to build as we look to the issues that hinder our efforts to kick out the code. It's been said that to know where you're going you must first know where you've been. I'll extend that a bit further to include where you are at the moment, which is a strange place, indeed.

# CHAPTER 2

# Business Is War.
# Meet the Enemy.

We know the symptoms of the problem all too well: endless hours of overtime, continual meetings with stressed-out management, and just crisis after crisis as software continually blows up in the field. These are but a few examples of what happens when the software development process goes awry. Any developer who has ever taken home a paycheck knows this cycle well. No matter how much we enjoy coding, this isn't the way we'd like to do it. It's just no fun being under this kind of pressure only to work in an environment that almost guarantees buggy releases. Because we'll never win the fight for the software development process if we're swinging at shadows, the next logical step is to grab the binoculars and get a good look at the enemy. If only they were really that far away.

## Unrealistic Deadlines

Ask any veteran programmer to name the biggest enemy on the job and chances are good that you'll hear about unrealistic deadlines. Exactly what is an unrealistic deadline? Simply put, it's a no-win scenario in which the game is lost before it's even begun because the software cannot possibly be developed, tested, and delivered in the allotted time. It would be much less of a problem if this resulted in software that simply wasn't shipped. Unfortunately, it always gets delivered. It's often unstable and almost never thoroughly tested, but it ships. As you might imagine, this creates more than one problem.

The first and most obvious bit of fallout from the decision to ship software regardless of its state is that of a customer paying for a buggy product. This makes for unhappy customers, which in turn makes for unhappy people at your company, all of whom are further up the food chain than you are. It's not difficult to figure out who will bear the brunt of the accumulated frustrations and anxieties that result.

The other more subtle and damaging problem that comes from shipping a product that wasn't ready has to do with expectations. It works like this. Management comes to you with a silly date. You argue that there is no way the software can be delivered in that amount of time. Your opinion is ignored, and the mandate is given that the software *will* be done by the aforementioned date, or else. You're expected to "do whatever it takes" to make it happen, or suffer dire consequences up to and including spontaneous loss of income. For those of you new to the business, "do whatever it takes" means that now would be a great time to rent out your house because you're not going to be seeing much of it until after the deadline. You will code, eat, and do everything but bathe in your cube for as many consecutive hours as you can manage to stay conscious. You will then sleep the absolute bare minimum required to prevent hallucinations and repeat the cycle, day after day. Of course, in this state of mind and alertness, you'll no doubt write your finest and most stable code ever.

The problem is that the software will indeed ship. Towards the end of the cycle, corners will get cut, bugs will be declared features, and printed copies of enhancement requests will mysteriously disappear, only to be seen many weeks later in the dumpster appearing rather well gnawed. (The watchman's dog, of course, will deny any involvement.) Any remaining issues will be deemed acceptable shortcomings that can be remedied by a patch that the customers can download from the Internet.

Why is this a problem? Even though you were correct in the beginning about not having enough time to deliver the software, you assumed everyone understood that you meant solid, full-featured, quality software. That's not what they heard, of course, so from their perspective you were dead wrong. It did in fact ship. This means that the next time management comes to you with a ridiculous deadline you'll have even less credibility, if that's possible. You said it couldn't be done the last time but, by golly, it shipped anyway. Consequently, there shouldn't be any problem with the next unrealistic deadline, right? That's why they call it a no-win scenario. If you hadn't met the deadline, there'd be the devil to pay. So you do your best to hack together something that they can call a release, and they see it as proof that they were right all along. It validates their practice of choosing arbitrary dates.

So far I've been referring to unrealistic deadlines as a rather vague concept. We know that they happen. However, to put an end to them, we have to know *why* they happen. One of the first causes is something that I refer to as "inverted project management." By this, I mean the time-honored approach of picking a release date out of the clear blue sky and then giving the project to the programmers. Even if they were inclined to take a reasonable and logical approach to arriving at the delivery date (and they're typically not), management simply lacks the technical skills needed to know how long the development process takes. That's why they hired programmers to begin with. They couldn't do it themselves. Fortunately, for all concerned, they typically spare us the pain and suffering of trying to justify in technical terms exactly why they chose December 7 as the release date. They don't have to. Remember the food chain?

Regardless of how and why they select the dates, however, it simply doesn't matter when it comes down to the coding. The dates are never even close to reality, and the ensuing chaos is a constant. Any time that your company selects a delivery date before the technical aspects of the project have been evaluated in full detail, you will either miss your deadline or suffer a poor-quality release. Any time, every time.

The next common practice that's sure to wreak havoc on the unsuspecting deadline is scope creep. If you're not familiar with the term, it means the addition of features after the product has been defined and the deadlines determined. Even if you've done everything right, evaluated the project in fine-grained detail, and come up with extremely practical and realistic dates, this will still nail you. The reason that scope creep is a problem is that, although the feature list changes midstream, the deadline doesn't.

The habit of adding features as you go tends to be an incremental process. Most people wouldn't dream of walking into the programming department and proposing a new feature equal in complexity to landing a man on the moon. Apart from the volley of whiteboard erasers that would inevitably result, it's too obvious that it wouldn't be possible in the time available. However, just one tiny little enhancement doesn't seem like a big deal, and developers are made to feel petty and uncooperative if they make a fuss about it. I mean, we're just talking about adding a new button to the program; how big of a deal can it possibly be? Leaving aside for the moment the mountains of code under the hood that could result from our hypothetical little button, the problem is really in the frequency of occurrence. One small change in a program is probably not going to blow the deadline. Over the lifetime of your project, though, there won't be just one of these incidents. There will be a continual stream of them that bears a close resemblance to a conga line in an all-night coffee house. Each enhancement is presented as no big deal because it's such a small matter. But, over time, these add up to the point that the Great Wall of China will look like a white picket fence in comparison.

It's tempting to blame this one on marketing, but, in truth, these requests come from anyone in the building who's even remotely familiar with the project you're working on. Even the night watchman will get into the act, reasoning that a motion detector and early warning system couldn't possibly take that long to add to your system. Simple math will illustrate the result when your feature list changes and your deadline doesn't. Something, somewhere has to give, and it's usually the developer's sanity.

Another reason that a project is destined to miss the delivery date from the very beginning falls squarely on the shoulders of the programmers themselves. If the developers have poor estimating skills, the timeline won't be accurate even if management is willing to let the programmers set the dates. When a programmer errs on an estimate, it is almost always on the side of optimism. If, at the lowest level, the person writing the code can't accurately estimate how long the development effort will take, then there's no way to come up with an achievable deadline.

This often comes about due to our desire to spend time coding rather than shuffling paper on what seems like dull, boring, and bureaucratic tasks. It's true that writing an estimate for the system you're going to develop is about as exciting as a judo tournament between two blades of grass. It doesn't matter. If excitement is what you're after, just wait until the last few weeks of the project. You may decide that boredom is a highly underrated attribute. Tedious though it may be, if we want to grapple with management for control over the delivery dates, we'd better be ready and able to back it up once given the opportunity. I'll take a few boring days up front any time if it means that the rest of the project will go smoothly and I'll have the opportunity to sleep on a regular basis.

Another area where we actually have some responsibility for bad dates is that of complicity. Programmers who are afraid to speak up are doomed to suffer from the poor choices of others. If there's no way to hit the deadline but everyone on the team remains silent, there's absolutely no chance of making it more realistic. It's true that management may still not change the deadlines no matter how vocal you are, but you can't succeed if you don't try. What typically happens is that a completely mindless date is given to the developers, but no one confronts management about it either out of fear of reprisal or simply a general distaste for doing anything other than coding. The date gets set in stone, the project moves on, and in the background you hear the constant grumbling of programmers grousing about how stupid the timeline is. Sorry, boys, but you should have spoken up when you had the chance. If you didn't at least give it the old college try when the dates were getting set, you forever lose your right to complain about them.

Of course, trying to convince management that you know best about the timeline is often about as easy as getting a coffee table to do the bunny hop. The simple reality of it is that, right or wrong, management does not take programmers' opinions seriously due to a number of reasons. First and foremost is the lack of a common language. Anyone who writes software for a living has a technical frame of reference and is consequently prone to geek speak. Business people have a completely different frame of reference centered on revenue, profits, expenses, market share, sales volume, and anything else that might contribute to the purchase of an exotic new sports car when they retire. Attempting to justify your reasoning with technical arguments will be met with the same results as trying to teach calculus to your cat. Even if it weren't for the natural indifference of felines everywhere, all those noises coming out of your mouth are simply unintelligible to the cat and are subsequently ignored. Of course, it has been noted that many managers lack the basic intelligence inherent in even the densest of house pets. This doesn't improve your odds for effective communications. However, no matter how correct the developers might be in technical terms, they are simply ignored by a management staff that doesn't speak the same language.

It certainly isn't fair, but the self-perpetuating cycle of missed delivery dates also contributes to management's resistance to the suggestions of their programmers. Once a team has a history of slipped dates on previous projects (and we all know how easily that happens), they have extremely little credibility with the higher-ups when discussing future deadlines. Management reasons that, because we couldn't hit dates in the past, then we clearly don't know what we're talking about. The fact that these missed deadlines are the direct result of poor management and the practice of ignoring the technical staff is always overlooked or denied. It's a tricky business saying "I told you so" to people who directly or indirectly have control over your paycheck. Their position on the food chain also allows management to simply stonewall programmers, denying any responsibility in the poorly considered schedule and placing all the blame on the development team. They outrank us, and therefore tend to get away with it. It ain't fair, but it's the way it is.

Business people also tend to dismiss the opinions of technical workers due to the backgrounds involved. Programmers rarely have MBAs. Management figures that, when it comes to business decisions, they're the ones who are trained to make such calls because it's their area of expertise. This is difficult to deal with because they consider everything to be a business decision. Consequently, software developers are treated like small children who just aren't grown up enough yet to realize that they don't know anything.

The "human wave" approach also causes its fair share of missed dates. Assuming that the company is large enough to have a good pool of coders to assign to a given project, many managers will often base their dates on the assumption that they can solve a problem by simply throwing more bodies at it. They don't really understand the nature of the dependencies that we deal with when coding on a large, multi-programmer project. Neither are they aware of the fact that it's often quicker and easier to have one person write a section of code than to try and share it among three. Instead, management typically sees the problem no differently than a factory production issue: if you have one person painting little wooden ducks all day, he can produce a reasonably predictable amount of decoys by quitting time. Therefore, if you have a hundred people painting little wooden ducks, by quitting time you'll have enough decoys to distract the entire migrating population of North America. If only it were so simple in programming. The fact that it's not matters little to the manager who ignores his techies. On the positive side, at least we don't have to make our software quack.

Abusive management is another project killer. When I was a younger man, I did a wide variety of things for a living, including working in factories and shipyards. I even flipped burgers. Most of these were little more than minimum-wage jobs. In my later days as a programmer, I noticed an interesting trend. Factory workers are very often managed by intimidation and abuse. They are made to feel inferior, yelled at, belittled, and driven like cattle. For the most part, you don't see this sort of behavior in professional circles. It struck me as an interesting curiosity that the more money I made, the less I was micromanaged and abused. And let me tell you, folks, if you think you catch some disrespect as a programmer, you need to do a tour of duty as a blue collar worker.

However, although this statement is true in general, it is not true without exception. People are people no matter where you find them in life, and managers are no exception. In our business, it's not hard to find examples of those who abuse their power and the people they control. Such miscreants will use threats, intimidation, and everything short of physical violence to cow the development team into doing their bidding. This is often an issue of unpaid overtime and a mandate of doing it…or else, although it may manifest itself in any area where programmers are forced to do that which they would otherwise avoid. Of course, we all know what the "or else" part means. Not only are such managers just not nice people, they're also not very smart. They assume that if they just demand loudly enough the deadlines will be met. That doesn't change the facts and realities of a poorly considered date, however, so the inevitable result is a slipped schedule and an unhappy group of developers. This type of manager never realizes that happy workers are always more productive than unhappy ones.

Of course, regardless of whether the date comes from highly accurate technical estimates or from a manager wanting to deliver on the birthday of his pet cocker spaniel, there is often little or no margin for error in the timeline for the unexpected. If our industry has any absolutes, the one thing that you can always count on is the fact that at least one thing will unexpectedly go wrong within the lifetime of a project. There is no way to predict it and no possibility of a contingency plan. You just have to wing it when it happens, put out the fire, and move on. However, no matter how adept a team is at managing the occasional crisis, if there's no room in the schedule for such events, the date will be missed.

The practice of casual estimates also creates problems for a project. One practice that both management and developers alike are guilty of is shooting from the hip. When considering either a full-blown project or a specific set of functionality, the estimating process is started and ended with the phrase, "No problem, that should take only a couple of weeks." I've also heard developers offer the equivalent: "Well, we've never worked with the XYZ technology before, but it looks pretty straightforward." The unpleasant truth of the matter is that casual estimating is often the result of laziness. Crunching numbers isn't nearly as much fun as coding the motion detector and early warning system that the night watchman wanted. So, the tendency is to say whatever is needed to make that pesky person asking for estimates go away. When the deadline crunch comes, and it will, the night watchman will no doubt be hoping that you got the early warning system coded at the beginning of the project. His trusty attack Chihuahua has already been updating his resume, keeping one eye on that fifth-floor window just to be on the safe side.

Many times, a marketing or management type will ask for "just a rough ball-park figure" at the beginning of a new project. Many an unwary developer has fallen into this trap. Even though the requesting party assures them that it's just a number to help them get a feel for the duration, the next thing you know, marketing has made announcements in every major trade publication on the planet trumpeting the new version of your product due to greet the masses on the date derived from your extremely rough and unresearched estimate. Once the date has been announced to the entire free world, management naturally considers it the gospel, and the developers are left to figure out how to make it happen. The local pizza delivery companies, who monitor the programming trade press with great enthusiasm, couldn't be more pleased.

A common mistake that in retrospect seems obvious to the point of simplicity is failing to factor in time for installation, integration, and other peripheral issues that must occur in the fielding of any software system. Programmers tend to think strictly in terms of coding, whereas management…well, we're not sure that they think at all when it comes to scheduling. It matters little, though, for in the end it must all be accomplished, and it all takes time.

In a similar fashion, there is almost never any time allocated for technical documentation, that is, the design-oriented documentation used by programmers for development and maintenance. Once a project is complete, most programmers don't want to deal with any of that boring documentation stuff, they just want to move on to coding the next gizmo. Actually, they usually want to get in at least one decent night's sleep, but that's another matter. Failure to update technical documentation may not hurt you on 1.0, but it'll impact 2.0 tremendously. Heaven forbid you should lose a critical developer at any point in the process before that section has been etched in paper. Of course, the maintenance programmers will also be extremely inconvenienced if they have to go on a bug hunt without a road map. I've heard some interesting stories regarding inconvenienced maintenance programmers, but it's worth mentioning that not all of them stockpile automatic weapons.

Merely having the initial design documentation—assuming you were given any time for that to begin with—doesn't get you off the hook. Something will change during the implementation to render it all out of date. An inaccurate road map is sometimes worse than no map at all.

Customer-driven deadlines are another source of difficulty for those of us trying to kick out a solid system on time. Following is a summary of a conversation that I've heard so many times in my career that it's not even funny anymore. "Well, I know you guys said it would take six months to build this system, but our most important customer says that if they can't have it by next month then we'll lose their business. So we told them no problem. It's no problem, right?" Note that these comments are typically delivered as the manager or marketing rep is walking steadily towards the door. Your protests are usually silenced by the noise of the door closing.

This theme has many variations, of course, and it's not always customer driven. It may be someone further up the food chain who declares an arbitrary date after they've asked you how long it will take to deliver. It makes about the same amount of sense regardless of the origination. It effectively boils down to your superiors telling you that they've decided to completely ignore everything you've told them regarding the timetable. They will then naturally expect you to embrace the schedule and be positive, enthusiastic, and motivated about hitting the deadline. Any other response results in your being declared "not a team player." At such times, I've reasoned that being a team player might not be such a bad thing after all if it gave me easy access to baseball bats.

## Vague Definition of Requirements

The next culprit in our lineup of seedy characters tends to appear early in the development process. While known by some less flattering names, we'll simply refer to it as the "vague definition of requirements" out of politeness. In the beginning, someone decides they want the software developers to create a program. That's all well and good, and of course programmers are typically quite enthusiastic about such things. However, asking them to write a system that allows the company to "take orders from customers via the Internet" is just a little on the fuzzy side for most of us. Unfortunately, the requirements are frequently not much more specific than that. Oh, you may get a little bit of detail, but it all too often ends up sounding like, "You know, get the customer information and the products they want to buy, and then charge their credit card." However, the interesting part of this is that, for many developers, that seems to define the requirements well enough to get started. They reason that quantity, product, price, billing, and shipping information should be obvious, and really now, how hard could charging a credit card via the Internet be?

As the seasoned programmer knows all too well, even the simplest of software has a host of details, with the answer to one question significantly altering all the questions that follow. Nonetheless, either through an optimism that knows no bounds or at the urging of management, many a project goes straight to coding with little more than these vague specifications. What follows is an extreme exercise in scope creep. Actually, it can't be referred to as creep with any fairness because the scope was never really defined to begin with. Instead, what you'll find is a never-ending stream of modifications to what the program should do, how the user interface should look, what the inputs and outputs need to be, and so on. In addition to the mess this makes of your schedule, it also makes a mess of your code. If you don't know what the program will do in the beginning, you will forever be wedging in little bits of code here and there in a completely undesigned manner. How could it be otherwise? The bit of code you're wedging in at the moment wasn't a requirement when you wrote the existing parts of the system. For that matter, it probably wasn't a requirement ten minutes ago.

The scheduling implications are obvious. It's almost completely unheard of in our business for management to ask us for a system without attaching a timetable of some sort. That means that this project has a deadline. As is the nature of deadlines everywhere, the requirements will change on you in an almost hourly fashion, but the deadline will not budge an inch. Deadlines are rather stubborn creatures and don't care much for being moved around once they're comfortable. Consequently, if you don't have your requirements etched in stone from the very beginning, you can give up any hopes you had of actually finishing the project on time.

Above and beyond our desire to just jump right into the coding, we end up with fuzzy specifications for a number of other reasons. One of these is again a matter of communications: domain experts are rarely technical, and programmers aren't always social. Someone has to do the translation, and there are very few in the company who speak both languages. In a well-organized shop, those who cook up the requirements aren't allowed to just grab a developer in the hallway and start requesting new features. Instead, they typically interface with the project manager through a series of meetings. The project manager then passes the requirements down to the developers. Sometimes select programmers are included in the requirements meetings, at least in the later stages, in an effort to get things spelled out in more detail. Ultimately, however, there must be at least one person who has both the ability and the responsibility to take what the domain experts are saying and translate it to geek speak. The fact that such a liaison is all too typically absent in development departments makes it extremely difficult to get the specifics required for a spec that won't move.

Impatience is another common reason that requirements gathering is given little serious attention. Management wants the program tomorrow if at all possible, and today by lunch would be even better. Explaining to them that there needs to be weeks of conversations before the software can enter even the design stage is met with little enthusiasm. In defense of management, though, the programmers aren't any better. Sitting around all day listening to a bunch of users talk about what they want is boring at best, and frustrating more often than not when the discussions venture into the unrealistic. Once again, we'd rather be coding. The end result is that no one, neither management nor development, wants to take the time required to really nail down the requirements in black and white. Because no one pushes for it, it just doesn't happen. Everyone is a loser as a result. Management won't get what they want, when they want it. And you know what's going to happen to the programmers about halfway into the project. Keep that sleeping bag by your desk. You're not going home any time soon.

All too frequently, even in shops with management willing to let the developers go through a fairly intensive design phase, a formal requirements phase is not taken seriously and is moreover deemed a waste of time. Those requesting the project will tend to speak in high-level terms, and any efforts by the programmers to get all the wagons in a circle and hash out the details meet with little success. As astounding as it may be to the professional software developer who has read all of the top design methodology books, most non-techies don't even know what a requirements phase is. The fact that it should be approached in a manner no less structured and detailed than the software design itself is equally alien to your user community. This makes it difficult to get people to commit time and effort to meetings, write formal documents, or do anything more labor intensive than standing around the water cooler dreaming up an ever-growing wish list of cool features.

Another reason that we meet with resistance when asking for formal and detailed requirements documents has nothing to do with impatience and everything to do with politics. The fact that they couldn't coax "Hello, World" out of a compiler does not make your user community stupid. They are far from it, indeed. In most cases, when it comes to internal company politics and maneuvering, they leave programmers in the dust, pocket protectors spinning idly in the wind. They're aware of the fact that anything committed to paper today could be trotted out to their disadvantage tomorrow. (The spoken word is much more difficult to prove.) A great many people in your company have an agenda all their own. Those who are savvy and determined about it take their business just as seriously as we take our debugging. Should things go wrong, a paper trail can be used to establish blame, and it can also give fair warning to an opponent with a different plan for your project. Either way, it's a political liability. Those who maneuver have nothing to gain by committing to paper, which gives them no reason to take on a potential liability. Although it may sound silly or paranoid to you that they wish to avoid putting things in writing, it's the reality far more often than you may realize. Because of this, we can add yet another obstacle to our need for a detailed and well-documented requirements phase.

Turf wars also contribute to problems of this sort. In all but the tiniest of companies, multiple departments are typically involved in the software you develop, particularly if it's for internal use rather than the commercial market. Each of these departments will, without a doubt, have their own agenda regarding what the priorities should be for your project. The development team is typically at the center of this struggle, as each party tries to convince either the programmers or the upper management in control of the project to see things their way. The ensuing conflict and politics do little to contribute to a well-ordered and balanced requirements document.

Of course, yet another entertaining aspect to the search for the elusive specification has more to do with being trendy than with practicality. Some of those involved in shaping your software may specify that particular technologies be used and promote this technology as a part of the requirements, regardless of its suitability for the task at hand. Never mind that choosing technologies has no place in the requirements phase in the first place. It's similar to inverted project management in which a participant decides that some specific network protocol or client-server architecture should be used because it's the buzzword of the day and then tries to force the rest of the project into whatever boundaries that this decision creates. If there's no one to stand up and firmly explain that requirements gathering is about *what*, not *how*, you may be stuck with this millstone around your neck from the very beginning.

## Inadequate Time for Analysis and Design

If it's hard to believe that companies would shortchange the requirements-gathering process, it simply boggles the mind that they're just as quick to dismiss the formal design phase. How anyone could be expected to deliver a solid, stable, expandable, and maintainable system without the benefit of an extremely well thought out design simply escapes me. Actually, I suppose that's not entirely true. Although we truly do require a sincere design effort to have any hopes of delivering a good system, I understand why we're expected to skip it all too well.

Probably one of the most common perceptions that prevent us from having the time we need for design is management's view that, if we're not coding, we're not really getting anything done. Consequently, time spent on analysis and design is considered a waste of good programming hours. I don't really understand how it is that they equate typing with work and yet relegate thinking to the equivalent of standing around the kitchen drinking coffee. As an aside, I might mention that I've solved a great many technical problems in my career doing just that, standing in the kitchen drinking coffee and thinking my way out of the sand trap. Nonetheless, a manager's typical mindset would lead to the quick conclusion that I must have way too much time on my hands and therefore need another project or two. As a result, I've developed hearing and instincts that leave gazelle in the dust. I can smell middle management three corridors away and be safely down the road before they hit the kitchen.

One of my programmer friends, not known for his diplomacy, handles things a bit differently. As a contractor at one of the large international corporations, he hit a technical problem that required some thought before any further coding took place. As is his style, he started wandering the halls. Having known him for many years, I recognize the distant look in his eyes and tend to just leave him alone when he wanders by in such a state. I know that he's fourteen levels deep in his brain working through the intricacies of the bit of code that he'll soon sit down and bang out with a ferocity reminiscent of a WWII machine gun nest. It's unwise to bug a guy in such a state. He also happens to have long blond hair down to his waist and probably doesn't look like the poster boy for Corporate America. So, he strolled slowly down the hallway, casually looking at the artwork because his eyes had to have something to keep them entertained while the mental process got all the attention. Suddenly, into the aisle pops a rather self-important middle manager who clearly assumes that some homeless derelict has stumbled in from the street and is trying to decide exactly which piece of art to steal. Clearly someone who was used to being obeyed, he confronted the distracted programmer. In a tone of voice that more clearly indicated the fact that my friend should clear out before he called the police, he huffs, "Can I help you?" The epitome of the classic, blunt programmer, my friend simply looked him in the eye, replied "No," stepped around him and kept walking as the manager fumed from behind.

Above and beyond the fact that the techie in question more closely resembles an invading Norseman than he does a high-level software professional, the message was reinforced quite clearly once more: if you're not coding, you're not working. Thinking doesn't count. It certainly doesn't seem to be a requirement in management, based on what I've seen at some of these companies. Because it seems that, the bigger the company, the more one encounters this mindset. It could even be argued that, in these circles, the absence of thinking is a precursor to financial success. As an aside, I'm thinking that another of my programmer friends who advocates a career change to herding sheep in New Zealand may be right on the money. At the very least, if you have a bad day at the office, the source of your irritation translates nicely into dinner and a warm pair of socks.

Why is it that thinking isn't considered a productive use of a developer's time? Maybe it's a trust issue. If you're banging on a keyboard and source code appears on the screen in front of you, it's obvious that you're engaged in a useful activity. However, because thinking isn't visible (and I'm sure the planet is the better for it), there's just no telling what you might be up to. You might be thinking about your girlfriend, if you still have one after the overtime from that last release fiasco, or you could be fantasizing about the latest cool video game. I suppose it's easier for management to picture us geeks doing something like that than having a girlfriend, anyway. The fact that you could be working through the various relationships necessary for the database system you're currently involved in never seems to occur to them. Regardless of the reason, it's a real problem. Show me a programmer who codes before he spends serious time thinking, and I'll show you a guy who's going to be working 22-hour days come release time.

Perhaps another reason that design is deemed wasted time is that management doesn't have an understanding of the relationship between poor design and the countless hours it costs in debugging, maintenance, and support. A computer program is not a physical structure with components that can be touched and examined with a magnifying glass, and so it's perhaps hard for some to draw the clear lines of cause and effect. When the Titanic struck an iceberg, it was obvious to those on deck who felt the ship tear against the ice that the resulting gash in the side meant a night treading water and hoping that the sharks had been fed recently. We have no such irrefutable proof available to demonstrate that giving us eight hours to design a software system that took a year to code is the reason that it's suffering the same fate in the marketplace as the aforementioned unsinkable vessel. Consequently, it is very difficult to hold management accountable for the disaster.

Not realizing that the correct and productive development of software is four parts thinking and one part typing, management is quick to dismiss our requests for a design phase with a response that seems an exercise in the obvious to them. "We don't have time for all this design phase stuff. We need this program now." In other words, instead of having fun and drawing all those pictures on the wall, it's time to get to work. So start typing.

Again touching on what is becoming a common theme, there's a failure to communicate. Programmers lack the ability to translate analysis and design deliverables into something meaningful to management. It would be nice if we could just ask management to trust us, but in reality that's not terribly practical. Ultimately, because no one can (or will) take the time to relate the results of an abbreviated design phase to corporate red ink rising from maintenance and support expenses, our request for adequate up-front design is simply denied. Although the company will end up paying the price in dollars and cents, the programmers will pay with fatigue and probably the occasional sleep deprivation induced hallucination. I'm sure that's why we throw monitors out of windows. That's my story, and I'm sticking to it. I've seen what that Chihuahua can do when he's agitated.

As is becoming apparent, though, it's never all management's fault. Coupled with our desire to dive into the code, programmers often fear that a lengthy analysis and design phase will give management a chance to change their collective mind and drop the project. If something's quickly coded and shown, the project's harder to drop because "it's almost done." If you've ever worked in a shop where middle and upper management were rather capricious in their approach to software projects, starting one only to cancel it and start another just a few weeks into the process, this won't seem like such a far-fetched defense tactic. Although it's true that this is often effective in saving a project from the scrap heap, it's rarely worth the cost. I think I'd rather just let them cancel my project every four weeks. At least that way I won't have to face the deadline insanities that are sure to arise in a shoot-from-the-hip project. The reason many programmers don't feel the same way is that we tend to get emotionally attached to our work, like artists. That's an easy trap to fall into, and a costly one.

We also fall short in another area. Once we've asked for time for a full design phase, management naturally wants to know how long such an effort will take. When we reply with vague answers that amount to the fact that we really don't know, it's not surprising that our request is denied. No manager in his right mind is going to sign a blank check. Would you?

As in many other aspects of life, often what we find is not a complete lack of time for design but rather simply an extremely inadequate amount. In the case of many formal analysis and design approaches, the time required to do the full-blown approach and all the charts, documents, and procedures is simply not realistic in terms of the time we're given. The choices are to either cancel the project or use an abbreviated analysis and design phase. If the team doesn't have experience using a condensed but effective design approach, the results are typically somewhat chaotic and of little value.

Of course, another contributing factor to our inability to get what we want when it comes to time allocation is the fact that management doesn't take programmers seriously when making business plans. Programmers (forgetting where their paychecks come from) also don't take management seriously and make little effort to speak management's language. We can't really afford that kind of attitude because our position on the food chain makes it obvious who will win and who will lose in these contests. However, programmers are technically oriented people, and rare is the developer who has (or is willing to develop) the skills needed to make management sit up and listen.

## Sometimes the Enemy Is Within

Poor project management is also a high-ranking officer in the enemy lines. Wouldn't you think that the project managers would be on our side? In fairness, while we all spent a considerable amount of time and effort to become competent programmers, those who find themselves in project manager positions, officially or unofficially, have often been drafted. Whether they migrate down from middle management or are the result of programmers who were too slow to keep from getting recruited, these are often people who end up in charge of a software development effort and yet have no real training in the process. The end result is often a project that's destined to implode due to poor internal support as much as for any other reason.

One of the first mistakes that those new to project management make is in creating timelines with the assumption that an eight-hour day means eight hours of coding. This even happens to those of us who got sucked into the position out of the ranks of programmers. Once you find yourself staring at graphs, timelines, and other such seemingly bureaucratic stuff, it's easy to glaze over a bit and start thinking in nice, tidy boxes such as eight-hour coding days and forty-hour work weeks. It happens. The reality, of course, is that we never get eight hours of coding in unless we're working thirteen or fourteen hours a day. The result is more missed deadlines, this time not because of the hours it took to do the job, but due to incorrect calendar projections.

Also included in this type of misfortune are not taking holidays, vacations, and sick time into account when laying out the milestones. The productivity of technical leads who take on a full coding load as well as project management duties is also suspect. Being the lead on even a small team results in far more interruptions to your day than you would have thought when you optimistically put yourself down for a full share of the coding workload. The only way such people get in eight hours of coding is if they do it when the rest of the team is at home asleep.

Of course, the absolute worst mistake to make with a timeline is to simply not have one. If you don't have a plan for where you're going, how you're going to get there, and what your progress is along the way, be prepared for some surprises.

Even worse than not having a timeline, however, is the habit of developing software by sequentially putting out fires, which is more aptly known as crisis management. The frantic and harried project manager, moving from one mini disaster to the next, follows an endless pattern of pulling the programmers from one task to the next without completing any of them. The conversation typically amounts to "Stop everything and do this!" only to be followed a day later by "Now stop everything and do this!" Naturally, nothing ever gets completed with this approach, with the possible exception of the programmer's résumé.

If the project manager lacks the necessary skills and ends up performing poor task partitioning or dependency ordering, the schedule will suffer as well. Another such issue is that of leaving integration testing between modules to the last minute. Sparks inevitably fly at such points, and a little extra time is required to smooth out the rough edges so that all the various subsystems play nice with each other.

Because so few shops actually have a testing team staffed by experienced professionals, keeping up with bugs, enhancement requests, and so on typically falls to the project manager. It's unreasonable to expect them to perform the same functions that a quality assurance manager would, but some projects are unwittingly sabotaged by failing to implement any form of organization in this area, such as a simple bug-tracking database.

A lack of general management skills can also hurt a team, such as the common scenario of frequent, long, and rambling meetings. Burdening programmers with unnecessary bureaucratic procedures just for the sake of the paperwork is another mistake common to those with a background in middle management rather than development. The project manager who operates in a vacuum, not taking the feedback from developers seriously, can also create deadline difficulties by making promises to management without consulting the programmers first.

However, one of the worst things that a project manager can do to a project is contributing to programmer burnout due to constant overtime. I actually worked at a shop once where the person in charge told me, with a straight face, that they didn't have any crunch time at the end of a project because they encouraged their coders to "do all the overtime up front." I think I managed to make it out of the room before the laughter came out. The line he was trying to sell me would no doubt result in my working overtime in the beginning of the project and once again at the inevitable crunch time. (They weren't immune to scope creep.) So, in other words, they were trying to sucker their programmers into constant, nonstop overtime. I didn't stay there too long.

Although a bad project manager can certainly throw things off track from the very beginning, it's possible for a seasoned professional to derail a perfectly good project even at the last minute. I once found myself as the de facto project manager on an effort that ran about a year and a half. I had a very small team, all of whom were top-notch, seasoned programmers. Early on we adopted a few systems to keep us organized, including a bug-tracking database, and for the first fourteen months or so we had an uncanny track record of meeting our milestones. No one on the team required any babysitting, and we all just followed the procedures we had put into place and got the job done.

Towards the end of the project, one of the other project managers who was an employee of the company (I was a contractor) decided to assume control of our project. I didn't bother to fight it as we were nearly done, and frankly I didn't mind someone else shuffling the paper for the last mile. This was a significant tactical error. Our code, which wasn't complete enough to be called beta, was given to our most hostile customer because they were screaming for it. The project team that ours had replaced failed to deliver to them even a year past the deadline, hence their demise.

What followed was a series of crisis management decisions as our coding schedule was disrupted and reduced to fixing bugs or implementing features that the customer made noise about. Further, the project manager expressly refused to utilize our bug-tracking database, for reasons that escape me to this day. Instead, each bug was distributed by writing up a document in a word processor complete with a screen shot. This was then printed out, additional notes were written on the printout in red ink, and this was then photocopied; the subsequent black-and-white copies were then distributed in piles on all of our desks. I'll leave the rest of the story to your imagination. This was at a period of time when the Internet was just entering the public consciousness, so in the end, of course, another team convinced management that our project should be scrapped and they should rewrite it from scratch for Web browsers. Given the disaster that had befallen our efforts, this was probably one of those rare moments when the irrational logic of Corporate America actually did some good by putting a wounded project out of its misery.

# No Time or Resources for Testing

Without a doubt my personal favorite target, though, is the lack of a professional quality assurance team in a shop. One would think that, with the incredible complexities inherent in even a moderate software system, companies would be extremely motivated to do a thorough and professional job of testing prior to fielding the system. But then, logic does not always drive the management decisions in our business. One of the most overwhelmingly consistent mistakes I've seen in shop after shop is the omission of time and resources for testing.

With the "logic" that I've just come to accept as normal in the business world, hiring professional testers is considered by most companies to be an unnecessary expense. How they justify the money spent on extended software maintenance and all those tech support calls is a mystery to me, but then I never was all that good at accounting. In general, management perceives programmers as a highly skilled set of workers, possessing the talents necessary to deal with any complex technical task. However, they don't view testing as a terribly difficult or technical undertaking and therefore reason that, if we were smart enough to write the program, then we should have no difficulty in testing it.

I will heartily agree that coding can be a complex task. However, most managers grossly underestimate the difficulty of comprehensive quality assurance. I'll take coding over testing any day of the week. The idea of forming an organized plan to exercise every aspect of a nontrivial software system makes me twitch. I wouldn't hire a plumber to tune up my car, and I'd certainly want a trained professional if the electricity in my house needed attention. Nonetheless, when it comes to the incredibly daunting task of regression testing, the business world sees no need for specialized talents. Why? Actually there's a herd of reasons, but they never seem to hold still long enough for a good group photo.

One of the best is the perception that the programmers can test it. I'm afraid the business people just don't understand the division of labor here. I'm adept at *creating* bugs. If I could catch them just as easily, well, I wouldn't be adept at creating bugs now, would I? Of course, management often takes the stance that anyone in the office who has a few spare minutes and can type at least seventeen words per minute can test it. How hard can it be? Failing that, of course, we'll just beta test it and let our customers find the bugs for us. Never mind what that makes the product look like to the outside world. Even though it's branded "beta" in big, bold letters, if the product flames out in the field it's going to get a bad rap. But, then, why bother testing it at all? If the customers find bugs in the release product, we can always just put a patch up on the Web site, right? These are only a few of the justifications for not hiring professionals to do a job that requires a high degree of skill and training. You'll notice that all of these solutions are approaches that don't require the spending of additional funds. I'm sure that's just a coincidence.

Still, these aren't the only obstacles to getting our software thoroughly tested before it hits the streets. Management, not being technical, truly has no concept of how tremendously difficult it is to exhaustively test all code paths. Often, they don't even know that there's a completely different discipline of technical workers who specialize in testing software. For those who do know, they often find that software QA is such a small field due to lack of demand that finding truly qualified testers is extremely difficult. I once was given the go-ahead by a company I worked for to hire a tester after much lobbying and fighting on the part of my team. Because we could hire only one, we looked for a senior-level person, and we had a reasonable budget to do so. This was in one of the major American cities with a good base of technical workers. In the course of a year, we went through three people. None of them even knew how to write a test plan. Writing up a bug with detailed steps to reproduce was pushing the envelope. This is an unfortunate side effect of supply and demand: with few jobs offered by companies, naturally very few people seriously enter the field.

Thus, much of the testing process is left to the project managers and teams. Even if you can find someone who understands how to set up an organized bug-tracking system (yeah, I thought it was obvious too, but apparently not), there are still many obstacles to creating some homegrown testing procedures. Typically, management doesn't want to spend the money for additional computers and the various operating systems and platforms that are needed to realistically test the software in all scenarios. Again, it's perceived as a business expenditure that doesn't bring any benefit in terms of dollars and cents gained. There's also the mantra of management when it comes to programming: they don't want to pay testers out of the development budget because, if it's not coding, it's not software development.

Oddly enough, another reason that we don't have better testing systems in place is that some programmers actually don't want people finding bugs in their code. It's probably just an ego thing, or the fear that if people find bugs in your code then maybe management will think you should be fired. I had a friend who worked for another of these large, international companies in an environment where they actually did pay for a QA team. Unfortunately, the system they set in place for motivation was a bit counter productive. The testers got points for each bug they found, and, for each bug that was found in their code, the developers lost points. As you might have guessed, these points translated to bonus dollars. Of course, there was a highly adversarial relationship between the testers and the programmers. I can't fathom why a company would want to foster that sort of confrontational environment. Personally, when someone finds a particularly glaring bug in my code, my first reaction is gratitude. It's going to show up sooner or later, and I'd much rather someone find it now so I can fix it. Found a bug? Thanks! Better here than in the field!

The biggest reason of all, though, that we don't have a professional QA department in every shop is that programmers simply don't fight for it. We fight for design considerations, technologies, tools, and even for nice, big monitors (not the cheesy little ones that tend to be flung out the fifth-floor windows during crunch time). What we don't fight for is testers, and we pay for it on every release. The business bottom line pays for it as well, although that's something that our MBA friends fail to recognize.

## Poor Company Management

In fact, although it's not really a technical matter at all, poor business management in general can have far-reaching effects on a software development project. Even though the Suits provide the paychecks and run the company, bad decisions at this level can sabotage a project before it even gets started.

Constantly canceling projects and starting new ones can make a mess of the occasional effort that actually does make it through to completion. More often than not, those programs that do see the light of day end up being some strange, mutated beast that's a hybrid of the fourteen failed projects that came before. It doesn't take much imagination to know what sort of a fiasco this can be. Perhaps companies that manage themselves in this manner think that they're showing nimble reflexes and an ability to quickly adapt to each new set of circumstances. I'm sure that sounded good on paper when they were studying for their MBA. However, out here on the streets, it's nothing more elegant than a well-ordered series of train wrecks. I've known of major corporations that reorganize their departments a couple of times a year almost as if by decree. The result is invariably a host of partially completed projects being canceled due to the restructuring. This in turn brings about the obligatory political activities as people vie for control of these orphaned efforts. Unfortunately, rather than just letting them die an ignoble death, the politically savvy often manage to resurrect a project and morph it into their own plan. This is more disastrous than the worst scope creep, as the existing code base is augmented with a new set of directives that may have little to do with the existing design and architecture. If you remember the old adage that a camel is nothing more than a racehorse designed by a committee, you've got the idea. For a developer who happens to be on one of these teams, it's an endless exercise in confusion and frustration of the highest degree. People always think I'm kidding about monitors and fifth-floor windows.

Following the buzzword of the week can also lead to frequent requirements changes. This has little to do with design or architectural issues, and programming isn't the only community with buzzwords. For the management-oriented worker, there is a never-ending stream of management trends promoted in the marketplace. Each of these is touted as the salvation of businesses everywhere and is eagerly embraced by companies that give more heed to talking the talk than walking the walk. If you're involved in meetings with these guys, you may have a hard time keeping a straight face. So many of the phrases you hear spouted with much seriousness sound so phony and shallow that even a first-grader would catch it. Others are pompous, overworded descriptions of an obvious fact. I encountered one example of this kind of thinking working for yet another large corporation.

I was to develop some communications code on the PC side of the house that would talk to minicomputers in a different department. The job was fairly small in scope, and all that I really needed to do was sit down with the communications guy who had coded the interface to which I'd be talking. This wasn't rocket science. So, a meeting with the other programmer was arranged. However, because it involved programmers from two different and warring departments, it just wasn't that simple.

My manager, sharp and politically savvy, knew what was about to happen and volunteered to come along and watch my back. I've learned to trust this guy in such matters and so readily agreed. Attending the meeting were my manager's boss (who was middle management of the most stereotypical kind), his counterpart in the other team, the upper-level managers responsible for both of these middle managers, and the vice president in charge of the upper managers. Five, count 'em, five levels of managers, including a vice president, all gathered together in a meeting at which I simply needed to ask another programmer for a couple of header files and the description of the interface API.

I had pretty much reached the end of my patience on this particular gig anyway and consequently wasn't feeling very diplomatic because my ten-minute meeting now went on for an hour as these managers all went through their dances and posturing while the two programmers just sat there listening. Finally, seeing a break in the action, I asked the room full of Suits what on earth they were doing here as I still hadn't had the chance to have the conversation I called the original meeting for. It was curtly explained to me (as if to a small child) that, although I certainly couldn't be expected to understand management matters, it was important for all concerned to "sign off on the process." That was one of their catch phrases. I don't remember if anyone other than my programming counterpart on the other team saw me roll my eyes. As I had finished the project for which I'd taken the original contract, I decided then and there that it was time for a new gig.

Bureaucracy and maintaining the status quo create a corporate culture in which the resistance to change takes on an almost fanatical pitch. Whether it's a set of procedures that were handed down on stone tablets from the company founder or it's a management style similar to the story I just told, keeping in step with the way things are done is mandatory for anyone wishing to climb the corporate ladder. You must look like everyone else, adopt the same mannerisms and procedures, and in general be seen as someone who follows the established practices, regardless of how unproductive or even disastrous they may be. In such an environment, excellence and innovation are not just discouraged. They're actively punished. We've all had to suffer through the proliferation of the phrase "thinking outside of the box," but the simple truth is that the minute you do you may as well paint a series of red concentric circles on your posterior, for you've become target practice. Anything that doesn't follow the norm is suspect and makes you subject to reprimand or worse. Should you actually follow the intent of the catch phrase and get *way* outside the box, things are not going to go well with your career.

I once worked on a small team that had the task of kicking out a database system for internal company use. Like any such venture, coming up with the perfect user interface to make it easy to grasp and manage a complex collection of data was a challenge. I worked for one of those guys who actually believed in pursuing excellence and didn't even own a box. In other words, he already had a reputation as a troublemaker, at least as Corporate America saw it. Being a video game enthusiast, he observed that in today's Hollywood-production-quality games that the user had to deal with a ton of information, all in a real-time environment that meant you either got the information you needed quickly or you were soon to be little more than a wisp of computer-generated smoke wafting to the heavens as your enemy stomped on to the next conquest. From that perspective, it made perfectly logical sense for him to show us one of his favorite games to point out the user interface techniques they used to accomplish this. So, here we are, three developers gathered in a cubicle around a monitor deep in the heart of Corporate America playing with a very conspicuous game. Naturally, my manager's boss chose that moment to happen by the cube. Needless to say, he wasn't impressed with our manager's initiative or original thinking.

Of course, while not a direct result of this incident (it was just one of a long string in this person's career), it probably isn't too surprising that he's no longer with that company. Ultimately, in the corporate world, those who promote change are labeled troublemakers and demoted to positions where they can't cause any more trouble. Although this guy was nimble enough to avoid demotions, neither did he advance and he was frequently the target for harassment by middle management. It's only natural that he would eventually seek greener pastures, and so a company loses yet another individual who could have made them more profitable. Worse still, when he left, the company probably felt that they were better off. It's a strange world.

## Internal Politics

If poor company management and business practices are the officers in the front lines of the enemy, then internal company politics is the common soldier. Decisions are almost never made because it's the best thing from a business point of view. They're made because they further the interests and career of the decision maker. These two concepts—doing what's best for the business or what's best for the career—are often completely at odds with each other.

As anyone who has ever witnessed a real shooting war will readily attest, such conflicts are a monument to pointless waste and destruction. There's little difference in the business world. Although we rarely break out the automatic weapons to solve our conflicts (well, if we forget about maintenance programmers for the moment, anyway), there is still no end to the amount of time and resources wasted in the petty struggles of departmental turf wars. In the end, it's all about individual grabs for power. Somewhere in the process, though, it seems to be forgotten that we were hired to develop software.

Consider a common example. Your team and another have both developed projects for internal use. A new company-wide software initiative is underway to consolidate all the functionality of the many disparate systems into one cohesive system. This, of course, will establish the team who develops it as dominant and relegate the other to a status of irrelevance, reducing it to perform the unpleasant tasks that no other programmer wants to do. The programmers may even be absorbed by the winning team to serve a similar function. If you work in either of these two teams, the outcome of who gets the project and who doesn't is an extremely significant factor in how pleasant your job will be in the months or years to come.

Every kind of business and even personal political tactic you can imagine get employed as the two teams compete. None of this has much to do with writing code at the moment, but it will most certainly affect the code you write in the future. If you don't believe it, just sit on your hands and wait for the outcome. If you don't fight, you will without a doubt lose and most likely find yourself relegated to life as a maintenance programmer in the deepest, darkest bowels of some system that no one wants to touch. Suddenly, politics have everything to do with the code you write. The fact that these obscure maintenance jobs are sometimes on systems that manage inventory control for automatic weapons may explain a thing or two, but you're still not going to have any fun with your coding.

Of course, similar struggles can arise within your own team as each member jockeys for a position that allows him to work on the sexy new technology, gain control over design, get concessions over which languages to use, and so on. The results are almost always the same. Those who are adept at political maneuvering typically get the juicy assignments while the technical prodigy who stood by silently gets the leftovers, regardless of who has the most appropriate technical skills and experience.

Maneuvering for promotions is another aspect of the same sort of thing. Middle managers with no technical knowledge often want to advance their careers by having control over your department. It expands their kingdom, and in such matters those vying for power consider any addition to the territory a good thing.

Sometimes project managers want to be middle managers and act more like Suits than programmers. Worse still, they forget their most sacred mandate: to protect their programmers from external politics and distractions so that they can code. Even at a lower level, team leads or programmers occasionally think they should be in charge of the current project instead of the project manager. This creates even more games and posturing. How do we ever get any code written in the middle of all of this? Well, sometimes we don't, which is why we should care.

Religious wars over technology and platforms are another common skirmish. Your team does PC development. Another works on mainframes. Each wants the company to use their team as the primary platform for software development. Just as in our example of the struggle for the internal software system project, these platform wars have similar fallout. Additionally, though, people in these conflicts are often true believers, those who sincerely advocate that their platform is superior to all the rest. If the general confusion of turf wars isn't bad enough, you can count on a lot of hurt feelings in this sort of struggle as such people are very emotionally attached to their positions. It may well have been in the midst of just such a scuffle that the first whiteboard eraser was thrown.

Even when we retreat to our secret hiding place of closed-door design meetings, we're still not immune to the effects of maneuvering. Think design meetings aren't political? Many is the poorly considered software feature that was an absolute disaster and yet made it to market only because a better technical solution had a weaker presentation in the meeting. Any time you have a room full of people, you have politics. The people who choose to ignore this fact are always the first victims.

## The Unexpected

Of course, no discussion of the enemy would be complete without mention of The Unexpected. It is one of the few constants in the universe. You can't control it, you can't foresee it, and none of your contingency plans cover it. It just happens and is as inescapable as the sun rising each morning, or the programmer who is still frantically coding away trying to hit an unrealistic deadline when it does. Although you can't adequately position yourself to be immune to it, you can strengthen your ability to cope with it. As simplistic as it sounds, this is often little more than making sure you always have margins in your plans to account for the time it will take when an unannounced little disaster drops by for dinner. Simple though it may be, it's amazing how often companies neglect to do just that.

It is both a truism and an exercise in the obvious to state that you can't really solve your problems until you know exactly what they are. The ground we've covered is by no means comprehensive, but it does bring to light the many factors that conspire against us in our efforts to be productive software developers. Ultimately, the very first survival skill that front-line programmers must possess is the ability to look at their own environments and recognize the dangers and obstacles to developing and delivering quality software. It is only with this heightened perception that we can hope to effectively combat the countless enemies of the professional developer.

# CHAPTER 3

# Good Coding Skills Are Not Enough

But I just wanna be a programmer! Why do I need all of these non-coding skills? Can't I just sit in my cubicle and concentrate on programming?

Sure you can. In fact, the overwhelming majority of programmers worldwide do just that. Of course, the overwhelming majority of programmers worldwide also have an extremely common set of complaints about their jobs. The simple reality of the matter is that your job is probably not anywhere near as good as it could be, and neither is your software. We've already identified a large number of culprits that appear to be responsible for the problems we encounter, but, when it all comes down to the bottom line, *it's your fault*. Ouch. Can I say that? Well, perhaps, if only because I'm safe for the moment from the sting of a whiteboard eraser.

How can all of the shortcomings in your software development shop—so many of which are typically caused by managerial decisions that exhibit about as much common sense as a lima bean—be your fault? Simple. If you sit on your hands and do nothing, then you're part of the problem when you could be part of the solution. Wait, that sounded a bit like one of those trendy catch phrases. Maybe I've been hanging out in Corporate America too long.

If I'm suggesting that you take a more active role in dealing with the issues you face as developers, I suppose it's not that different from asking you to storm a machine gun nest. Of course, all those years of dealing with maintenance programmers has undoubtedly prepared you better for such a task. Still, to be practical about it, anyone taking risks should have a reason for doing so. In other words, what's in it for you?

## What's in It for Me?

Probably one of the biggest hassles in any full-time programmer's career is sacrificing your life to countless hours of unproductive—and very often unpaid—overtime. It's bad enough that you're given a situation where you can't get the job done working forty hours a week. The way most businesses are run, the end result may well be yet another release disaster even if you put in eighty hours a week.

That's not exactly a rewarding experience, particularly if you have to give up your life for it. When we fire up the editor, what we're reaching for is the next killer app. We are artists as much as anything else. To put blood, sweat, and tears into a project (okay, maybe not the former if you don't have to interact with the maintenance programmer) only to have management ship it in a half-baked state can be downright infuriating, and that's with a full night of sleep. I have no desire to work day and night as it is. Doing so on a project destined for failure adds insult to injury.

Along those lines, one of the things that are in it for you as an artist is the ability to ship a better-quality product. Whether your name is in the About box or not, your signature is on every piece of software you ship. We all tend to take a great deal of pride in our accomplishments, so who wants to be associated with anything other than a spectacular success? Do I work for money or for ego? Both. (In that order, for the record, but definitely both.) If you want to be involved in projects that make you proud, you have to do your part to help them survive in the wild.

Actually, I've always had a pretty bad attitude towards companies that take advantage of programmers and expect them to dedicate their every waking minute to the job. Maybe it's because I've been a musician all my life and have seen how nightclubs and other aspects of the music industry tend to pay almost nothing. They get away with this because they know we love music so much that we'd probably play for free and are usually happy to take whatever we can get. A low-paying gig on the weekend is more fun than no gig. Because of this, bar gigs pay today almost exactly what they paid twenty years ago. Really. It's an unfair and predatory practice but is so common that it's become the accepted norm. If you push for more equitable pay, you're simply told that they're not doing anything different than every other venue in town. That's typically true, but it doesn't make it right.

Many software development companies employ this exact approach in dealing with programmers, and for the exact same reasons. We got into this business because we were passionate about programming. We tend to do it at home in the evenings and on weekends just for fun. With the same predatory attitude, these sweatshops take advantage of our love for development and make continual overtime an accepted norm.

I have a friend who is a programmer working in such an environment. In fairness, I must say that he was told up front in the interview that, due to the stock options giving the employees a sense of ownership in the company, they hired only those people who were willing to dedicate above-average hours to the job. Nonetheless, he's been killing himself the past few weeks working late hours. I made some of the usual jokes with him regarding end-of-the-project crunch time and asked when the release date was. His answer floored me, even though it's nothing new. He said there was no deadline; it was simply a corporate culture. If you weren't putting in all the extra hours, you just weren't working hard enough.

When there's an honest-to-goodness crisis, you can count on me each time, every time. I'll be the guy with the sleeping bag next to my desk. Obviously, my friend sees it as worthwhile, and he's a pretty sharp guy for whom I have a lot of respect. However, this sort of open-ended abuse of programmers constitutes a gig that I wouldn't touch with a ten-foot pole.

Consequently, for years now I have employed a somewhat unorthodox tactic for avoiding sweatshops. I live in a major city, and there always seems to be plenty of work out there for my particular skill set. Consequently, when I go out for interviews, I do so with the desire of landing a job that I really want. By the time I actually get down to the normal face-to-face interaction with the company, we've already done a lot of the dance and it's a foregone conclusion that I'm potentially a good fit. They wouldn't bother to interview me otherwise. So, we go through all the normal motions where we each do our best to convince the other that we're something that life is just not complete without.

When it's just about all said and done and things look good, I ask about the kind of hours that they're working on average and if overtime is a frequent flyer in their world. I've found that a good many managers don't want to be honest with you about this because they figure it would be harder to get people to sign on. They're certainly correct. So, just to make sure that I'm not being suckered into a sweatshop environment, after they've assured me that they don't work much overtime I happily agree with the philosophy, telling them that I have enough going on in my life that I like to get my job done in forty hours a week. I then tell them that as a seasoned developer it's my personal conviction that, if you're unwilling to pull the occasional all-nighter at crunch time, you should get out of the business. However, I feel that any company that has a crisis every week and that requires constant overtime is a company with extremely stupid management, and I have no desire to work for such morons.

The truth is that, if the conversation has indicated to me that I'm not the only programmer in the room who curses like a sailor, I use much stronger language than "extremely stupid" because I really want to make a point. Having done so, one of two things usually results. Either they were telling me the truth in the first place about little overtime, in which case we've agreed on yet another topic, or they're lying to me. If the latter, I have just terminally insulted them and there is no way in heaven or earth that they will hire me. Which is exactly my intent. When times are tough, you take whatever gig you have to in order to survive. However, under normal circumstances, there's plenty of work in our business, and life's too short to work for abusive companies.

Does all of that sound patently unprofessional to you? Perhaps it is. Nonetheless, ask me how many sweatshops I've worked in. Now, I spend my nights and weekends living my life while others toil away hour after hour, pushing themselves closer and closer to burnout. I'm a decent programmer, but many folks in this business are much, much better than I. And yet, I get paid as well as the next guy and I work forty-hour weeks. Why? Because I realize that, to have a gratifying career, good coding skills aren't enough.

The ability to consistently meet your deadlines is indeed another benefit that we can gain by looking beyond our technical abilities. Above and beyond the obvious fact that, if you're hitting your goals in a well organized fashion, you're not killing yourself with pointless overtime. Being successful and productive tends to lower your stress level and makes you less likely to be harassed by management. We get up each morning and spend a very significant portion of our days working for a living. If that experience is unpleasant, then simple math tells us that a very significant portion of our lives is unpleasant. Who wants to live like that?

Of course, if you regain control of your programming life, you can spend more time coding and less time putting out fires. I realize that, technically speaking, coding is coding, but that doesn't mean that I enjoy it all equally. My personal preference is to sit undisturbed writing new code on a project that sparks my interest and enthusiasm. I can assure you, I've spent many, many hours coding in scenarios that were nowhere near my preference. So have you. I could have gone to school and learned to do a great many things for a living. I became a programmer because it was a way to pay the rent that was actually fun. If I'm not having fun, I feel cheated. Consequently, I care a great deal about any aspect of my job that could interfere with the enjoyment of my work, for when I'm enjoying what I'm doing I'm giving it heart, body, and soul. That's good for me, that's good for the project, and that's good for the company. I believe strongly in win-win scenarios.

Naturally, one of the things we want to do is work on the cool projects instead of the stuff nobody wants to touch. Who cares if you're using the programming language and environment of your choice if the task you've been given is dull, tedious, and probably destined to never see a real, live user anyway? The cool projects, as you have no doubt observed, tend to go to the people who make an effective effort to get them. That sexy new project has to go to someone. Why not you?

I once worked a contract with a friend doing development on a data entry product that had an extremely complex list of input validations that were different for each state in the country and for each new customer's needs. The approach that they were taking when we got there was to create a new dynamic link library for each customer/state modification. This struck us as a little cumbersome. We then found that their method of doing this was copying the entire source code base for one library, pasting it to a new directory, going into the code and manually changing anything that needed alteration. Above and beyond the volumes of duplicate code, they even approached the positioning of images by changing magic numbers in the call to display the image, compiling, viewing the image, taking a guess at how much it needed to move, and repeating the process.

My friend, being a serious veteran programmer, observed the obvious that what this really called for was a custom screen editor and code generator, coupled with common code libraries. Of course, we could have solved this problem in other ways that didn't require a code generator, but in talking to the other developers we encountered massive resistance to the idea. They felt that, if there wasn't a lot of code floating around, their job security might be threatened. We both take a dim view of such poor ethics but were realistic enough to know that we were swimming upstream in trying to fight it.

We approached the project manager, who was himself a programmer and a good guy. He was newly arrived to this project and not responsible for the mess of his predecessor. He enthusiastically embraced our idea and told us to get to it. In the end, while the rest of the team slogged away copying and pasting code (my friend also observed that .cpp clearly stood for *Copy-and-Paste Programming*), we were off creating a cool new app using the latest version of the operating system, all the new UI gadgets, and anything else that we wanted to play with that we felt would make a better tool.

When it was complete, work that took several programmers three months to accomplish was done in a week or two by a single developer. After we had moved on to new contracts, we heard that the project manager was promoted. When a new manager came in, the developers got together, scrapped the system we built, and returned to the old ways of copy-and-paste programming. Who cares? We didn't. I've long since spent that money. It's my responsibility to conduct myself in an ethical fashion and do quality work; what the company does with it is its own affair. The point is that, although everyone else was working on dull, boring, and tedious tasks, my friend and I were having a blast kicking out a cool app and earning the high regard of the project manager. Why? Because we both pursued talents beyond the technical.

The last reason I list in terms of what's in it for you is no doubt one of the most important. The ability to make better money has a lot to do with non-coding skills. You do work for money, don't you? I suppose I could have pursued different avenues of programming that might make me a buck or two more, but I like what I do. That's a big deal, and without it I think I'd just go back to playing guitar in smoky bars. Life's too short to spend it doing something you hate, no matter how much it pays. Nonetheless, I've been broke many times in my life (many of which had a curious relationship to the amount of time I spent playing in smoky bars), and I don't care for the experience. Money ain't a bad thing, and, if you want me to write code for you, money is required. How much? Every last penny that I can negotiate, of course. The goal is not just to do what we love for a living, but to get paid extremely well in the process. To accomplish both, you're going to need more than just your technical prowess. If you can code in technical utopia and also have enough money to keep yourself stocked up on the latest bleeding-edge gadgets, isn't that worth a little extra effort?

## Who Needs These Skills?

How do these various skills fit into the structure of the development team? You may be thinking that much of what we've discussed thus far is of limited use to a production coder and applies more to those who pursue a management career path. Actually, it's never really that simple. I've never met a programmer whose job could be neatly packaged into one tidy little category. In the real world, throughout the course of the project we end up wearing different hats at different times, even if the job description when we signed on was supposed to be nothing but a coder.

Whether your part of the project is large or small, the same requirements apply if you're to successfully deliver your software. Chances are good that you have some additional responsibilities beyond making sure that your code compiles without warnings and doesn't cause smoke to pour out the back of the box. (It's true, though, that I once came back to my desk in the middle of a debugging session to find a fire extinguisher in front of my keyboard. I can assure you that there were no hardware problems. Honest.) If that's the case, you're going to need skills beyond the technical. However, even if you're fortunate enough to do absolutely nothing but code week after week, you still have other responsibilities. At a minimum, for your project manager to be successful in shielding you from the insanities of the corporate world, he's going to need your support.

You're also going to be involved in meetings. If you never go to meetings, drop me an email and let me know who the human resources person is at your company. In any event, you're going to find that you spend much of your workweek doing things that don't require compiling, debugging, or uttering the occasional programmer's expletive.

The size of your team may shift the types of skills you need, but whether it's large or small you've got to be able to cope with the business world in one manner or another. Small teams with a lot of individual autonomy require individuals with good organizational and navigational skills. If you're working in an environment where you're given a task and are then left alone to make it happen, you actually end up doing a lot of project management whether you realize it or not. (You can think of it as just being organized and focused in your work if the "project manager" part makes you twitch.) Whatever you call it, however, you have many of the same duties. You still need to be able to define your requirements clearly, perform adequate design, and arrive at an achievable timeline with milestones arranged along the way, just to name a few. Your compiler won't help you with any of this.

When working on larger projects with multiple teams, you'll often encounter as much corporate fumbling from within your team as you do from without. You will likely have a dedicated project manager and perhaps a structure of technical leads as well, along with a hefty complement of programmers. Political considerations will be much more a factor in this environment, as will issues such as how well meetings are run, the competency of your project manager in partitioning tasks, how much interference you get from middle and upper management, and many of the other things we've touched on thus far. Remember, you're at the bottom of the software development food chain. Very little happens higher up that doesn't have an effect on you, one way or another.

You may also find yourself working in the capacity of technical lead from time to time. Although it's a testament to the confidence that others have in your technical and organizational skills, this can be a thankless job with great potential for burnout. A technical lead is often nothing more than a project manager with limited scope who carries a full coding load. In other words, not only do you get to do all the work you normally do as a developer, much of it technical and therefore enjoyable, you also get to handle the managerial tasks that are relevant to your team. If it sounds like you just inherited a considerable amount of overtime, you're probably not far from the truth. The trick to working this position with any degree of success, which includes avoiding burnout, is to realize that you can't be a manager at any level, not even the team lead, and get a full day's worth of coding in. Depending on how large your team is and how much organizational work you'll have to perform, you should take your normal level of coding assignments and knock off a quarter or perhaps even half. Unfortunately, technical leads are not always given the power to make such decisions, which is why it's often a real burnout inducer.

Of course, if you have a one-programmer project (and that happens a lot in the business world), you're the project manager, team lead, and coder all rolled into one. If you thought that technical leads had a workload, you'll just love this one. Of course, there are some significant benefits to being a one-programmer team. With no other team members to distract you or call you into endless meetings, you might actually get some coding done. However, never forget that there are always going to be managers above you. What they're called is irrelevant. Any way you shake it, they're managers and that involves all the normal issues of politics, bureaucracy, their effectiveness in dealing with their own management, and all the rest. Additionally, just because you're the only programmer doesn't mean that it's wise to short-circuit the requirements gathering, design, or estimation phases. The rules don't change based on the size of the project, although experience tells us that, if you're a one-programmer team, the chances are good you work in one of those places where they expect to see code flying off your fingertips nonstop. Trying to get a process in place is even harder when you're the only one there.

# Taking Control of Your Time

To be successful—and, even more importantly, to be recognized as such by those you work for—you have to get the job done. This sounds too obvious to mention, but sometimes it's easy to overlook the obvious. It's important to keep in mind that business people pay you because they want you to produce something. If you really want to be good at your job, there's more to delivering the goods than coding. You have to keep in mind the end goal of the system you're developing and what it's supposed to accomplish, and do everything within your power and the scope of your position to see it through to completion. You may or may not be recognized for your extra efforts. You may not even want to be recognized, for a variety of reasons. Nonetheless, your ultimate reward will be in delivering quality software, on time and within budget, without overtime, without stress, and without any other nonsense you can avoid. Make this happen, and you put yourself in a better position for the next project that comes up. Everyone loves a winner.

At every level of development, one of the constants is the need for effective time management if you wish to meet your deadlines. Approaching software development in a scattered and disorganized manner is going to significantly diminish your results and increase the amount of time it takes you to get them. Along with that comes a higher level of stress as you've never really quite got a handle on what's going on. This tends to leave you feeling rather breathless and with the nagging suspicion that you're always running behind. It's probably a correct assessment.

I once knew a project manager that actually oversaw several development efforts. This person always seemed to have several balls in the air at any time. His office looked like a whirlwind of file folders, stacks of paper, and various boxes of uninstalled software, and there were probably a couple of chew toys from his dog in there somewhere as well. He constantly had a harried look about him as if he were somewhere on the border between not being able to cope with it all and the sheer terror that someone else was going to come yell at him. All of his projects were behind, and he spent half his time dealing with customers who were upset about it. This, of course, didn't help free up any time for him to solve the problems.

In short, this was one of the most disorganized managers I've seen. Little wonder that his projects were a mess. In fact, what thread of cohesion that actually did run through his various teams was the result of the personal initiative of his developers, who wisely saw that they would get no support from their manager and consequently took matters into their own hands whenever possible. The interesting thing about this guy is that, not only was he overbooked as it was, he never hesitated to take on a new project whenever he could get his hands on one. Could he have handled this kind of workload efficiently? Probably not in forty-hour weeks, but it didn't have to be the disaster that it was. It all comes down to organization. He didn't know how to keep his own ducks in a row, had no skills at planning or running a meeting, and interacted with his developers only in a crisis-driven mode, dashing out in a panic to tell them of the latest fire that they had to work late to put out.

With better time management skills, he could have taken control of the various projects, avoided being yanked from one crisis to the next, and perhaps even have delegated a little. Such things would have settled his projects down tremendously. What's that you say? It's not your problem because you don't want to be a project manager? You're just a programmer? Well, who do you think he had working for him? If your manager is a mess, and many of them are, you're going to need all the skills you can get purely for self-defense.

## Enhancing Design

System design is another area in which it's handy to have some facility in something other than compilers. It is certainly not a given that a good coder is naturally a good software designer as well. Although obviously related, they are two completely separate disciplines. However, you don't have to know how to code to work in an architectural capacity, and you don't have to have design skills to write source code. However, you do need to have a grip on the design side of things before you start writing that source code. If you just shoot from the hip and don't think your way through things on a small scale the same as you would for larger tasks, you're likely to encounter difficulties either halfway through what you're coding or the first time someone else has to interface to your code. We typically think of design in terms of mapping out the entire software system, but, when you get down to it, you should always think before you code. Even if management is inclined to believe that you're daydreaming rather than working.

One of the many reasons you need some facility with design is that, to meet your deadlines, you're going to have to have some skills in estimating as well. It's true that an estimate is of little importance if you're given the date before you're given the assignment, but sometimes you'll have a manager who asks you how long a task will take and actually pays attention to what you say. If you can't cook up a good estimate, you're not only setting yourself up for failure, you're doing it to your manager as well. I've found that in general it's a bad thing to make the person who is responsible for your paychecks look stupid to their own boss. People are funny that way.

## Improving Interaction

One of the significant benefits to possessing more than merely technical skills comes when you learn to improve your interaction with others. Sometimes it's courtesy, sometimes it's being able to deliver the goods, and sometimes it's just plain old politics, but it's always a beneficial thing that comes back to you. When you come in to the office each morning, you don't deal with a highly specialized class of sentient office furniture. You deal with people. Okay, I did once know someone who spent an inordinate amount of time talking to his furniture but I gave him the benefit of the doubt and chalked it off to sleep deprivation. If you keep in mind that you're dealing with real, live, flesh-and-blood people instead of nameless, faceless coworkers, you're going to have a much better time of it in the business world. The better your people skills, the better your chances of getting what you want, whether it's a new computer, a new project, or more money. If you can also learn to be bilingual and speak the language of business people, there's no end to the enhancements your programming career can experience.

For those of us who take our programming seriously, sometimes just the ability to bring better software to life is reward enough. Interpersonal skills help tremendously in this area as well. If you have great new ideas on how your software should be designed or how a particular chunk should be coded, you still have to be able to sell it to others if you want to make it a reality. Proposing new ideas successfully requires more than flowcharts and whiteboards. Decisions are often made not because the facts overwhelmingly pointed to a particular solution but rather due to the charisma of the individual making the presentation, whether it was a formal meeting or just a persuasive conversation in the hallway. Don't feel as if you're really overflowing with charisma? You'd be surprised how much of that can be an acquired skill. We weren't all born movie stars. Many times, attention to the details of how things work in the business world and learning a few navigational tricks are all the tools you need to gain the respect and admiration of your peers and management. Many programmers feel that they'll never have much luck in the persuasion department because they weren't born natural orators. However, if you learn to speak the language of your audience, understand the things that motivate them, and position yourself appropriately, you'll be surprised how often you win. We'll be going into these things in more detail later, but I'll touch once more on a recurring theme here: you can't win if you don't try.

Probably the bane of programmers and cubicle dwellers everywhere is the dreaded meeting. Some weeks it feels as if all you've done is travel from one meeting to the next. Sometimes it's true. Ironically enough, many of those meetings will be rants from higher-ups who wonder why the heck we're so far behind on our schedule. You're probably not in charge of most of the meetings you attend and therefore have to suffer through someone else's poor skills at organizing and running such gatherings. There's only so much you can do in that scenario, but you can help expedite the process at least a little. Further, if you decide to get serious about your skills in meetings, others will notice and a small groundswell may result. A meeting run by an inept manager can be put back on track, shortened, and made more productive when just a few of the attendees understand some of the basics and are assertive enough to help the process along. If you're actually responsible for reducing the number or duration of meetings at your company, you'll probably become a folk hero among your peers. (Who knows? They may even name a conference room in your honor.)

## Getting What You Want

Something that's not really as obvious as it seems is knowing what you want out of life. The truth is that a very large number of people in this world just don't know exactly what they want. Just as it's impossible to meet all the expectations when developing a piece of software with poor or fuzzy requirements, so too is it true in life. That includes your career. If you don't know very specifically what you want, you'll have difficulty achieving it and probably wouldn't recognize it if you did.

My observations have led me to believe that a large majority of programmers got into this business much as I did: I started programming for fun, got hooked, and decided that it would be a cool way to make a living. I then went out and got a job. What exactly was I looking for in a programming career? In retrospect, I had absolutely no idea. I just wanted to get paid to write code.

Having put a number of miles behind me by now, I have a much better idea of what I want for two reasons. First, I've had enough experience to see what's out there, what I like, and what I passionately wish to avoid. Secondly, and I think even more importantly, is the fact that at one point I sat up and realized I was working with fuzzy requirements and decided to do something about it. I actually spent time and gave serious, detailed thought to just exactly what I wanted in my programming career. I then set out to accomplish it.

Naturally, it's much easier to get what you want when you know what it is, and I have had a very enjoyable career thus far. I've spent time doing the types of things I wanted to do and have been paid well for it. This is not because I'm any kind of superstar, one-in-a-million programmer. It's simply because I detailed my goals and desires and then set out to accomplish them in exactly the same way that I would approach turning a requirements document into a good design and ultimately an implemented product. That involves little more than taking one step at a time, always with an eye to the future. Of course, from time to time, I revisit my desires and tweak the spec where necessary, as what I want tends to change. I also spend a fair amount of time reviewing where I am, where I've been, and how things are going so far in my efforts to meet these goals. That helps me to make the necessary course corrections.

Many of us tend to spend our lives on automatic pilot to one degree or another. I'm sure if you took a little time to yourself and gave it some thought, you could come up with a pretty decent list of things you'd like to change about your current job and perhaps your career or life in general. That's a step I'd encourage you to take. Be specific. Be very specific. What you're defining is the perfect world. Don't leave anything out, even if you think it unlikely to accomplish. Once you've done this, you'll have a decent requirements document from which to work.

The next step is to come up with a decent design doc. Take a look at where you are in your career and start brainstorming, just as you would in a design meeting, about how you might get there. Unlike as in software design, in this exercise it's acceptable to leave some questions unanswered. You may not see the solution at the moment, but new input or opportunities could come out of the clear blue sky at any point in the future to help you chart a course for that particular goal. Keep it on the requirements list. For all the other items, you'll end up with at least a beginning strategy and plan of action. Although this doesn't agree with all of the true software design methodologies, in the real world design tends to get tweaked as we go, benefiting from what we learn and steering around problems as we encounter them. So too will your design doc that you create for your programming career be modified as time goes on. I've heard it said that no battle plan survives contact with the enemy. Allow for that flexibility.

Once you've got a good design (which in any business is simply a detailed road map for how to get where you wish to be), it's time to give some attention to implementation. You now know, in great detail, exactly what the perfect programmer's life is, at least for you. You have a strategy in place to make this a reality. The next logical step is to start taking the necessary steps to realize your desires.

When you have both your requirements and design docs sitting in front of you, you'll quickly realize that to meet your goals you're going to need a few more tricks up your sleeve than just knowing how to avoid compiler and runtime errors. That's where we're headed next. You already know how to code. You're good at it, or you wouldn't have a job. Now it's time to hone your skills in all of those other areas so you can effectively combat the insanities of Corporate America and achieve your objectives. With any luck at all, the result will be more coding, more fun, and fewer encounters with nervous little dogs. The last time I saw him, the watchman's partner was sporting a camouflage collar and jacket and was having a whispered conversation with the maintenance programmer about inventory control.

Part Two

# Guerilla Tactics for Front Line Programmers

# CHAPTER 4

# Preventing Arbitrary Deadlines

For a host of reasons, software projects either fail to be delivered on time or are released in an embarrassingly buggy and unstable state (and there's actually an even more common scenario that combines these two). The most frequent reason for these disasters is probably the arbitrary deadline.

Developing software is a highly complex pursuit with many interacting considerations. One small change in a seemingly isolated area can have consequences that ripple through the rest of the project like a stadium full of beer-consuming sports fans doing the wave. It's difficult to stop once it gets going, and it won't take much for things to get just a little out of hand.

We already encounter enough surprises throughout the course of a project to make any specified delivery date an exercise in fortune telling to one degree or another. However, meeting deadlines and delivering solid software is indeed achievable, but only if all of the complexities and interdependencies of the development process are considered when determining the delivery date.

Unfortunately, this is almost never the case in the business world. Instead, programmers are handed drop-dead dates by which a system must be delivered. Of course, these dates all but ignore the intricacies involved in bringing a new piece of software to life. The dates chosen by management are, in a word, arbitrary. This is certainly not the only way to sabotage a project but it is without a doubt one of the best. Unless the final delivery date and a well-considered set of interim milestones are selected with the same attention to detail as that required by the coding itself, there's little chance of your project surviving as an unqualified success.

To remedy this situation, we must first acknowledge something that, although seemingly obvious, is categorically ignored by the software industry as a whole: *reliable and achievable delivery dates can come only from developers who have made a detailed and realistic assessment of the effort.* No matter where you sit in the food chain and no matter what your personal agenda, this statement is the unblinking reality in the world of professional software development. The facts do not change based on whether you like them. Were it otherwise, I can assure you that my first step would be to address the escalating difficulty of getting a decent and affordable pizza these days.

Only a disciplined approach to the software development process can put an end to arbitrary deadlines and the excitement that they invariably cause. In this chapter we're going to define that process. Many of the major steps encompass sufficient detail to merit subsequent chapters of their own. Consequently, what we'll focus on at this stage of the game is the overall approach that will lead us to consistently accurate delivery dates with a more reasonable workweek. What you do with all those overtime hours you don't have to work is up to you. Personally, I'd recommend a little extra sleep. You're starting to look a bit like the maintenance programmer.

## Defining the Process

As any veteran of the business world already knows, it's one thing for us to declare a process, but it's another matter entirely to persuade management to follow it, particularly because these guys somehow have the impression that they're in charge. The tactics and techniques we'll need to employ to win management over to our way of thinking constitute a large topic in and of itself. Before we can sell anything to management, though, we must first understand the details of the process that we're promoting. Consequently, we'll leave for a later chapter the methods we'll employ in convincing management to follow our lead. I'll leave graphic visualizations of the ensuing conga line to braver souls.

A software development project has a number of facets, requiring efforts from people of many disciplines to bring it to the intended audience. However, we're going to narrow our focus to just those issues that have a direct effect on programmers. Consequently, whereas you might have guessed that we won't be including marketing strategies, we also won't be touching on user documentation. The technical writer's part in the project tends to run a somewhat parallel path to that of the programmer. Other than the meetings that we must attend from time to time to explain the software, it has little effect on our code or our hours. What we will give our attention to is the dance between management and programmer and the steps that each must take to ensure a successful project. Because debugging is a part of the programmer's typical day, we'll be looking at the testing process as well. After all, it's much easier to have a debugging session when someone has scared up a bug to chase.

First, let's take a quick look at the overall sequence of events required to bring a new software system to life, from the initial phase when management decides they want a new program to the very end when the software is delivered to the target audience. To keep it simple, for those tasks that fall on the software development side of the fence, I'll just refer to programmers as the group responsible for the task. In reality, some of these duties may be performed by project managers, and others by team leads. Of course, in many shops the project manager, team lead, and production programmer all occupy the same spacious cubicle and type with the same set of fingers.

So then, what are the steps that we must take to generate reasonable deadlines and high-quality software? A well-behaved software project should follow a certain sequence of events, but our project is not a straight-A student, mind you. It has to exist within the confines of the corporate world, amid all the distractions and inefficiencies that line its corridors. Consequently, it will no doubt cut a class here and there, but, when you have time for nothing more than the essentials, the following steps are a summary of what you really need to make it to release day in one piece.

1. Management states high-level requirements.

2. Programmers formalize the requirements in detail.

3. Management approves detailed requirements.

4. Programmers identify testing resources.

5. Management approves testing resources.

6. Programmers estimate duration of design phase.

7. Testers estimate duration of test plan creation.

8. Management approves design and test plan efforts.

9. Programmers perform design phase.

10. Testers begin development of test plan.

11. Programmers estimate duration of estimation phase.

12. Management approves estimation phase.

13. Programmers perform task partitioning.

14. Programmers perform detailed estimate in hours.

15. Management may allocate additional programming resources.

16. Programmers define timeline with incremental milestones.

17. Management approves the timeline.

18. Programmers begin implementation.

19. Testing begins when software deliverables are available.

20. Programmers complete implementation.

21. Testers perform full regression testing.

22. Programmers define integration procedures.

23. Programmers implement installation program.

24. Testers perform full regression testing including installation and integration.

25. Testers approve beta release.

26. Beta testing begins.

27. Testers perform free play testing in parallel with beta.

28. Beta testing complete.

29. Testers perform full regression testing including installation and integration.

30. Testers approve product release.

31. Management or marketing begin distribution.

32. Programmers collapse in corner and sleep for three days.

As you can see, our list has quite a few steps. Chances are good that some of these steps are absent in your environment. Shucks, for that matter, some of the players (notably testers) may also be absent from your environment. Don't worry; one of the most important aspects of a successful development process is realism. It doesn't matter how great a plan looks on paper if there's not a snowball's chance that it'll fly in your actual corporate environment. That's where many strategies fall short. It may sound great at a technical conference to mandate that you generate a pile of design documents large enough to ensure a visit from your local "Save the Rain Forests" committee, but the minute you try to implement such a procedure you may find that management is less than supportive of the time required. Consequently, flexibility is key in all of our subsequent endeavors.

Additionally, although it would certainly be nice to simply post the list on the company bulletin board and declare that all steps will be followed, you'll more typically find that an all-or-nothing approach to restructuring your development process translates very quickly to nothing. In other words, it's going to take time to change the way things are done in your company, and for a variety of reasons. Not only do you simply have to fight the status quo that prefers to do things the way they've always been done, you must also establish credibility before you can gain control. That's perfectly natural. Everything looks good on paper. It's your job to convince management—not only through persuasion but, more importantly, through results—that life just goes better when the programmers are in charge of the programming. Therefore, you must be prepared from the very beginning to fight a longer battle with incremental successes eventually leading to a completely restructured software development process. This may very well span multiple projects, with management giving in more and more to your approach with each improvement that they see. It's a longer road, to be sure, but you weren't planning on giving up programming anytime soon, were you? Let's take a look, then, at the steps we need to take on the road to the mythical stress-free release.

## Commissioning a New Software Project

In the beginning, management decides that the company's life is just not complete without the addition of a new software system. At this stage of the game, it's unrealistic to expect a highly polished, detailed set of requirements. For all their faults and foibles, pointy hair notwithstanding, it is indeed the job of upper management to think in terms of the big picture. In fact, when you have upper or even middle management trying to direct the minute details of your daily job, it's called *micromanagement*. That's the sort of thing that sends maintenance programmers scurrying to review the inventory control program. To upper management falls the task of charting a general course for the company to follow. They are aided by input from both marketing and middle management, of course, and together they will arrive at a set of loosely defined requirements that justify the time and expense of a software development effort. This is a good thing. Most of the beneficial software we have in this world started out life in the conceptual stage as ideas of a general nature.

Of course, not all programs have their genesis in the hallowed halls of upper management. They may be proposed by marketing or even deemed desirable by those in middle management. In fact, while we'll touch on this in more detail when we start looking beyond projects and more closely at the individual programmer's long-term career, many a software project is conceived and proposed by the actual worker bees of the software environment, the front-line programmers. Left to their own devices, programmers would probably just sit around and write new software anyway, so it's not much of a stretch of the imagination that they would come up with proposals for projects to benefit the company as a whole.

Regardless of the origination, however, the requirements are expected to be loose and general at this stage of the game. The emphasis should be on identifying the problem to be solved or the benefits that the new software bring to the party. An idea must survive this phase of the process on business merits alone. The proposed new system must either generate revenue directly or enhance a business process that translates to increased profits, either through reduced expenses or the ability to more efficiently generate revenue. If the program won't do at least one of these two things, then no matter how cool the technology or how trendy the approach, the idea should make its way into the nearest recycle bin with all due haste. Our purpose in being here is to benefit the company, no matter what we would prefer to be doing with our time.

Such decisions are the responsibility of management. Should they choose to field a new piece of software that doesn't meet one of these baseline requirements, it won't affect your life in terms of the development effort. A stream of such decisions that generate expenses without enhancing profitability will, however, eventually kill your company. Even though it's not your job to run the firm, always maintain an awareness of the business decisions made in your company. It's much better to update that résumé *before* your company files for bankruptcy or is acquired by another firm that knows more about manufacturing dog food than it does software. Certain members of the security staff may greet the latter scenario with enthusiasm, but it'll do little for the care and feeding of the local programmers.

Once the decisions makers have decided that there is sufficient justification to kick off a new development project, it's the programmers' turn to take the field. This is a crucial area that is all too often skipped, particularly in smaller shops. It is a great temptation to take the general requirements announced by management and begin working on the design or code. In fact, this is what will most likely happen by default. But, to start developing some discipline in your company, this is where you must take your first step and make your presence known.

## Identifying the Requirements

Once given the general directives regarding the new system, the programmers should then begin asking questions. The types of questions are bounded by the fact that the requirements phase, high level or detailed, can be summed up by a single notion. At every step of the way and every level of detail, you must ask for specifics on exactly what the program must do. This requires the persistence to ask again when the answer is vague or ill defined. Sometimes you'll find that the people you're asking don't really have a clear picture themselves. They may not even realize this until you start asking very precise questions. Nonetheless, you must dig in at this point and resist moving forward until you have a very explicit definition, in writing, of what your software is expected to do.

The importance of this phase of the process cannot be overstated. Your ultimate success is judged by your ability to deliver the software requested of you by the agreed-upon date. If you don't have an extremely clear definition of what the software must do, there's no way for anyone to know if you succeeded in your task, even if you do make the deadline. Furthermore—and even more dangerous to those of us who will roam the halls at three o'clock in the morning—should the project fall behind schedule, if the software requirements are not chiseled in stone tablets and hung from the highest ceiling beyond the reach of meddling hands, your task list will grow while your date remains unchanged. This is how the death march begins, and it is to be avoided at all costs.

Not only is it the programmers' responsibility to lead management by the hand in generating a set of detailed requirements, it also falls on our shoulders to set some boundaries. Once you've managed to define the requirements (a step that we'll detail in a subsequent chapter), you must then identify the ultimate authority over the project and get that person to sign off on the requirements document. This signed document gives you a task to perform that, albeit large, is explicitly defined. It is to this signed requirements document that you will link the delivery date for the project that you will determine after the estimates are done. That delivery date is the *when* part of the equation, the requirements document defines exactly *what* is to be done, and the design document (which we'll also look at in a future chapter) states *how* it is to be done. That's the contract.

Having made the requirements document a publicized matter at the beginning of the project, you have some ammunition further down the road when someone comes along and wants you to add additional features. You are then able to state in an unemotional and businesslike manner that the current deadline is tied to the approved project requirements, but you'll be delighted to add any new features that they desire. However, because we've changed the requirements from which the date was originally derived, the date must naturally be reevaluated as well. Either the requesting party backs off, or you update your stone tablets and delivery date and life continues in an orderly fashion. Reasonably speaking, if you have sufficiently detailed requirements and you've done a good job of designing and estimating your effort (including time for the unexpected), there's no reason why you shouldn't meet your deadlines every time. Of course, the more deadlines you meet, the more credibility you have with management, which means that they're more likely to allow you to do things your way in the future. It's a process that tends to snowball as you continue to succeed.

# Building Your Testing Environment

Now that management has signed off on the detailed requirements document, your project is an official reality. If you work in a company that already has a well-defined and -staffed quality assurance team, you're way ahead of the game. For most of us, though, the company has been unwilling to put money into building such a capability. What this means is that, in the end, your software will hit the streets with very little testing and most of that being fairly haphazard. Thinking ahead at this stage of the game can help save you from such a fate. Just as there's no way for you to provide an accurate estimate without detailed requirements, so too are your testers at an extreme disadvantage without a detailed plan. Furthermore, if you don't have trained professionals, it's not fair to expect them to know what to do in the first place. This is another area where you can step in and act proactively.

Chances are good that, when management decided to authorize the project, they envisioned the coding and debugging and maybe even a little beta program. That's about as far they can see, and it's certainly as far as the testing considerations typically get. Just as it was the responsibility of the programming department to take the initiative and create a detailed requirements document, so too is it our task to create a quality assurance process where none previously existed.

Again, you start by identifying the person with the authority to allocate such resources and asking questions, with an ultimate goal of identifying which individuals will be available for testing, what their availability will be on an ongoing basis, and what their level of computer experience is. You might find the last statement a bit curious, but I can assure you that from time to time you will encounter people chosen to test software who think that a mouse is a rodent requiring an underfed feline and that a keyboard is something you see on the stage of the better-equipped rock bands. Even with such limitations, you're often consigned to either take what you can get or take nothing at all. It's best to know what you have to work with up front so that you can factor into your own schedule the additional hand holding that they'll need. A tester you trained yourself is far superior to no tester at all.

Questions about testing at this early stage will frequently surprise management, just as detailed requirements did, and so it is critical that you nail down your testing resources up front. Parallel to your development efforts, testers will need to devise a test plan so that it's ready to go when the software is available to test. No resources means no test plan, and that means no testing of any dependable nature.

In addition to identifying the individuals who will be available for testing, this is also the time to get hardware commitments. Depending on the specifics of the system you'll be putting together, you may need an isolated network, a certain class or combination of computers, particular types and versions of operating systems, external computer hardware or hardware simulators, and many other such items. Failure to acquire these resources will mean that the first testing in these environments will be by your customers, which is guaranteed to generate stress and increase consumption of antacids. It's also much harder to debug something from a customer's description than it is in the relative safety and comfort of your own lab.

It's a good idea (if it's at all possible) to get these resources committed to you in writing. The future is always uncertain, and there may come a time when you need to defend your claim to the people or hardware involved, as other departments will almost certainly be vying for control of them as well. Although having it in black and white doesn't mean you won't end up arm wrestling for it anyway, such a signed agreement gives you more ammunition when you get down to the nitty-gritty. And you can never have too much ammunition out here on the front lines.

## Entering the Design Phase

Now that you have identified your testing resources, the next major task for the programmers is the design phase. This obviously takes some time, but, without having done sufficient work in this area, there is no way to accurately estimate how much time it will take to deliver the system.

It's unrealistic to expect management to casually sit back at this point and wait on you to finish the design at your leisure. They have a business to run, and other departments are affected by your release schedule. Additionally, programmers cost money, and every week you spend on design adds to the overall expense of the project. It's certainly a justified expense, but no manager in his right mind is going to sign a blank check. Neither would you, in their position. Consequently, you not only need to perform the design phase, but you must first give management an estimate of how long it will take. Such an estimate allows them to coordinate the other departments and the flow of the development effort in general. It also keeps them in control of the expenditures, and managers like that sort of thing.

It's worth noting at this point that the word *estimate* gets used a lot in our business. The truth is, if you look up the word in a dictionary, you'll find that it's tantamount to an educated guess. If you take your car to the shop and ask for an estimate of the repair costs, the final bill may indeed be more. No one likes these kinds of surprises, but the mechanic will be quick to point out that what you were given was an estimate, not a guarantee. This is all true enough, but in our business it's also completely irrelevant. At every level of the food chain, an estimate—no matter how rough—is understood to be a commitment rather than an approximation. I have tried over the years to educate management about the difference between an estimate and a hard and fast guarantee; I would have spent my time more productively had I taken up knitting classes. At least I'd have something warm to wear in the winter. No matter how loudly you say it, the bottom line is that, in our business, an estimate is considered a commitment. That's just the way it is. Consequently, I've become more creative in my estimating process to give me the room I need to cope with this fact.

At the same time that the programmers are estimating the design phase of the project, the testers (assuming such creatures actually exist in the wild) are creating similar numbers for the time required to write the test plan. If you don't have professional testers available, and most of us don't, then the people who will ultimately perform the testing must come up with the estimates for developing a test plan. In the common scenario (wherein you don't have trained testing professionals), this means that the testers are going to need a fair amount of help from the programmers. This does increase your work load, but anything that you can do to improve the testing process ultimately yields tremendous benefits to you personally, so it's well worth the time and effort it takes to support the testers. Consequently, you'll need to determine how much time and effort on your part that they'll need and add it, as a separate line item, to your estimate for the design phase. No, it doesn't really fit there logically, but it is during this same time that you'll be helping the testers, so this is the estimate you bundle it in with.

Having delivered time estimates for the design and test plan phases, you once again appear at the doorstep of your favorite manager's office, pen and document in hand. In addition to getting the required approval, we're also doing a little conditioning here. After a while, management will become accustomed to your asking for specific documents and signed approvals. As it becomes the norm, you'll have to fight a bit less for it each time. That's one of the benefits to an incremental approach. I'd toss in a metaphor about old dogs and new tricks, but I'm not sure how much legal representation the canine portion of the security force has. I understand that night watchmen have a pretty good union, and it's never a good idea to tempt fate.

Now that management has actually agreed to allocate time for the design phase, a major victory in and of itself, you're back in familiar territory. Although we'll be covering the details of a compressed design phase in subsequent pages (because you won't ever get as much time as you want), programmers are generally comfortable with this part of the process because it concerns actual programming issues. However, at the same time that you're performing your design, you will most likely be helping your untrained testers develop their test plan. The reality of this is that you may well have to all but write the test plan yourself until they get the hang of it. As a result, your design phase will be interrupted a bit more than usual. It's also worth nothing that preparing the test plan continues beyond your design phase. That's because, although the requirements doc drives much of the test plan, the specific test cases themselves will have to be written in terms of the user interface you provide. Naturally, the details of the user interface won't be available until you complete the design phase, which means that you must also factor in time for helping the testers as you move into subsequent stages of the process.

## Estimating the Effort

Having completed the design of your new system, you're now in a position to give a legitimate, well-considered, and accurate estimate of how long it will be before management can wrap their fingers around the mouse and take the new software for a spin. You may notice that I intentionally avoided referring to how long the implementation phase will take. That's because there are more steps to delivering the software than simply calling its code complete. There will be installation programs, integration issues, and rounds of regression testing and beta testing, all of which must be performed before the software can be shipped. You need to factor these into your estimates as well.

Just as we've done in prior steps, the next duty for the programmers is to deliver to management an estimate of how long the estimation phase will take. Yes, even the estimation needs an estimate. It's going to take some time to do it right, and this is actually the point we've been building up to all along. I'll bet you thought that the coding was the part we'd been building up to. Actually, the point of this entire process, at least from a programmer's perspective, is to do the organizational work up front and arrange life so that, when we actually do get to sit down and fire up the editor, we can have as much fun and as little stress as possible. To do that, however, we have to take the estimating phase very seriously. If we do this job properly, from this point out we'll be dealing with realistic deadlines and maybe even normal business hours. I'm not terribly excited about staring at a spreadsheet all day, but, just as women have told me that the pain of childbirth fades quickly from memory, so too is this task quickly forgotten and even appreciated once we fall into a smooth coding groove.

Once management has signed off on the time that it will take us to perform the estimate, we must first take a look at task partitioning before we can start crunching numbers. In all but the most trivial systems, there's going to be more than one programmer involved. As it will ultimately fall to the individual developers to do the lowest-level estimates, it's only common sense to give them the piece of the puzzle that they will end up implementing. Although management may allocate additional programming resources to you after reviewing the estimate, you typically start with at least a core team of senior-level developers. It's a good idea to remind them when doing their estimates that the actual coders who perform a given task may well have less experience, so it's a good idea to temper the numbers with the realization that you won't be able to count on a senior programmer's productivity in all areas. We'll get into more detail later when we come to the chapter on estimating, but for now it's sufficient to know that all estimates are done in terms of the actual hours it takes to perform a task, not in calendar days. Calendar days, and their derivative dates, are calculated based on these hours.

Once the programmers have turned in the estimate, written in detail for the programmers but summarized appropriately for management's consumption, the brass may determine that additional resources will be required to move the project along at a rate consistent with their desires. This may also happen after you've delivered the timeline. If it does, you will of course have to rework the timeline, but management will be happy to give you time to do this, as an earlier release date is what they were after when they gave you the additional resources.

In any event, once you have the hours and know what resources you have to work with, you're in a position to extrapolate actual milestones and delivery dates. You need to consider a number of other factors when creating this timeline, including vacation and holiday schedules, the number of coding hours per day, and other such practical considerations. Nonetheless, giving attention to these details, you again show up on the doorstep of your manager. He's probably already reaching for his pen.

This is the big moment and one you most certainly want documented in indelible ink. This is where you hand your manager a timeline complete with delivery dates and he approves it. Get it in writing. Get it in blood if you can, providing that doesn't violate any state or federal statutes. Attach a copy of the signed requirements document so that the two are inextricably linked. Once he's put his name on the dotted line, make a copy of the signed documents and take them home. Think I'm kidding? Not even a little. I'm also not wanting to appear cynical or paranoid, but Corporate America is a strange and sometimes bizarre world in which rules and codes of good conduct just don't always apply. Some people change their minds, others pop up from different departments with their own agenda, and not everyone operates in an honorable or above-board fashion. People frequently try to weasel out of commitments or even deny altogether that they ever made them. Signed documents are a little harder to deny. However, things sometimes mysteriously disappear in the cubicle world and believe it or not, there are times when the watchman's dog is truly innocent. You've busted your tail to get a signed copy of the requirements and the timeline for the project. Protect your investment.

You have now made a commitment to deliver a very specific piece of software on a very specific date. After all that I've been through in this business, this is one situation that I'm actually quite comfortable with. If you blow the deadline after these steps, it's because you didn't do a good enough job somewhere up to this point. However, you've been given a fighting chance, and that's all that most developers have ever really needed. The date bearing the manager's signature—and yours as well—is one that was carefully considered and based on reality as you know it in your company. I would venture to say that, if all programmers were given this opportunity, the state of the software industry would change dramatically for the better.

## Coding Bliss

In the time that all of this has taken, you'll probably want to order the upgrade to your programmer's editor that was released while you were nose deep in all of these non-coding tasks. Then it's time to fire up the espresso machine, put on the headphones, and enjoy some time in coding bliss. However, you won't work without interruption. In Corporate America, there's always a meeting or two that you get dragged into (kicking and screaming, no doubt). There's also the likely reality that your testers are not professionals and will consequently require a fair amount of support from you just to give you the support that you need in the form of thorough testing and well-documented bugs. Even so, you're now doing what you signed up for. You're coding. Enjoy the moment.

Without a concerted effort on your part, you wouldn't have spent all the time leading up to this point doing non-coding tasks. This process will not be in place by default; rather, it is something you have to work for. No matter how much time you spent on it, however, you'll more than make up for the hours you spent away from the compiler between here and the release date. Your software will ship on time, you'll sleep on at least a semi-regular basis, and you will be able to hold your head high and be proud of the quality when your product reaches the users. Who knows, the maintenance programmer may even take you out to lunch. Time will undoubtedly heal any rifts between you and our trusty attack Chihuahua as well, but don't count on that happening anytime soon. He's still in therapy from those monitor incidents.

## Testing the Candidates

You still have a few steps to take before you're home free, though. Testing will proceed as soon as you have software deliverables available. There will be bugs, and this means the standard test-debug cycle with which we're all familiar. This will actually be a more pleasant experience than usual, however. If you've trained your testers properly, and you no doubt have, then they will be giving you bug reports with detailed steps to reproduce the bug. That, my friends, is programmer's heaven. As we all know, reproducing the bug is the hard part. It's all just coding from there.

Although the testing is an incremental and ongoing process that follows the software along as it progresses, the programmers will ultimately reach the point of being code complete. At this point, the testers will run a full regression test, which is effectively a process whereby they run every test case in the entire test plan. Should any deficiencies be encountered in this process, the bugs will be fixed and the appropriate tests performed for the specific problems identified. When the last of the individual bugs have been fixed and the relevant tests are run, the testers will once more run the full regression test, top to bottom. The goal is to make it through the entire regression test from beginning to end without finding any deficiencies. Once this is accomplished, the software is ready to move to the next level. Resist the temptation to just run the tests that verify your bug fixes. You know full well how one part of the codebase can influence another. Running the entire regression test from top to bottom is the only way to know for sure that the system is solid and that the bug fixes didn't create other problems.

## Addressing the Installation Issues

Now that the product has been certified as solid and without known issues by the testers, it's time to turn your attention to the installation and integration issues that will need to be addressed prior to actually shipping the software. Although at a minimum there's typically an installation program to write that was no doubt included in the original programming estimates, additional steps often need to be performed to field the system.

The installation program, and any other programs and scripts that the installation procedure requires, must be tested like any other program. This means wiping out the computer and starting with a fresh operating system or environment from scratch, installing the program, looking for any defects in the installation procedure, and documenting the deficiencies in the exact same manner as was done for the software system itself. This can get a bit tedious as for each pass the operating environment must be certified to be completely fresh and representative of what the end user will have when installing your product. Nonetheless, the installation process is considered complete only when the program can be installed in a stable and dependable manner on a fresh system and the integration scripts are certified bug-free. Of course, the same must be done for any uninstall programs. (This is why you can't just run uninstall each time instead of refreshing the operating environment. You can't trust the uninstall program to provide the baseline for testing, because it, too, is a program under test and therefore suspect.)

When both the installation and uninstall procedures have been certified by the testers, the full regression test must be run once more on a freshly installed system. Any defects found at this stage of the game will set you back a couple of steps. You must fix the bug, run the individual tests, and then perform the entire regression test before moving on to the installation test. Once that passes, you again perform the regression test on the newly installed system. Seem like a lot of extra work? Perhaps, but this is the only way that you can be absolutely certain that the user experience will be a solid one from the first moments of installation all the way through each feature of the software. Any shortcut in the process only leaves you vulnerable to bugs in the field. Nobody wants that. Especially after the maintenance programmer was nice enough to buy you that cheeseburger.

## Managing the Beta Phase

Once the testers sign off on the system, again in writing, your system is now ready to move to beta testing. If you have any control over the matter at all, you should choose beta participants with great care. Remember that, when a customer sees your product for the first time, it makes a lasting impression. It doesn't matter that they know it's a beta release. It doesn't matter that seasoned developers every-where know that *beta* is probably an acronym for *Bugs Expected To Appear*. The customer will run the program, somehow manage to trigger a code path that no one caught in testing, and crash the system.

This experience leaves a sinking feeling in the customer's stomach that your system just isn't stable or trustworthy, and that feeling never completely goes away. "Well, of course it's not stable," you might reply. "It's in beta testing." That doesn't matter. Although nothing may even be said, that impression will live on in their minds, and it will be reflected when they speak of your product. Further-more, if the customer doing the testing is one who has experienced any degree of dissatisfaction with your company in the past, it could trigger an entire series of events that in the animal kingdom would look very much like a small, hairless canine gnawing on someone's ankle.

In other words, although you want to get your software field tested in the very harshest of real-world environments, you should not ignore certain political and image considerations. When at all possible, choose customers who love you and who can be counted on to actually test the system rather than bet the farm on it. If your beta testers put your system into play in the real world where they have real live dollars and cents at risk, you can count on some very unpleasant experiences. Chant it to them over and over so that they can reflexively recite it to you on demand: *Don't get attached to any data created in a beta system. It will go away.* In a perfect world, you won't have to make such tradeoffs, but, if push comes to shove, you should choose a less-demanding beta participant over one who could shake down the software better but would cause bad publicity or much gnashing of teeth. It's not fair to subject your software to the criticisms of the real world just yet. You haven't released it.

When the system has made it through the full cycle of beta testing and no more bugs can be shaken out of it, it leaves the hands of the customers who were kind enough to test it for you, and the focus moves back to the testing department. Again, if you have any control over the matter, all traces of the beta product should be obliterated from existence on the customers' computers, leaving not so much as a smoking floppy disk on which it once resided. Take a magnet to the floppies. Break the CDs in half. Walk through the customer sites and reformat their hard drives. Burn the documentation. Erase the name of the product off any stray whiteboard where it may have been written. You want every last vestige of the test system to be nothing more than a fleeting memory. Hopefully a pleasant one.

Why get so nuts over wiping out traces of the beta? If you don't, then somewhere, somehow, sometime, when the customer is at their most critical moment, your system will crash in full, living color. Perhaps even a very striking shade of the color blue, depending on the operating system for which you develop. Some time later, probably around three o'clock in the morning, it will be discovered that the crash was caused by some incompatible or buggy piece of the beta that was left lying around and somehow got mixed in with the production system. Worse still, it'll be the maintenance programmer who finds it.

Now that your program once again exists nowhere in the world other than in your own software development lab, to the testers falls the task of running the full installation and regression test one last time. By now, it's probably going to be a seamless experience. However, if it's not, now's the time to find out. When the software leaves the testers' hands at this point, it will do so once more in writing, for this is your certified release, ready for deployment. It's time to open the champagne, or at least fire up the cappuccino machine, and celebrate. You've just done something that few developers ever get to participate in. You've released a solid, full-featured software system, on time and under budget. Now go home and get some sleep. All that racket from the celebration is keeping the night watchman awake.

# CHAPTER 5

# Getting Your Requirements Etched in Stone

The *Curse of the Casual Requirement* is a classic thriller guaranteed to scare the pants off of programmers everywhere. It's a bit of a sleeper, though, as the scary stuff doesn't happen in the beginning. Unlike most mysteries with the good guys winning in the end and the blame falling on the butler, in our little story the good guys lose and they never really could afford a butler to begin with.

The software development process begins with an idea for a program. This idea is typically about as fuzzy as those socks that get lost behind the washing machine. When the programmers first get wind of management's desire for new software, only two paths can be taken. The first is the default direction, in which the programmers do nothing and begin designing or coding based on whatever nebulous requirements they were given. The second direction is more arduous: the programmers must fight, scratch, and claw for every single detail that they can get and make sure it's documented in explicit and unwavering language for posterity. In other words, this entails getting the specifics and generating a paper trail to be used at the end of the project, or at any other point in which the developers need to defend themselves.

If you already follow an organized, structured, and effective requirements-gathering process, you don't need guerilla tactics. Instead, you should probably spend more time hanging out in the coffee shops that programmers frequent, as you're sure to get the local hero treatment. For the rest of us, trying to get management to cough up the details and commit to them in any form more tangible than the spoken word is harder than trying to herd a corral full of greased pigs into a room for a bath. And, no, I'm not going to draw any further parallels. My own management may be reading this, and I've grown rather fond of my paychecks arriving on a regular basis.

Make no mistake: if you leave room for people to wiggle on the interpretation of a requirement at some future point in time, they will. At the very last minute. Furthermore, an imprecisely worded requirement is an open invitation for scope creep. Even if you do everything right from this point onwards, either of these can throw you into a frenzy of overtime when you're one week away from the deadline. The requirements will suddenly change, and of course your deadline won't.

You might be tempted to argue that you were hired to write software, not manage the company, and so therefore it's not your job to make the requirements specific. The requirements should be that way when they come to you, and whoever wants the program has the responsibility of making this so. In terms of the world I'd like to live in, you certainly won't get any arguments from me. However, it's also a well-documented fact that the world I'd like to live in entails much more money, offices with real walls, and the complete absence of middle management by federal decree, just to list the ones that can be printed. In the world that we step into each day to do our jobs, things work a little differently. Because we're at the bottom of the food chain, we rarely have the luxury of demanding much of anything. And, because the requirements for the software we write comes from those who outrank us, we typically receive them in a wide variety of forms, with none of them organized and very few of them detailed. Consequently, it *is* in fact our job to make sure that the requirements are explicit and well documented before we begin our design. It simply won't happen otherwise, and we are the ones who will ultimately pay the price at the end of the show. Where's a good butler when you need one?

## You Don't Have to Like It. It Just Has to Be Clear.

Another thing that should be considered at this point is that, even though we tend to get a little possessive about our programs once we start working on them, when it comes to requirements it doesn't matter if we like them or not. The only thing that matters is that they are precise and unwavering. Whether you're a mercenary or a full-time employee, you're a hired gun in management's eyes: they brought you on board to write the software that they needed or wanted and your job exists for no other reason.

I worked for one company that tasked my group with writing a database system to manage customer information. As this was a national firm, part of our requirement was to keep the data up to date in thirty cities. The decision was made at a higher level that this should be done with a replicated database with each city having a copy of the data. When any one city would update information, databases in all other cities were to be instantaneously updated via the corporate WAN. We implemented this system and delivered it, on time and under budget. It was at this approximate point in time that *Internet* became a household word, which of course meant that it was one of those trendy things that middle management felt we should be using. Therefore, mere weeks after we finished installing the system that they asked for in thirty cities, the word came down to us that all the data should reside on one computer at a single location and access should be provided to the thirty cities via a Web browser interface. Consequently, the system that was now installed and serving its purpose was to be thrown away and completely rewritten from the ground up to provide the exact same functionality. I don't count beans for a living (unless you want to include coffee in that equation), so I have no idea how much money they threw out the window on this project. But it makes me feel a little better about all those flying monitors.

We should note a couple of important points from this example. First of all, it's obviously incredibly wasteful to implement a system, field it, train the users in its operation, and then immediately scrap it just to do the exact same thing on a different platform (and for no other reason than to be trendy). However, that's not my problem. I'm hired to write software, not manage companies. Furthermore, if they want to pay me twice to write the same system, my bank makes little distinction when it comes to the deposits. In other words, because it's not my company, choosing which programs to implement or what their requirements should be is not for me to say. If I feel strongly about the matter, I need to quit and start a company of my own. Otherwise, it's my duty to implement the decisions of the people who hired me.

That being said, the second thing to note here is that the amount of money this company wasted was probably enough to keep me on a beach with a full margarita glass for a good year or two. The reason this money was pointlessly spent was due to a fundamental mistake in the requirements process. In the very beginning, before a programmer had even heard of the project, they were specifying *how* it should be done, when the requirements phase is about *what*, not *how*. They threw suitcases of money out the window simply to change *how* something was done when the business needs had already been met. Unfortunately, the evening that the money went flying out the window the night watchman and his partner were on vacation, which is truly a shame. It might have paid for all that therapy.

If you want to spend your time coding a system that inspires you personally, you may have to hang out a shingle and go into business for yourself. I've been asked to write a lot of things that I didn't find particularly riveting. I can live with that. All I ask is that, if you're going to bore me to tears, please go about it in a very precise manner. If you'd like for me to write your system twice, that's just fine with me as long as the second iteration is just as explicit as the first. I will give these folks credit for one thing: they had no idea what they were doing, but they could explain that to you in great detail.

## Where Does the Power Lie?

Regardless of how much sense it makes to implement a particular software system, when it gets to our desks the question is not "why should we write it?" but rather "what exactly should we write?" If we can get satisfactory answers to the latter, preferably in writing, then we've got a fighting chance at meeting the deadlines that will eventually await us. The first step to take in getting these requirements nailed down may seem like an exercise in the obvious unless you've been wandering the halls of Corporate America for a while. As programmers, we are not in a position to declare that a piece of software is complete. Rather, someone above us in the food chain must sign off on the system and call it done. Who is the person who has that authority? Is it one person, or is it some formal or informal consortium that must be satisfied before we can put the code, and ourselves, to bed? In short, who makes the decisions?

Until we have identified this person or group, we don't know who to turn to both at the end of the project when we're done and in the very beginning when we want to get the requirements etched in stone. It's a common mistake to assume that, if our boss comes to us and tells us to write a program, then he must be the decision maker. I can assure you, particularly if he's middle management, that he has about as much authority over the definition of the project as you do. If you put your fate in his hands when it comes to the requirements phase, you may as well stock up on espresso. You're going to need it. The way it typically works in any company large enough to have a layer of middle management is that people positioned above your boss are the ones who truly need to be satisfied with the programs you write. Chances are good that the manager you directly report to is not a programmer. Consequently, he has neither the training nor the motivation to press his managers for more detail on a project. In fact, he's likely to avoid just that sort of thing, as people who make too much noise in the business world are often put on the slow track when it comes to promotions.

If you work in a smaller company, you may not have much middle management to deal with. This doesn't mean, however, that the person who asks you to write the program is the only one who needs to be satisfied when the coding is done. People from other departments may be involved. If you work in a vertical market, there may well be important customers who have a say as well. Basically, anyone who wants to put their finger in the pie and has enough political clout to gain entry to the game must be taken into consideration.

No matter what your company's structure, when the word comes down to your team that there's a program to write, the very first and most crucial step to take is to quickly and accurately identify who the people are who have the final decision-making authority over your system. Once again, you may be tempted to shrug this duty off to your project manager and turn back to your compiler. However, you must bear in mind that you're on a team. In our business, the fate suffered by one is shared by all. If your project manager is stressed out and living in overtime city, it's a pretty safe bet that you will be, too. One of the nice things about working on a team, though, is that you have more people to apply to a task.

This will come in handy, because identifying the major players can require a bit of detective work and you won't have much time to figure it out.

Know up front that there are times in our business when you must make a choice between taking action that involves some political risk or suffering the consequences that are sure to befall your project if you don't. If there were a simple prescribed set of rules that every company recognized that would allow you to operate within your normal chain of command and accomplish all that you need to deliver your software, you wouldn't face this dilemma. These rules don't exist. If you're a good boy, you'll trust those above you in the food chain and simply do what you're told by your immediate superior. You probably won't get yelled at much, I'll grant you. However, if one path offers a little political risk, the other guarantees the evils that we suffer on every release. I decided long ago that I've had enough of pointlessly chaotic releases.

## Politics Are an Inescapable Reality

In fact, I also made a decision about politics in general many years ago. I used to have a philosophy that many programmers share: I just wasn't going to get involved in any of that political nonsense. I was a programmer, I was there to code, and, if everyone else wanted to stand around the water cooler and play little power games, then fine. I had serious work to do. I eventually ended up in a small company on a project that required only a couple of programmers. My project manager, who was the head of development, was actually a solid database programmer. So solid, in fact, that he kept his head buried in a database and actively avoided any project management duties.

The programmer initially assigned to this project was a sharp guy, but he was one guy too few for the deadline that was dictated. The manager was pressed to beef up the team a little, and I wanted on the project. It was technology I wanted to play with, and I liked the guy that was already on it. However, a new guy who didn't have even the most fundamental grasp of the programming language itself, let alone the technologies, was available. Not to be uncharitable, but let's just say that no amount of experience was every going to make this guy a good programmer. Some folks have it, and some don't. Nonetheless, having to deal with the issue at all was a distraction that kept the manager from enjoying his database programming, so the new guy was quickly assigned to the team so that he could return to his fun.

Naturally, the project's progress deteriorated rapidly as the original coder had to not only do his own job but baby-sit the new guy and clean up after him as well. Several weeks went by, and the manager was pressed to get the project back on track. Obviously, the solution was more bodies. This time, due in no small part to the lobbying effort of the lead programmer, I was assigned. We decided that the first thing that needed to be done was to lighten our load by one body so that we could get some work done. I was a very vocal person, and the lead programmer was much more politically savvy. So, I confronted the manager without so much as the slightest regard for diplomacy and had the guy reassigned to the equivalent of scraping gum off the bottom of chairs. In retrospect, I may have made some comments about how stupid it was to have assigned this clown in the first place. I was also rather forceful and demanding, because we were already working over-time and this guy was making matters worse rather than better. As I said, I wasn't interested in politics and I saw it as a simple, cut-and-dried technical matter. This wasn't a particularly bright thing for me to do, but I didn't realize it at the time.

In the end, we delivered the project two weeks late after many all-nighters. That's not on time and under budget. However, in our business, being two weeks late is also a little better than the average. Nonetheless, when it was all completed, I suddenly found myself in the manager's office. By the time I got back to my cube from the conversation, my network login and my job were both history. The stated reason was because the program was late, but curiously only one of the two pro-grammers was fired. The truth of the matter was much more simple: I ticked off the wrong guy, and I paid for it.

Incredulous, particularly after I had just killed myself with overtime in the name of being a dedicated employee, I went to one of the company owners. He was a good guy, and just told it like it was. He agreed that the situation was bogus but pointed out that my manager was the head of development and, unless there was an extremely compelling reason to override him, he had to back him up. He then told me something that lives with me to this day. He said that I knew as well as he that, while technically I was being treated unfairly, politics were just as real and valid a consideration in business as any other aspect. He was half right. What he said about politics was true, but I didn't know that at the time. I decided then and there that although in the future I may lose political battles from time to time, I would never, ever again lose because I didn't play.

The lead programmer, who had much more common sense than I, continued to rise in the company. He's still a friend to this day, and he continues to do well in the programming business due to the unbeatable combination of good technical abilities and good political skills. And, although I certainly haven't won every bat-tle I've fought, I have never again ignored political realities.

The example I've just given has nothing to do with defining the requirements for a software project. However, it has everything to do with how you get them. As we were considering, chances are good that the people who must be satisfied before you can stop coding and get some sleep are further up the food chain than your immediate manager. This poses a dilemma. If you go over your manager's head, you risk ticking off the person who can eliminate your source of income. On the other hand, if you don't, you're not going to have any time to spend your money anyway as you'll always be at the office coding away to ever-changing requirements. We'll discuss some ways to communicate directly with the decisions makers in a moment. For now, it's sufficient to say that our first step is to identify the people who truly have sign-off power on the software. Between you, your fellow programmers, and a bit of asking around, you'll find it's usually not that hard to figure out once you decide to look.

## Identifying the Other Influential People

Having made note of where the power lies, the next thing to jot down is less of a political issue and more of a practical one. Any system is going to have some domain experts, that is, those people who have the business experience relevant to the system being developed. For instance, one of the projects I've worked on involved software for air traffic control. A couple of the guys at the office used to work as controllers, and they were considered domain experts because they had worked the position and knew what a controller needed out of software. It's important to know which domain experts will be involved in defining the requirements of your system because these people bring a very practical perspective to the software you will develop. In the end, people will use your program to accomplish a set of goals. The more input you can get from domain experts, the better your software will be. It's also worth mentioning that these people typically have some degree of political clout, or management wouldn't have let them participate in defining the software to begin with.

If it's possible for the type of work you're doing, it's also a good idea to list some actual users as well, the real people who will be using the system. They often have a perspective that's very different from anyone else, and they can also help you clarify the requirements. It's better to hear their voice now than to wait until the software is fielded, they don't like it, and you find yourself redesigning the thing in the beta testing phase of the project. It happens.

I realize that I often paint a picture of Corporate America as a place in which common sense is never a priority and people are always scheming, unreasonable, or just plain hard to work with. Although this is the case often enough to make it foolish to ignore, a great many programmers live in an environment that's more accurately a combination of this sort of nonsense and groups of smart, practical, and dedicated people. If I emphasize the bizarre aspect of the business world, it's only to make you realize that there's a little bit of that in every company. Actually, there's a lot of that in some companies. Therefore it's counterproductive for you to ignore it.

We're going to assume for the moment that much of the chaos in the development cycle is due not to people who are unwilling to make the necessary changes, but rather to the fact that those in the upper ranks of management simply don't understand that their approach is causing disaster after disaster. This is very often the case. Because business people want to succeed, we have a fighting chance if we approach things in a sensible manner.

## Selling the Process

So far, we've identified the decision makers, the domain experts, and the people who will actually use the software. The next thing we need to do is insert a pause in the process. Frequently, we're given fairly high-level requirements and expected to start coding. The fact that the project starts into the design or implementation work at this point is due to no one making the suggestion that there's a better way. That's what we're going to do now.

Development efforts come in all sizes, from one programmer to large groups with multiple teams, and so there's no one right person to whom you should make this suggestion. If you're a coder on a team, enlist the support of your fellow programmers and your team lead and go to the project manager. In smaller groups, there may be no officially titled project manager, in which case your group simply talks to the next level up on the food chain. In any event, you'll have more success if you can first convince your peers and enlist their support in your efforts. If there's one among you who would make a better spokesman, get him up to speed on what you're trying to accomplish and then by all means utilize his abilities to further the interests of the team.

After arranging for a little time with the appropriate manager to talk about the requirements, first briefly go over what you have at this point. Because you wouldn't need to go to this trouble to begin with if you had detailed specs, you should have little difficulty in pointing out the ambiguities in the requirements you've been given. You probably don't need to do anything more than touch on a few high-level requirements and start asking the manager, quite innocently, exactly what they mean. It will quickly become evident that you have insufficient details. You're not looking for anything more than his acknowledgement at the moment. Once the manager has agreed that yes, things probably should be spelled out a little more clearly, you have an in.

People are always much more prone to lending an ear to someone who both has a problem as well as a proposed solution than to a person who just wants to complain about the problem. Now that the manager has agreed with you that it would be difficult to code from the existing requirements, you simply mention that you have an idea that might help in this regard. If you could get together with a few of the people involved and ask for a little clarification, you could answer your questions and get right to work on the programming. Chances are good that this won't seem terribly unreasonable, and you'll be given the opportunity to proceed.

How much of the process you lay out to the manager is going to fall to your instincts and common sense, based on the level of support and cooperation you're getting. To a manager who is truly supportive of anything that will improve the software development procedures, the process we're about to walk through will seem logical and productive. On the other hand, if you're having to fight every inch of the way to make changes, you need to employ what's known as incremental selling. In this case, rather than overwhelming a less-than-enthusiastic person with all the details of a decent requirements-gathering phase, you instead speak more generally about "just a meeting or two" with the relevant people to clear matters up. That's easier for them to commit to than some big, fancy, and time-consuming process. It gets your foot in the door, and once you're there it's fairly easy to keep having "just one more meeting" until you get the details you need. A little underhanded? Maybe. But, hey, they've been doing that sort of thing to us on software requirements for years. For now, let's proceed with the assumption that you have at least a little support and can put it all on the table.

## The Definition Questions

At this point, we're going to define a set of questions to which we'll occasionally refer for the purpose of defining a requirement in greater detail. These are the *requirement definition questions*, or simply the *definition questions* for short. They are,

- What is the desired action?

- What initiates the action?

- What data does it operate on?

- Where does this data come from?

- What action is performed on the data?

- What supplemental data does it need to perform the action?

- Where does the supplemental data come from?

- What are the visual requirements?

- What are the audio requirements?

- What other systems or subsystems are affected by this operation?

- What are the effects of the other subsystems on this operation?

Most of these are obvious in their intent, but a couple of them require clarification. The questions regarding the visual and audio requirements can easily drift into issues of user interface design. That is not the intent. We still want to focus on what, not how. At times, however, part of the requirement will be visual or audible by nature. For instance, air traffic controllers need to know if data being displayed on the screen is out of date and consequently invalid, regardless of the reason. For example, the figures displayed on the screen for the current runway visibility may indicate a clear day with no visual obstacles. However, if the equipment that gathers this data has malfunctioned, the controller may not be aware of the fact that a fog bank has rolled in and the pilot couldn't see a Chihuahua if it scampered across the runway right in front of him. Not all controllers have windows. Consequently, it may be fairly stated in the requirements that the controller needs to be given a visual warning indication that the current data is bogus. There may also be a requirement that some sort of audible event take place to get their attention. Both of these accurately state *what* the software needs to do without getting into *how* this is accomplished. It's crucial to keep this in mind at all times. When in doubt, simply ask yourself if the topic being discussed is about *what* or *how*. That will keep you on track. Following is an overview of the process we're going to be using.

1.  Identify the decision makers and key participants.

2.  Create data entry forms and a database to gather individual requirements.

3.  Have a series of meetings to clarify issues on individual requirements.

4.  Collect and organize the individual requirements and formalize them in a document.

5.  Have the decision makers sign off on the final requirements document.

Seems pretty straightforward, doesn't it? Actually, it is. Requirements gathering, stripped of all the pomp and ceremony of the big-ticket design methodologies, is nothing more complicated than holding meetings with the appropriate people and asking precise questions about the needs of the system.

# Preparations for Effective Information Gathering

Although we have our key players identified and we have a set of concise definition questions, we still need to do a couple of other helpful things in preparation for the requirements meetings. First, set up a database that has, at minimum, a record for a single requirement and fields for the data gathered from the definition questions. If there are a lot of major categories or subsystems, it would be a good idea to include fields for those as well. Whoever is most comfortable with databases in your group can easily go to town from there, but these are the basics. Create data entry forms that will make it easy for nontechnical users to enter this information in plain text and normal language. Make this database, or at least the data entry mechanism, available to all attendees via your company network.

Using this data entry form as a guideline, create a document template as well using whatever word processor is prevalent in your company. It's helpful to have two versions of this, one that the user can type directly into and another that is designed to be printed out and written on. A constant in any enterprise is the fact that the easier you make it for someone to give you what you want, the better your chances of getting it.

Set up a couple of projects in your version control system to house two types of documents. One project will hold the documents that describe a single requirement, and the other will be the repository for the actual formal requirements documents that will be the output of the entire process. Yes, yes, I know, it would make much more sense for everyone to just enter the individual requirements into the database. For a variety of reasons that rarely make sense, this just won't happen with some folks. Having both the documents and printed forms gives you a fallback strategy for those who can't or won't use the database. You need the information more than you need to stand on principles of how they should get it to you. Frankly, if they won't use the database, the document templates, or the printed forms, but they will answer the definition questions on a cassette tape, *take that instead*. What we need are results, so take the input any way you can get it.

Now that your infrastructure is in place, if you don't already have a document that details everything you currently know about your requirements, now's the time to gather one together. Once you have this, it's time to arrange the first meeting. As a general practice for all meetings, it's not only common courtesy but much more productive if you distribute the documents with which you wish your attendees to be familiar a day or two prior to the meeting. In other words, give them enough time to read and digest it before the meeting. A lot of people won't read it anyway, but it'll be easier for you to diplomatically ask them to hold questions that were covered in the document if everyone had time to read it beforehand. You'll find that the other attendees will be supportive of this, by the way, because no one likes going to meetings, and anything to speed them up will make you popular among your attendees.

Another general practice for productive meetings is to always have someone who will be responsible for taking the notes during the meeting and generating a summary document afterwards. Designating such a person makes it easier for everyone else to give their attention to the matters at hand, and also helps to avoid conflicting perceptions of what took place.

At a minimum, in this first meeting you need to have the decisions makers present. If at all possible, you also want to include the domain experts and anyone else who is a power to contend with as far as the requirements go. If you need to work a little harder to arrange a time that everyone can live with, it's more than worth it if you can get all the major players in one room. Everyone should have had a chance to read over the general requirements of the project as you currently understand them.

## Defining the Requirements

The first thing you want to accomplish in the initial meeting is a bit of partitioning. For any nontrivial system, you can usually divide the requirements into some major categories or subsystems. The next step is to build a focus group for each of these subsystems. You may find that some people will need (or want) to be involved in more than one group. Although it defeats the purpose to have all participants work in all groups, this is at times a legitimate need and should be allowed. You may find that there also may be a political need, which is just as important. Identify a leader, preferably by group consensus, for each group. This person will serve as the moderator for the focus group meetings to keep them organized. Of course, you'll need someone to take the minutes for each group as well. That's not a terribly gratifying job, so it's best to get a volunteer if you can.

You now want to give these focus groups a task to accomplish and turn them loose. From the issues in their subsystem, they are to put together two lists: the first is a feature list of all items that they agree by majority vote are desirable, and the second list contains those features that were mentioned but didn't claim a majority. The focus groups should proceed by first going off individually and making their wish list of features. Detail is encouraged, but it's not required at this point. They simply need to be able to identify the features in such a manner that everyone in the meeting understands what they mean. After a reasonable amount of time, typically a day or two, the focus groups reconvene and the weeding-out process begins as people lobby, bribe, and argue their way through the wish list. It's a good idea to remove all the whiteboard erasers from these conference rooms.

As each focus group finishes the two lists, they should distribute them to all members of the complete group. When all focus groups are done, it's time to reconvene the complete group. At this point, the leader of each focus group walks through the list and lets the group vote on it at large. The same rules apply: majority rules. However, at this point, any decision maker can override the group decision and accept or reject a feature. That's one of the reasons that the decision makers must be present at these meetings. They're going to do this anyway, and you don't want it happening after you've already coded the darned thing. After the list of agreed-upon features for each focus group has been covered, the list of features that got only a minority vote is reviewed. If a majority of the overall group decide that it's a keeper, it moves to the feature list.

If your project is large, you may want to stagger your effort by a series of meetings, one for each subsystem. All-day meetings are tedious and a waste of time by the second hour. If you truly care about keeping everyone's attention, no meeting should ever go past the one-hour mark.

The output of this meeting or series of meetings is the definitive list of features for the system, albeit loosely defined. The next step is to drop back down to the focus group level. These groups reconvene in their individual meetings armed with their list of features and the definition questions. The output of this process is a record in the database for each requirements, with answers to all the definition questions. How it gets into the database is a matter of what works best for the people you're dealing with. For some companies, it's viable to have a workstation in the conference room so someone can enter the data as the questions are answered. In other environments, printing out the forms and filling them in by hand may be the most likely approach to succeed. Even if they do it on a cassette tape and someone transcribes it into the database, it doesn't matter. Just get the questions answered.

When the focus groups have finished, the information in the database is then used to generate a draft of the full requirements document. Depending on how formally your company likes to do things, this can be as simple as a database report or as tedious as taking the information and creating a separate document in a word processor. The important thing is to do it in a fashion that contains all the details and is in a format that works for the decision makers. It's a draft of the document you'll eventually want them to sign. If they're formal and officious people, you must create a document in the same spirit or it won't be taken seriously. It may sound dumb, but that's human nature in the corporate world, and in the end it's critical that this document—and you and your ideas—be taken seriously.

After the draft requirements document has been distributed, it's time for another meeting or series of meetings, depending again on the size and the number of subsystems. This time you want some of your top programmers involved as well. There's an advantage to having all of your programmers in on it if you can manage it, but at a minimum you need the key players for the subsystem that they'll be working on. If the decision makers want to skip out on the next meeting or two, that's fine, but the focus group members have to stay because they're the ones the programmers will question. The same procedure is repeated, and each requirement is visited. This time, in addition to input from anyone in the room who feels the requirement in question isn't as clear as it should be, the programmers have a chance to review each feature and verify that they have the information they need to design and code from.

Here's your chance, folks, so don't be shy. If it's not clear to you now, it won't be when you fire up your editor, either. This is one of those rare times in life when it's okay to put words into other peoples' mouths. You may hear vague descriptions of functionality that you must help translate into strict and specific statements. An approach that I find helpful is to take the fuzzy statement you heard and repeat it back to them in precise terms, asking for their agreement, such as, "I see. So what you're saying is that we need to <replace vague ramblings you just heard with a precise description of functionality>. Did I get that right?" Remember, many of the participants aren't techies, so you may need to lend your skills in that area. Diplomacy is very important when doing this because you want to build allies, not adversaries. Believe me, I learned about diplomacy the hard way.

Although the programmers don't have veto power regarding which feature stays and which feature goes, they do have the power to flag a requirement as incomplete, meaning that it needs further clarification before it can go into the requirements document. Of course, the more specific they can be about what additional info they need, the better the focus group will be able to comply. Additionally, programmers can flag a requirement as impossible to implement in its current state. For instance, if a feature requires Internet access but the program will be run on some machines that lack that connectivity, it's a no-go. This does not mean that the feature is dropped from the requirements document, but rather that it is placed on a list for the decision makers to ultimately review. They are the only ones who can make the call to either drop the feature or to ensure that it's possible to implement (such as, in our example, by including Internet access as a part of the product requirements).

Additionally, the programmers can flag a requirement that turns out to be a design issue rather than an actual requirement. If people have properly answered the definition questions, you shouldn't see much of this. If it does happen, though, it needs to be noted so the programmers can address it with the appropriate people when it's time for design.

## When the Party's Over

When all of the requirements have been worked through and there are no more issues to resolve, the draft requirements document is updated once more and distributed. One last meeting is convened with the decision makers and the full group. The goal of this meeting is to get all concerned to figuratively "sign off" on the requirements, but, literally, there should be signature lines for all of the decision makers and the leader of each focus group. The leader of the programmers will also sign. The signatures of the decision makers are mandatory because that's the point of the entire process – getting the people in power to make a firm and public commitment to a very specific set of features. Getting the focus groups to sign off on the document is simply good politics, indicating that everyone involved has agreed that these are, in fact, the gospel requirements. You never know when this sort of thing is going to come in handy.

Check the document into version control, label it as the final requirements document, and distribute a copy of the signed document to all participants. It's a good idea to have everyone sign two or more copies at the last meeting if any of the decision makers want to keep an original. You certainly want one with ink on it for yourself. Store it where it's safe from the gnawing teeth of any stray canines.

Once it's approved, the requirements phase is officially over. For any future feature requests, there's a simple response. You can have anything you want, as long as it's in 2.0. But what if a decision maker requires a new feature? If so, and this may happen, then it must meet the same stringent guidelines outlined by the definition questions, and the subsequent design and estimation phases must be revisited. The bottom line is that the dates *must* be adjusted accordingly. However, having bought into a process of specific dates tied to specific deliverables, you'll find that this will be much easier to accomplish.

While the meetings are in progress, encourage the use of email for question-and-answer sessions among members of the requirements team. People have different schedules, and email is the most considerate way to ask questions without interrupting what they're doing. Of course, email is also the easiest way to get ignored. If you find that some people are prone to doing this, encourage the others to simply camp outside their office door if they have to. Consideration works both ways. Also, remind the team that, as far as the official proceedings go, hall meetings don't count. If it's not in writing, it doesn't exist.

## Coping with a Hostile Environment

So far, we've been working on the assumption that you'll get the participation and support that you need from the decision makers to follow this process. Due to politics, resistance to change, or any of the other reasons that people do stupid things in the business world, it may not work out this way. In fact, you may encounter active and extreme resistance to any or all of this. In my opinion, a process is completely useless if it doesn't fly in the real world, no matter how impressive it looks on paper. If the decisions makers, who are ultimately the only ones who count, won't allow or follow through with this process, then a couple of things are clear. First, you're in a pretty bad environment, and frankly you might want to dust off that résumé. Any management that is resistant to a procedure that will help them get the software they want on time and in good working condition is just going to be trouble at every turn. The second thing that's clear at this point is that, if this is your reality, any help you can get is going to be better than what you have. So, let's take a look at some shortcuts. It won't yield perfect results, but any degree of detail and accountability is better than vague feature requests from people who position themselves as untouchables.

No matter what, you must still identify the decision maker. In this particular case, you want a single person, the ultimate authority that can veto everyone else. This shouldn't be hard. He'll be the one telling you that he's not going to support or allow the requirements meetings. This is the guy who you ultimately need to coerce into making a commitment. It's crucial to know who this person is and to verify that he indeed has the power to sign off on the software system. It's also still important to round up, or at least to identify, as many of the relevant domain experts as you can.

Forget about the formal document templates for the individual requirements, but keep the database. Just realize that you'll have to do all of the data entry yourself. It's tedious, but worth it in the end.

In this abbreviated process, you're going to follow some of the same steps, and it still starts with your creating a document that summarizes the requirements given you by management. You still need clarification. Because the decision maker doesn't want to support a legitimate process, you need to target this person with your questions. We're now on touchy political ground, so be very wary. Use the person on your team who has the best people skills and doesn't mind storming that machine gun nest. If you don't have anyone on the team willing to do this, you're toast. Normal, logical approaches have failed, and you must now decide whether it's worth taking some risks to try to improve your lot in life. No one can make that decision but you. Your only choices are to update your résumé or get out the sleeping bag.

You want to ask the questions in person. The tactic here is a tricky one, but the idea is to make it clear to the manager that you can't write the software until you get answers to your questions. If you're not allowed to have the meetings you need with the parties concerned, you can't get your questions answered. However, because this is the person who's requesting the software, he can obviously answer them because he ultimately is the one who must be happy with the system. Your only hope of success is to be pleasant, positive, nonconfrontational, and impeccably logical. If you approach it with a seemingly naïve innocence, it's harder to get nailed. Gee, you need to write software but you just don't know what you're supposed to write, so naturally it's okay to ask these questions, right?

The implied statement here is that if the manager wants the software but doesn't want to allow you to go through the common sense steps of defining it, you're going to be a pain in his behind until you either get your questions answered or he gets irritated and delegates the matter. The danger in irritating a superior is obvious, which is why you want your least-irritating person to perform this mission. The interruptions will be irritant enough. You don't want one of your guys coming back with the pink-slip equivalent of a Purple Heart. With any luck at all, you'll at least get some definition out of this guy. You probably won't have much time each time you corner him, so have your questions prioritized, well thought out, and ready to go. If this is as good as it gets in your world, then, in addition to getting the information, you've also been conspicuous enough in your approach that he'll remember having committed to the details you asked for, if only because he found it annoying.

Another thing that can be helpful in this scenario is to use one of the small pocket cassette recorders rather than trying to take notes. Just be sure it's obvious to him that you have it, or it looks like you're trying to pull something over on him. There are also legal implications involved in recording people without their knowledge or permission, and you just don't want to go there. Simply explain the fact that you appreciate how little time they have so you don't want to waste it trying to take notes, and then put it in your shirt pocket so it's not waving in anybody's face. This makes it a little less threatening. The wise bunny rabbit does not threaten the Bengal tiger. Also be prepared to be told to turn it off. Some people are uncomfortable with being recorded for a number of reasons. If the person expresses such sentiments, comply quickly and with a good attitude. Have a small notepad handy as a backup.

If the person gets irritated enough to delegate, that's an opening. Pounce on it. If he was previously resistant to the meetings you proposed, probably because he didn't want to fool with it himself, you can now suggest once more "just a quick meeting or two" with the people he's trying to delegate to, which is tantamount to agreeing with him. However, you might casually suggest at this point that it might help speed things up a bit and be less of a hassle for the people he delegated to if you bring in "just a couple of other people" who might be able to answer some of the questions. These couple of people are the domain experts you've already identified. No need in announcing how many or who unless you're pressed for it. Even then, there's no need to admit to the full complement. Mention the person or two least likely to cause resistance. The rest just get invited to the meeting. It's always easier to ask for forgiveness than to ask for permission.

Be prepared when you hit the meeting, but don't distribute the documents prior to the meeting as you normally would. Remember, if you're here, you're in a hostile situation and need to think a little differently. Any little bit of fair warning you give offers the opportunity for someone to screw it up for you. So, show up to the meeting with copies of the high-level document you prepared and hand it out. What you do at this point depends largely upon the feel of the group. You may find that, even though the decision maker is an inflexible pain in the posterior, the people to whom the work was delegated are actually reasonable and supportive.

You'll have to play this one by instinct. If you get a good attitude from all concerned, you might try suggesting that you break it into subsystems and letting each of them gather a little information, perhaps getting together with some users or other people that they feel would help with their area. Further, you offer an approach that will help them, that is, the two-list system we've already covered, and you slide each of them a list of the definition questions that you were holding on to just in case. In other words, if you end up with a good group, you just slide right into the procedure, quietly and with little fanfare. Don't push them to do any data entry or any other tedious task. Your main priority is to collect information, and your secondary priority is to establish allies whom you can count on when it comes time to get the requirements document recognized by the decision maker. Your team can handle any of the grunt work needed. You just don't want this alliance to unravel, so do whatever you can to keep things rolling smoothly.

If you get to the delegated meeting and you don't have a supportive group, then you simply fall back on the same tactics you used with the decision maker: innocence, logic, charm if you've got it, and an overriding goal of getting as many questions answered as you can. Towards the end of each meeting, for as long as you can get away with it, casually ask one or two of the key players if they'd mind getting together with you briefly a little later in the week to "just answer a couple of questions." Target people that you need the information from the most. If you can pull it off, you can use this approach to hold a series of mini-meetings with a couple of people at a time. In a similar fashion, you can drop by a person's office (email is useless in this context) and ask if they could spare a minute or two for a couple of questions. In other words, your mission is to gather information, even if it breaks down to house-to-house fighting. All of this is a real nuisance, but still not nearly as much of a pain as trying to cope with deadlines and pressures when you've only been given the vaguest of requirements that you know will continue to change on you.

What if you simply don't have physical access to the decision maker? This is a hard situation. At that point, shoot for people directly under them in the food chain and work the same tactics. The bottom line is that, if you don't get some cooperation or access at a reasonably high level relative to the people who make the decisions on your software, you're pretty much done for. However, I've worked for large, international corporations, and, although the general directive to go forth and create software may come from the CEO, in reality the people who will approve your software as being finished are typically not too far from you in the general scheme of things.

In a similar fashion, regardless of which of the preceding tactics you're forced to employ, your ultimate goal is still to get an official approval of your detailed requirements from the decision maker. It's best to get one in writing. However, if you're in a hostile or unsupportive environment, that just ain't gonna happen. In such a case, you take the finalized requirements document—the best that you could put together under the circumstances—and make it available on the network after having labeled it in version control to prevent someone from tinkering with it later. You then send an email that this document exists and how to find it to anyone with any clout in the decision-making process, in other words to all perceived decision makers, as well as all domain experts. In your email you state, diplomatically of course, that to the best of your understanding here are the *only* things you're aware of that you need to implement in the software and that, unless you hear otherwise, it's all you're *going* to implement. The language should be nonconfrontational and more along the lines of telling them that you'd be grateful for any clarification or input that they might have. If you get any takers, try and walk them through the definition questions on any features that they may want to sneak in. After a round of that, update the document and repeat the email. When you send an email and you don't get any response back for a day or two, then that's as good as it's going to get. However, when the release crunch comes and people start trying to wedge in new requirements or wiggle on existing ones, you've got a paper trail (print out and save at home all of the email responses you get) to help fight off the last minute changes. It's not as good as a signature from the decision maker, but it's a little more ammunition than you would have otherwise had.

## Politics Are Never Far Away

Even though we've run the gamut here from a constructive and cooperative environment to one that is hostile and unreasonable, some of the basic concepts remain unaltered. To define a given requirement, you need to ask specific questions. To tie requirements to a date, you need to formalize the final requirements and have the decision maker acknowledge them. As important as all of the issues we've covered here may be, perhaps the most critical consideration is realizing that, if you get anything less than full support when trying to nail down your requirements, you're dealing with political issues. This is a double-edged sword. Although politics are unsavory to most of us and certainly dangerous if ignored or handled poorly, programmers can also employ them to get what we want. This is most prevalent in the requirements-gathering phase, as you have people with their own personal agendas jockeying for what they want. That's politics, pure and simple. However, you're going to find that, although we talk about practical, nuts-and-bolts programming issues regarding condensed design approaches, low-level estimating techniques, and so on, political considerations will never be far behind. If you make your living in the business world, it's an inescapable reality. In the end, the programmer who successfully delivers his software is most often the person who has good technical skills, good organizational skills, good political skills, and is willing to use each when called upon.

# Effective Design Under Fire

If the realities of the requirements-gathering phase are a combination of politics and trying to pin down slippery product definitions, the design phase in most programming departments is typically an exercise in making the best out of the time you're given. In many shops, management doesn't even understand the concept of a design phase and are consequently not too generous in their time allotments. The end result is an implementation phase that often starts with little more than a meeting or two gathered around a whiteboard before the programmers scurry off to their corners to begin coding against an already impossible deadline.

With that in mind, let's take a look at some of the essential realities. First of all, when it comes to design, you're not going to have time to do it The Right Way. I'm sure you've read about it though and probably even have a few excellent books on the software design process lining your bookshelves. Personally, I've learned a great deal over the years from such approaches and they have doubtless made me a better programmer. I've just rarely been in a shop in which management gave the developers even a fraction of the time necessary to fully implement these methodologies.

That's a shame, too. I actually worked in one shop where they followed the rule that software development is 80% design and 20% coding. We literally designed the entire system on paper, down to the function level, complete with all parameter passing, and debugged it in peer meetings before we ever got near a compiler. Seemed like it took forever at the time, but in retrospect the design and coding phase together took about half the time it would have taken with the typical shoot-from-the-hip-and-debug-all-night approach.

When (and only when) the overall design finally survived a gathering without red ink, we started coding. The design was so detailed we could have almost hired typists to do that part of the work. When the last compile was complete, we plugged four independently developed modules together for the first time, and it just worked. No sparks flew, there were no major or minor rewrites, and we found an extremely small number of bugs. We're talking around two or three per module, and this was a nontrivial codebase. Everything that they tell you in these methodology books about the benefits of following an analysis and design approach thoroughly, in great detail and by the book, is true. I've seen it work.

## Design? What Design?

Sadly, however, that was a unique experience in my career. I've been at this for a little more than twelve years. Never before or since have I been given anywhere near that kind of time in the design phase of the project, if in fact I was given any time for design at all. Remember, in management's eyes, if you're not coding, you're not working. The way they handle the development teams in most of the shops I've seen is chaotic and extremely short sighted, and they pay for it with every release. You'd think that they would eventually figure it out, but they never quite seem to catch on. Nonetheless, it is what it is. No matter how much better life would be if they'd let us do it The Right Way, you're just not going to have the time you need to design in complete and thorough detail before you're expected to start coding. As such, we must either adapt or be dashed upon the rocks of corporate reality.

I'm not going to teach you how to design software, nor am I going to introduce another design methodology to the world. I'm sure you're already familiar with many approaches, and there is a wealth of excellent books available at your nearest bookstore. Instead, what we're going to focus on is how to cope with design in the compressed timeframe that we're typically forced to live with. You should know right up front that the things I'm about to suggest will doubtless destroy my reputation as a serious systems architect and software engineer in the eyes of credible and respectable professionals everywhere. However, I've got deadlines to meet and I've always been more interested in that than looking respectable, anyway. It's probably just as well. The black leather jacket tends to give me away every time. Don't ask about the earring.

So, brace yourself. We're going to do everything backwards here. We'll be basing the way we approach our design upon the available time instead of declaring the amount of time we need based upon the design philosophy. That's because, as in every other aspect of our jobs, we simply don't have the authority to say how long we're going to take on a task. Rather, management tells us how long we have and will hear no arguments to the contrary. Consequently, the design document that we'll come up with is not a 400 lb. college research paper. It's a computer-generated cocktail napkin to help you get the job done.

You need to keep a couple of other things in mind as we go along. First, design specs are not the same as technical documentation. When the implementation is done, it will not match the original design. It never does. Along the way, things will change here and there as you encounter unexpected and undocumented problems and are forced to come up with solutions on the fly. You won't have time to go back and redo all of the design documents that these changes affect to keep them up to date with the implementation. You'll simply make some notes that are relevant to the remaining work and keep moving. The sole purpose of these design documents is to aid you in your quest to write the code. They are not sacred scrolls. Scribble on them, put your coffee cup on them (provided you can still read the text around the coffee ring), and don't sweat it if a printout or two gets torn. They're cheat sheets. Nothing more. Additionally, you're going to find that you'll need more than a typist to code from them. A programmer's interpretation will be required, although that won't be much of a problem because it will typically be the programmer who drew the given diagram in the first place.

## Estimating the Design Effort

Before any design effort can begin, we have to get the time to do it. Consequently, the first task of the project manager (or whoever happens to be in charge) is to secure this time. As in all other phases of the project, management will want an estimate of how long the design phase will take. Being a reasonable kind of guy, your project manager will be happy to comply. At this point, he asks management to give him a few days to put an estimate together. How many days is "a few"? That's going to depend on the climate of your company, your project manager's experience in dealing with the management, and his bargaining skills. In general, asking for a month to estimate how long the design phase itself will take will never fly. Asking for half an hour is too little. Somewhere between two days and a week is probably in the ballpark, depending on the size of your project. In the end, of course, you'll take what you can get.

You might think that the purpose of the days you've just bought for estimating the design phase is for figuring out how long the process will actually take, right? Well, no, but thanks for playing and we do have some lovely parting gifts for you. The goal of this estimation process is not to determine how long the design will take, but rather to put together the compressed design approach itself and then do the highest level of design. Did I mention that we might be bending a couple of rules ever so slightly here and there? To however many days or weeks you'll ultimately be given to do what will have to pass for system design, you just snuck in a few more. Hey, they don't play fair, so we don't play fair.

We'll touch on the actual estimate that gets forked over to management in a moment. For now, let's take a look at what we're really going to do with the day or two we've just been given. Before we can do a design at any level of detail, we need to get organized. In addition to the fact that we'll generate some degree of design documentation that will need a common set of symbols, definitions, and so forth, we'll also need a common language and point of reference to use when discussing the design issues. Which design methodology should we then use, Brand X or Brand Y? Actually, we're going to roll our own. If having an official name for the design approach makes you more comfortable, you can think of this as Incremental Design, for reasons that will soon become apparent. Or you can just call it Brand Z.

What we're going to do is build a composite methodology that leverages the existing knowledge of your team. To do so, quietly gather your developers together in a small little conference room on the bad side of town where management can't find you, and make a list of all the design methodologies that you know of. It doesn't matter how old the approach is, whether or not it's object oriented or even if anyone's ever heard of it before. We're looking for building blocks at this point, and we want to pour them all onto the table before we start building anything.

From the list of methodologies you've now assembled, make a list of all the diagram types in each, along with the purpose that they serve. Duplication is okay and is in fact expected. Most design systems overlap in a number of areas, varying not so much in content but rather in the style in which things are approached. Nongraphical representation is okay as well. We're building a list of ways to present design information, and the printed word is perfectly valid, if sometimes verbose. If you see holes when your list is complete, declare a new diagram type and define its purpose. Don't worry about the representation for that particular diagram type just yet because you'll address it later. Keep in mind that you're short on time here, so don't go crazy and get into tons of detail. Keep it simple and concise, and remember that your ultimate purpose is to build a customized design methodology for this specific project that you can actually take into battle with you. Leave all the theoretical stuff for those ivory tower guys in the white lab coats. It weighs too much in your backpack and will only make you tired.

Next, break the software system down into its major modules. Although this partitioning often falls along some fairly obvious boundaries, the size of the modules may be in question. If so, think in terms of the size of a team and how large a chunk they could handle. Before you can perform this partitioning, however, you're first going to have some discussions of the overall system itself, what you're trying to accomplish with it, your vision of the overall architecture, where the major interaction points are, what the high-level flow of data is, and other such familiar topics that are necessary to make an initial pass at system architecture and high-level design. Once you have this level defined, break these major modules down into successively smaller submodules until you have a module size that one programmer is capable of handling.

By the way, remember that estimate that we were supposed to be working on? Here's how it works. When all the justifications are made and your team has explained the various benefits of any given design approach to management along with how long a proper effort will take, you'll find that they really just don't give a rat's patootie. They didn't understand a single word you just said, and they already knew how much time they were willing to lose on all this design nonsense long before you started talking. Yes, in their mind design is frequently considered lost time. You're not coding. Bear in mind that you're getting any time at all only because you made a fuss about it.

So, once again, based on his previous experience with management, the project manager determines the amount of time, in calendar days, that he thinks management will realistically agree to in terms of the design process. This is typically a matter of weeks, not months. It's important to be realistic about this number regardless of your personal feelings on how much time you'd like to have. Once this number has been determined, he then multiplies it by 1.5 and gives this new estimate to the team. The individual teams will use it as a boundary and work under the assumption that this is the amount of time they have to do the complete design once the design phase starts. This helps them to determine how much detail they can afford to pursue.

This will also be the estimate that the project manager presents to management as a starting point, once you've chewed up all the days you were given to do the estimate, of course. Because it's half and again more than he expects they'll accept, they will most likely balk at the figure, and so he bargains for what he can get. As a general rule, if they say yes to your first offer, you could have gotten more. If they say no to your first estimate and proceed to haggle you down from there, you can rest assured that you squeezed every last day out of them that you were ever going to get.

You already know that you won't be given the time that you really need to do a complete and detailed low-level design. However, if you can get a good high- to medium-level design laid out in the design phase, then, as you're doing the low-level estimating that will be required later on to determine the implementation timeline, you'll actually be doing the low-level design. It just won't be obvious to management. Keeping this in mind will help you maintain your focus at this stage of the game. You don't need to go into minute detail in the design phase. You need to go only deep enough to provide the framework that you'll use later when you actually are ready to go into fine-grained detail.

As you can see, what we're doing is taking the true, overall design phase and surreptitiously spreading it out over a couple of estimation phases as well. In such a manner, you can come close to doubling the amount of time that you have to design your software. Furthermore, you'll probably impress them on at least one level because management respects people who can give estimates, manage time, or perform any other function that somehow works out to numbers. While you're in the process of getting what you need to get the job done, you're also gaining credibility because you're speaking the language that they understand. In the end, everybody wins. Now that we have the estimate safely scribbled away on the back of an old gum wrapper somewhere, let's get back to using up those days we were given to conjure up the aforementioned estimate by doing some more design work.

## Rolling Your Own Design Methodology

You have both your modules and teams defined, so now you need to assign the major modules to the individual teams that will ultimately be working with them. Their first task will be gathering the information you need as you build your customized design approach for this project. When doing this, don't worry about the next project or trying to come up with an approach that will be perfect for all needs and all times. While you obviously won't forget what you learn on this project and will of course tend to keep things that have worked for you, it's important to note that this customized design methodology is disposable. You'll use it for developing this project, and then you'll simply throw it away once the post mortem has been done and you glean all the information you can from it to roll into technical documentation. Remembering this will help you keep it simple, concise, and to the point. If you weren't short on time, you wouldn't need to take this approach in the first place. However, because these are the waters you find yourself in, you have to maximize the effectiveness of every minute you have, which means cutting out the fluff whenever and wherever possible. Marketing has an acronym about simplicity: KISS. Buy them a drink sometime and ask them what it stands for.

Previously, we built a list of all the different diagram types we could come up with from our pooled knowledge of various methodologies. Each team is now going to determine which diagram types it needs in order to design the module for which it is responsible. Just as the overall group had high-level discussions on overall system architecture, now the individual teams have similar conversations regarding the architecture of their major module.

As you start to make this list of diagram types, you need to keep a couple of important questions in the forefront of your mind, remembering that we're doing only high- to medium-level design and that time is short. How deep do you really need to go to have a workable framework for future low-level design, and how much time do you have? These two questions should continually bound your efforts. As you consider this level of design, approach it with the perspective that the interfaces are more important than the internals. The latter will be fleshed out in more detail later. The interfaces should consequently be given more attention.

Additionally, what level of experience does each of your developers possess? The level of design detail can vary on each programmer-sized submodule, based on the experience of the developer who will be working that piece of the puzzle. This is acceptable because, in the end, each programmer will be coding largely from the design specs he created. Because each will know what they're capable of in terms of filling in the blanks on the fly, the diagrams and design documents that they will use can reflect that. Thus, you can save time when working with seasoned developers rather than going down to the lowest level of detail for every module whether it's needed or not. That's one of the benefits of using disposable cocktail napkins for design.

Each programmer now proceeds to create his own list of diagram types that he'll need to develop the portion of the code for which he's responsible. From the overall diagram types list, he'll make a list of only the diagram types he needs to communicate the program design both to himself and other members of the team. The goal is to take a minimalist approach that efficiently covers the bases, as it leverages the experience of the individual and leaves part of the communication of the design to a verbal process that can often be much quicker than a large stack of detailed drawings. While it's true that a picture can be worth a thousand words, sometimes a few well-chosen words can save you the arduous task of generating a thousand pictures.

To derive this individual list, the programmer will have to think through the major aspects of the portion of the system he is to design. Although I've been loosely equating a design methodology to a set of documents, we all know that it's really not that simple. A design methodology is not just a way of documenting things; it's also a way of analyzing and organizing a software system for subsequent coding, be it an overall project or the one small part that's managed by the given programmer. Once again, what we're doing is leveraging the strengths of the individual. Each programmer will naturally gravitate towards the methodologies with which he's familiar. As a result, when he sits down to look at his part of the system, he will instinctively apply these approaches as he breaks his work down into progressively smaller pieces and defines the interfaces, states, interactions, data, and procedures that are required for implementation. Thinking through these issues and conceptualizing the work enough to determine the types of diagrams that are necessary represents the next initial stages of high-level design, even if you're not writing anything down just yet.

Now that you have a list of the diagram types that you'll need to code your portion of the system in the time given to you by the project manager, make a second list of diagram types that you would use if you had only half the time. It can be a subset of your first list or a completely different list if you find that you really need different types of diagrams for such an abbreviated approach.

Having covered the procedure that we'll follow, let's look in a little more detail at the process of rolling your own design methodology. Those of you who have watched the occasional Bruce Lee movie may have heard mention of Jeet Kune Do, the system of martial arts that he developed. One of the fundamental principles, which can be applied to many aspects of life, has to do with stripping away formalities that appear to exist for the sake of formality alone and instead gleaning from any martial arts system you encounter those basic techniques that work for you personally. Although this brief statement is obviously inadequate to describe an entire system of martial arts, it's sufficient for our purposes as it relates to software design, as that's just what we're doing here.

In every major design methodology that you encounter, you're going to find many useful techniques and ways to represent information. It's not unusual, however, to find that even going by the book you don't need all of the tools that they provide for you to properly describe your system. This isn't a matter of taking shortcuts in the given approach. Rather, it points out that a methodology, to be complete, must be able to cover all the bases for all systems. From this basic set of tools, you follow the prescribed procedures and use those elements that are relevant to the system under development.

What we're doing here is loosening the rules somewhat. We're expanding our toolset to include every design technique known by the group as a whole, and we're removing the constraint that a strict and particular set of steps and procedures must be followed. Instead, we will utilize the strengths that each system brings to the problem at hand and simply leave the remainder unused. This applies not only to documents and diagrams but to methods of thinking, analyzing, organizing, and every other aspect of the design process that's covered in those books you bought. Although following the entire process as outlined has definite benefits when you have the luxury of that kind of time, a great many aspects of each system are strong enough to stand on their own. We'll take advantage of that.

Just as we'll avoid going through procedures for the sake of formality alone, we also want to avoid a scattered approach if a more contained one is available. If you can use the graphical representations from a single design methodology with which everyone on the team is familiar, you're off to a good start. You have a single point of reference, a good source of documentation on the symbols themselves, and a group of practices and diagramming techniques that were meant to work together. Even if not every person on your team has experience in the given design approach, take a look at the numbers. Is the group small enough that it would be easier to bring them up to speed than it would be to roll your own? What is their general level of experience and mental agility? Is it such that they would quickly grasp things? If they have a background in any methodology at all, they should be a quick study.

What you're taking advantage of in this case is existing common knowledge. If you decide to use a single approach in your efforts, make sure that your motivation for doing so is the prevailing knowledge base of your developers. Do not—I repeat *do not*—force a particular approach down everyone else's throat because you have an emotional attachment to what you consider to be The Right Way. That's counterproductive and will also make you the target of many whiteboard erasers. The one and only justification for using a single methodology in our situation is to save the time it takes to roll our own. If overwhelming numbers don't make this a no-brainer, there is no benefit and we go back to picking and choosing the best of all worlds.

Assuming that you don't have a team trained in a single method of design, we'll continue with our considerations of creating a customized subset of many approaches for our own use. In the beginning, as you're considering the types and definitions of your diagrams and documents, there are no rules, only the goal of coming up with your set of tools for this project. This means that you are encouraged to make up the rules as you go along, creating or borrowing them from the methodologies you've seen in the past as is appropriate, and always working to boil things down to their essence. The end result we're striving for is the simplest, shortest, quickest, and most efficient method that we can come up with to describe this software project. In the end no one, particularly management, will care what brand of box you drew on your design charts. They'll only remember if you made the deadline and that the software works. In short, results count. Purism for its own sake is to be avoided like an attack Chihuahua who's had one cup of espresso too many.

You'll be defining only the diagram types that you need and for which you have time. Are you approaching things in an object-oriented fashion? Then you'll probably want some manner of describing your class hierarchy. However, you may or may not need the equivalent of a state transition diagram. Flowcharts? They take a great deal of work to do in low-level detail, but would they be useful in showing the overall process for a given module?

Don't forget the user interface. Now that we've passed beyond the requirements-gathering stage, we're no longer asking *what*. We've moved on to *how*. Consequently, there are times when you may want a quick and easy way of communicating UI design without having to kick out a prototype. I've seen some standard business drawing packages that made it pretty easy to drag and drop a quick screen representation together. If such tools aren't available to you, it's actually easy to convey a lot of UI information using nothing but rectangles of various sorts. Do you need to go to this trouble? That's going to depend on the target audience for the software (particularly the decision maker over the entire project) and the amount of time you have. If you've seen examples in your company of people constantly redoing the user interface to a program, it might be a good idea to at least hit the high points and put them in front of the decision makers for approval. That's no guarantee against their waffling on it later, but you can at least get a few rounds of that nonsense out of the way on paper, where it's quick and easy. To do this, you'll of course need a diagram type or two to easily represent such things.

If you have concepts that you need to represent that are not covered by a given methodology, take a diagram from another methodology or simply make one up yourself. It's worth mentioning that making up a diagram type of your own should truly be used as a last resort. If you create it, then you have to make the legend, explain to others how it works, and give them the information that they need to be able to use it or interpret it themselves. That's not really a problem, but, if you use a stock one out of an established methodology, all you have to do is hand them the book. That saves time, and saving time while doing effective design is what we're concerned with here.

Wherever possible, try to map your design diagrams and verbiage to the programming languages and technologies that you'll be using for implementation. One of the advantages of this crude, homegrown approach to design is that you're not creating a generic, reusable methodology. You're defining the tools that you need for a single, specific piece of software. Whereas a standard design methodology must remain absolutely generic in terms of platforms and programming languages to be of benefit to the development community at large, you have no such constraints. Consequently, you're able to speak a more specific language that relates directly to the environment in which you'll be coding as well as addressing the particular business issues for which the software is being created. That does wonders for improving communications both among your team and when you want to convey something to management or your user base.

Now that each programmer has created two lists of diagram types for his own piece of the puzzle, the overall team reconvenes and compiles two global lists of diagram types, one for the allotted time and one for half the time. Because the entire team is assembled, it's a good idea to discuss interactions and interfaces between modules to determine if additional diagram types are needed. The two global lists are then updated accordingly.

You now know exactly what types of diagrams or other documents you need as a group to perform the high- to mid-level design of your system. It's now time to clarify and formalize each diagram type. For each one on your list, a decision is made on a common representation that everyone will use. In other words, you determine exactly what boxes, arrows, circles, and the like that will be used on a diagram of a given type, and what each of these symbols will represent. Then, a legend is created for each diagram type, and these legends are summarized in a document and made available on the network.

I've certainly done this sort of thing by hand with pencil and paper, but there's no reason to suffer through that these days. You should also decide as a group which pieces of software you will use to generate the documents and diagrams. If possible in the time you have available, create document templates for these diagram types if your software supports such things. If not, you can accomplish the same thing in a less elegant fashion by creating blank documents the same as you would a template and storing them, as read-only, in a common directory on your network. To create a new document you simply make a writable copy of your virtual template and go from there. It's a bit clunky but nonetheless effective and worthwhile in terms of the entire team exhibiting some consistency in the look and feel of the design documents.

You now have a design approach that's customized for your particular project and that uses a minimalist set of diagrams and documents. It leverages both the overall group knowledge of various design methodologies to broaden your design options as well as benefiting from the individual programmer's experience level to reduce the amount of documentation you have to deal with. Additionally, you've talked through the high-level design of the entire system as well as the internal architecture of the individual modules. Each programmer has also given thought to his individual part of the project and has performed a similar level of conceptualization and high-level design on his area of responsibility. In other words, you have just performed the highest level of design for your system, and the clock hasn't even started ticking yet. Having used up all the days you were given for estimating the design effort, the project manager now presents the 1.5 estimate to management and bargains for what he can get. We want to squeeze every hour out of this that we can, but make sure that you deliver the estimate by the time you said you would. It doesn't matter what the deadline is for; it's critical to your credibility that you meet each one. Having done so, a duration for the design effort is now set and the official design phase commences.

## Hitting the High Points

As discussed earlier, the goal of the design phase is not function-level detail but rather to think through the system as a whole, consider the interactions and interfaces, and prepare a design of sufficient detail to use at a later stage in performing the function-level design. The fact that the function-level design happens during the time you're given to estimate the implementation effort is immaterial. It's simply the third step in an incremental approach to design. When you're done with the official design phase, however, you should know how the major components of the system work together. At a programmer level, you should have a grasp of what objects or their procedural counterparts you'll need, along with a good idea of what the internals of these will consist of in terms of data and routines. You'll also have thought through which of these will be used internally and which will be exposed externally. The overriding question that should drive this process is very simple: when you're done, will you have the information you will later need, whether explicitly detailed or implicit in form, to figure out what needs to be done in terms of coding?

This is usually a fairly easy distinction for experienced developers to make. To take a very simple example for illustration, consider a requirement to print an invoice. You know that you're going to need data pertaining to customer account information, inventory, pricing, and the relevant tax information. You may need the ability to both retrieve this data and update it. Given this data, you'll perform some fairly straightforward calculations. Eventually, of course, you'll also need to format your results and send them to a printer. How much detail do you really need at this stage to prepare for such a task? Let's take a slightly closer look.

Assuming that you will ultimately need to provide a method that someone else can call to print the invoice, you must first know at least in a general sense where you're going to get your data. You will also be taking data as parameters to let you know which particular invoice to print. This may be as simple as an invoice number. Because the mathematical calculations in this example are trivial, the only other piece this leaves is the printing routines. You'll doubtless need to select a printer, and then you'll make formatting calls and output your results.

At this level, you simply define the type of data that you'll need to work with, such as customer information, inventory line item data, and so forth. You don't have time to spell out all the fields and data types in painstaking detail, so a certain amount of trust is required in this approach. By stating that you'll need customer information, you're saying to whoever is handling that part of the project that you need an interface to obtain this data. The minute details such as what type of variables you'll be using will be handled in real-time discussions when you get down to actually doing the coding. The same applies to the printing routines. You define the basics of the services you'll need, which serves notice to others that these interfaces will be required.

With this in mind, how many pounds of design documentation do we need to convey this in a manner sufficient for the programmer at hand to later think through the details of the functions? Not even a fraction of an ounce. By drawing whatever lines and boxes you've agreed upon to represent the input needs, data gathering, calculations, subsequent data updates, and printing options, you're going to have a pretty good idea of what your coding tasks will be. It doesn't take much to represent that if you don't get caught up in drawing a bunch of stuff just because you feel like you're supposed to.

Later, when you start doing your low-level implementation estimates, you'll take a look at what you've done here. At that stage you'll start thinking through in a bit more detail the steps required to, for instance, retrieve the customer billing information. This framework will provide adequate boundaries and mid-level conceptual design to enable you to do this. As such, the design work you perform at this stage doesn't have to be pretty, fancy, or official looking. It just needs to be effective. Nothing else matters.

## Effective Prototyping

Many times, it's useful to do a little prototyping in the design stage, particularly if management wants to be involved in the overall look and feel of things (or simply has to meddle to feel like they're managing). Of course, this has tradeoffs. Prototyping can do wonders for settling down the user interface before true coding begins and therefore save many hours of rewriting UI code again and again. However, no matter what tools you use, prototyping takes time. If you spend a significant portion of your design phase prototyping the system, you may well end up with a lot of great-looking screens and absolutely no idea of how you're going to handle the internals of the system.

In general, prototyping should be avoided unless you truly need to convey UI design concepts to someone outside the programmer group, such as management or your users. If you're in a situation wherein either your higher-ups request it or you know from personal experience that without this sort of direct user and management interaction you're doomed to an endless series of rewrites, it's best to present it as another stage of the process. In other words, when the project manager is bargaining for time to do the design phase, he will also bargain for a prototyping phase as a separate entity.

The first rule of presenting this is to avoid the temptation of bargaining for both design and prototyping time together. Instead, the wily project manager will simply ask for time to estimate the design effort as we've already covered. Several days later, when the bargaining is complete for the design phase and you're a day or two into it, the project manager returns to management in a casual manner. With the duration of the design phase already defined and indeed underway, you simply approach management as if this thought has just occurred to you. Observing the degree to which they like to be involved in all things related to UI, you ask if they'd like to see and approve some simple prototypes and screenshots before the actual development begins. This, of course, also makes you look much more responsive to the needs and desires of management and your user community, which is always a good thing. It also communicates in subtle language that you recognize their authority and are happy to cater to them. A lot of sales are made in the business world by going for the ego.

Once you have their interest and enthusiasm, you briefly get a feel for the level of detail that they'd like in the prototyping. Do try to remind them that a prototype is not the foundation of the ultimate system but rather an empty house with screens on the outside, and try to keep them from going nuts with details. A prototype is little more than a moving sequence of screenshots. Further, make sure you emphasize that *absolutely no prototyping code will be used for the production system*, as that tends to cause a lot of rewriting, creates bugs, and makes missing the deadline that much more likely. This should scare them off. If it doesn't, make sure that the prototyping tool that you use is not in the same programming language or in any way compatible with the development environment already accepted for building the system.

Once you've got some boundaries set on the prototyping, you'll also have made it plain in your conversation by implication that this isn't something you can kick out in ten minutes. You then mention that you obviously can't begin the prototyping before the design phase is complete because you'll have to take the design information into account in your prototyping. Following that, you make the observation that of course you'll need to put together a "quick estimate" on how long it will take to kick out the prototype.

Right about now you'll see the light bulb go off over their head as they realize that the prototype isn't free. At this point, you do what your marketing brethren would call "assuming the sale." This means that you tell management that it'll take roughly the same amount of time to put this estimate together as the design estimate did, so you'll have the numbers back to them in that amount of time. If you're lucky, they're still staring at the headlights just a bit and will agree. If not, it's back to bargaining for the amount of time you'll get to do the estimate for the prototyping phase.

Of course, you'll follow the exact same process with the prototyping estimate as you did with the design phase estimating. Take the days you've just materialized, gather your team, and work through all those high- to mid-level design issues that you would have liked to have addressed but just didn't have the time previously. You should, however, give some thought to the level of effort required by the prototyping. That will tell you how hard you should fight when you go back to bargain for the prototyping phase. Otherwise, the tactic is the same. Propose 1.5 times the duration that they gave you for the design phase and bargain from there. If you honestly think, because of the degree of prototyping they want done, that you can get more time, remember to ask for 50% more than you expect them to accept and go from there.

When the design phase is done and you're moving into the prototyping stage (assuming that you're using one), build only those prototypes or screen mockups that are absolutely necessary to convey a concept or get approval. If this sounds familiar, yes, it's the exact same attitude with which you approached the design phase. Prototyping can be an excellent communications tool provided you don't let yourself get bogged down in unnecessary detail. Use rapid development tools and as much smoke and mirrors as possible to provide the maximum visual feedback with a minimum of code. Remember, there are no user serviceable parts inside. In fact, if you don't have to show any actual processing, consider using a desktop publishing package, slideshow presentation software, or any other such tool that makes it easy to put together sequential screenshots without coding. Keep your focus on the goal of the exercise, communicating with your management and users, and leave the coding to the implementation phase of the project.

Another benefit of having no code in your prototype is that you can't use it in production. You want to avoid code in your prototype at all costs. If you do have to code but you know from the beginning that it's a throwaway effort, then you won't waste a lot of time on the details. You'll simply hack something together that gets the point across using whatever cheap tricks you can come up with. You'd never do that in production code, of course, but for prototypes you don't care about how solid or maintainable the codebase is. You only care that it works and meets its

purpose. Remember, the prototype is a tool for clarification and is ultimately
for the recycle bin. Fortunately, the maintenance programmer will never see it.

## When You Can't Get Even This Much Time

By now, anyone who has the luxury of doing things The Right Way is doubtless
shaking their head and clucking their tongue over my proposing such an unso-
phisticated approach to software design. Don't get me wrong; I'm with you all the
way. This is not my preferred method of operation either. Rather, it's simply how I
deal with life when I'm painted into a corner by unreasonable management.
Nonetheless, don't bother trying to explain this to anyone who lives in the ivory
towers. It's a foregone conclusion that they won't be inviting me to any of their
parties. However, while they're turning up their noses at this down-and-dirty
approach to developing software, I'm busy meeting my deadlines, which is what I
get paid to do.

Of course, the ironic part is that, although the ivory tower types would quickly
dismiss such a slash-and-burn approach to design, many of you are doubtless
shaking your heads and wondering what planet I live on that makes me think
you'd get anywhere near this much time from your management. As hard as it
may be for some to comprehend, there are shops out there where even spending a
week on design is considered a ridiculous request. I was once on a project with
three senior-level developers. We created a system that took the full extent of our
talents and a year and a half to implement. We were given two weeks to design it,
and only then after some serious bargaining. Furthermore, the only reason we got
anywhere near that amount of time was due to the fact that the head of the company was also a programmer. Heaven only knows how long we'd have been given
if we'd had to bargain with a Suit.

For any of you who may be new to the programming business, I'll state it
plainly: two weeks to design a system that required a year and a half to implement
is insanity of the highest order. It's an exercise in the absurd and any highly paid
design consultant would probably walk out of the meeting and not take the client
if those were the terms of engagement. Nonetheless, that was the time we were
given and that's what we therefore had to work with. I don't define reality. I just
have to cope with it.

So, what if you can't get enough time to do even this much? Give up? Not me. I
may go down, but I'll go down fighting. Ultimately, some of the basic principles
remain. The amount of time that you have for design is more a factor of your
negotiating skills than anything else. What you must do after you know how much
time you're given is make the most efficient use of what you have.

The things we've covered here can indeed be scaled down even further. If
you're in an extreme situation that may involve only a day or two of design, the

first thing you do is ditch the printed documentation. You don't have time for it. In a similar fashion, whether you were creating documents or not, you don't have the luxury of a lot of the concepts, such as completely detailing your class hierarchy. In times like these, ask yourself one simple question: what would you draw on a whiteboard?

When I say to ditch the printed documentation, I naturally don't mean that you should leave no written trace of the design. Rather, I simply mean that you don't want to try to draw detailed diagrams or create densely worded documents. Although you may indeed jot some of this down for posterity in your favorite drawing tool, they will be sketches. Think framework, not blueprint. Simpler does not mean less structured; it merely means that you eliminate a few levels of detail in an organized and consistent fashion. In terms of the diagrams and such that you come up with, you can also forget all but the most basic of symbolism. That might not be quite the limitation that you would expect. It's amazing what you can get across with two rectangles and a few arrows. If you can make it work while standing in front of a whiteboard, you can make it work on paper. Just remember that it's easy to get carried away with details when you're in front of a computer. You'd never draw all that stuff on a whiteboard, particularly in a meeting with a lot of erasers handy.

If you indeed find yourself in such dire straights, I would recommend reviewing the approach we've covered here and then mentally making a checklist of what levels of detail you can eliminate from the process given the amount of time you have to work with. Just as we cover only the high- to mid-level design here because it provides sufficient conceptual boundaries from which to do more-detailed work, so too is this true in progressively higher levels. If you think of a hierarchy drawing that is fifty boxes at its widest and ten boxes at its deepest, you'll quickly see how you can eliminate a few of the middle layers and still have an organized chart. In fact, I've made similar suggestions over the years regarding middle management, not that it ever did much more than get me banned from the meetings where the really good donuts were served.

## Onward to Implementation

No matter how little time you're given for design, if you keep the end goal of delivering software firmly fixed in your consciousness, throw out the rule book, and trust both to your common sense and to the experience of your team, you can put together something that will be the foundation you need for meeting your deadlines. As much as it is a tool for developing software, the design phase is also the springboard for a good estimating effort. In the end, no matter how long the project takes, if you do what you said you would in the time allotted, you're going to look good. To meet that objective, you need to know how to put together estimates that you can meet in a consistent fashion. Our next step, then, will be to move beyond the collective bargaining tactics we've had to use thus far and start digging into the details of truly estimating the implementation phase. Of course, we'll be sneaking a little design in while we're at it, but you didn't hear that from me.

# CHAPTER 7

# Practical Estimating Techniques

The dreaded estimate is at the very heart of the software development cycle and the individual programmer's efforts to meet deadlines. No one likes doing them, and most developers have a hard time projecting an accurate estimate for even the smallest program. If so many software professionals all have difficulty with this aspect of the development process, clearly the problem is not a lack of aptitude on the part of the programmer. In the minds of many, estimating a software development effort is simply one of the hardest aspects of our jobs.

Much of this problem exists not because we are unable to determine how long it will take to code a particular task but rather because we have insufficient information with which to work. Even a fortune-teller is going to need a good cup of tea before she can read the tealeaves. For many things in life, you simply must have a foundation upon which to build if you wish to have any hopes of achieving success. So too is it in our profession. To offer truly accurate estimates upon which we can base a realistic delivery schedule, we must perform some preliminary steps. Fortunately, we've actually been working our way through these crucial prerequisites as we've put forth the effort to nail down requirements and knock together a good design framework.

You simply cannot know how long an effort will take if you don't know exactly *what* that effort is. We now have those requirements spelled out. In a similar fashion, you won't be able to determine how long it will take to code a given task if you don't know *how* you're going to do it. We've addressed the larger part of that question as well. Because we intentionally avoided low-level detail in the design phase, we'll be working through the rest of *how* we're going to do things as we estimate. In the end, however, we will have answered the two fundamental questions without which we would never be able to render an accurate estimate for our project: *what* are we going to do and *how* are we going to do it? For those of you who played the murder-mystery boardgame *Clue*® as children, these questions may trigger visions of butlers, libraries, and pipe wrenches in the back of your mind. Believe me, I've fantasized about a few of those things myself over the duration of my career, but management and cubicles typically replaced the butlers and libraries. For what it's worth, however, I never could seem to find a good pipe wrench when I needed one.

## Understanding the Process

Armed as we are now with the answers to the fundamental questions of the estimation process (if not a good pipe wrench), we're in a position to kick out some numbers that actually have meaning in our less than perfect world. Let's quickly review all of the steps in the estimating process that are required in addition to the information we need about what we're creating and how we're going about it. The following list summarizes the steps required for a dependable delivery schedule.

1. Estimate everything!

2. Estimate the duration of the design phase.

3. Estimate the duration of the implementation phase.

4. Estimate the effort for the install program and integration issues.

5. Estimate the duration of the release candidate testing/debugging cycles.

6. Estimate the duration of the beta testing phase.

7. Estimate the duration of the post implementation technical documentation.

8. Estimate the duration of the post mortem phase.

9. Finally, estimate how long will it take to do the estimating steps.

The first step is perhaps the most important and the most frequently overlooked. If you don't estimate every step of the process, from the time management dreams up a new project to the time you hand them the keys and walk away, you have a window of vulnerability. This single window can be enough to blow your deadline. The last step is a summary of some of the individual steps we've taken thus far as we've offered estimates to management of how long it will take us to give them a particular estimate. It's easy in the rush of the development process to dismiss small issues as unimportant and not worth the time to consider. However, everything takes time, and time is always cumulative. The little steps you don't account for can add up to a very big cup of coffee as you work around the clock to meet a deadline.

You may notice that there isn't a step to estimate the requirements-gathering phase. In an ordered and organized shop with a company that is willing to let you go through an orderly and detailed approach to the requirements phase, you would want to start by estimating the duration that this phase would take.

However, that's also only necessary if the clock begins ticking before you begin defining the requirements. In a shop with management that actually possesses the common sense to listen to the programmers, that's probably not going to be the case. The clock really shouldn't start ticking until you know what it is that you're creating. In an imperfect world, though, the clock usually starts running the moment management decides they want a new piece of software. As you'll recall from our focus on requirements gathering, because this isn't a shop where common sense prevails that phase is the result of bargaining and political maneuvering as much as anything else. We're not given the luxury of a requirements-gathering phase as an official cycle. Consequently, there's nothing to estimate.

We've also given them an estimate of how long the design phase will take and have now performed that task, bringing us to the point at which we estimate the implementation effort. This is the next area that we focus on, but you may have noticed that there are quite a few steps after it. These are also areas where confusion can get a foothold in the development cycle. If indeed an estimate for the implementation phase is even formally constructed, it's often the last thing considered before the coding begins. The coding, however, is not the last thing that happens before you polish the bumpers and hand them the keys to their shiny new high-performance software vehicle. Once again, failure to estimate and account for these efforts will leave windows of vulnerability through which confusion and missed deadlines can enter. We'll be touching on these in a bit more detail following our discussion of the implementation phase.

## Avoiding Common Mistakes

Before we get into the steps we'll take to deliver our implementation estimate, let's first take a quick look at the way it's normally estimated in the always-under-the-gun world of the professional developer. I like to think of this as the Guess Times Two method. When asked how long a particular program or piece of code will take to deliver, we're typically not given any time to consider the details. If management is not standing there waiting impatiently, they will at least expect us to get back to them before the day is out. What tends to happen, therefore, is that the programmers take a wild guess at how long it will take, scientific or otherwise. Then, just to be on the safe side and make sure that we have a little cushion in case things go wrong, we multiply that number by two and give it to the project manager. He's no fool, of course, and knows that programmers are typically a bit optimistic with their estimates. To avoid giving management a date that runs the risk of failure, he then multiplies the numbers he was given by two and turns the estimate in.

One would think that with all that padding it would be a pretty safe estimate, but in truth these almost always fall short of the mark. That's because without truly thinking through the details of what needs to be done you'll always overlook a great many issues, many of which can be extremely time consuming. It's worth mentioning as well that in such an environment the programmers have also not nailed down the requirements or had the opportunity to do any sort of significant design phase. This weakens their chances of a good guess even further.

However, at times the estimates are so overly generous that when multiplied by two a couple of times they end up representing far more time than is actually needed, and the project finishes way ahead of schedule. Great, right? Nope. Now you have no credibility. Ultimately, for you to gain more control over the development process from management, you must be able to deliver accurate estimates and timelines. Then and only then will they be able to believe what you tell them and have sufficient confidence in your opinions and abilities to trust your recommendations on the best approach to developing software.

## The Myth of the Eight-Hour Day

Another common mistake made when estimating software development centers on the myth of the eight-hour day. If you've compiled your estimate figures in terms of hours, which in and of itself is rare enough, many project managers will then convert these numbers to calendar days by simply dividing by eight. Although that's a nice convenient number to work with, it's simply not realistic when you're trying to put together a timeline for software deliverables. Whether you're designing or coding, you never get eight hours of it done in an eight-hour day. A significant portion of any normal business day is consumed by many non-coding activities: scheduled meetings, hall meetings, administrative work, unexpected tasks, and a host of other distractions. Consequently, any timeline based on the assumption that programmers will be coding every single minute that they spend at the office is doomed to failure before it even begins.

To convert hours to days, you need to determine the percentage of your day that you actually spend coding and apply that to your calculations. A realistic modifier is to assume 62.5% productivity, or five hours of coding in an eight-hour day. Management may balk at this, call you into a meeting, and ask just what the heck you're doing with the rest of your time. It's unwise to retort that you spend it in just such pointless meetings. Nonetheless, this can sometimes be a bit intimidating. However, if you think that at the very best you'll get in more than six hours of coding in an eight-hour day, you're dreaming. The six-hour coding day is optimistic in many environments, particularly larger corporations in which bureaucracy is rampant. Consequently, you should start with six as your absolute best-case scenario and adjust it downwards to reflect your corporate reality.

Whether you come up with 6, 5.5, or 5 hours of coding per day, when you try to communicate this to management and factor it into your timeline, some fur will fly. Regardless of how unpleasant the conversations may be, it is absolutely critical that you hold your ground and establish this figure as a constant to be used in all estimates and projections. Let's look at how much of a difference this can make in your ability to hit the deadline. For the sake of example, let's assume that you work in a fairly busy and bureaucratic environment and consequently only get five hours of coding in during your eight-hour day. Management, however, insists that your timeline be based on eight-hour days. You have five programmers on your team, and with the calculation of eight-hour coding days per programmer, your project will take six months to complete. To keep it simple, we'll call six months exactly 24 weeks and we won't account for vacations, holidays, and so forth.

Here's how the numbers come out. You have five programmers working eight-hour days. Your original estimate was 4,800 hours for the project. Divide that by eight-hour days and you have 600 programmer days. Divide that by the five programmers that you have on the project, and you have 120 calendar days. Using five-day workweeks, that tells us that the project will take exactly 24 weeks to complete, hence the six-month deadline that will loom over our head.

Now let's take a look at reality. In our hypothetical environment, programmers are actually coding five hours a day. Divide 4,800 hours for the project by five-hour days and you find that it takes 960 programmer days. Now divide this by the five programmers you have on your team and it translates to 192 calendar days. Using the same five-day workweek, our project will actually take 38.4 weeks to complete. Using simple four-week months for illustration, this means that, instead of the six months that management insisted upon, this project will actually take 9.6 months to complete. What we have now is a project that is due in six months that will be 3.5 months late. Somewhere down the line, someone will figure out that you're running really, really behind. At that point, the overtime death march begins. So, you'll probably spend the last three months of the project killing yourself, but it won't be enough to offset a difference of 3.5 months. You'll still miss the deadline. The only thing worse than being screamed at by management for being late on a project is to have to listen to this nonsense when you haven't had a decent night's sleep in months. It's somewhere around this time that the night watchman starts getting a little nervous and spends a lot more time away from his post under your fifth-floor window. Don't worry about his Chihuahua, though. He's switched his therapy sessions to evening hours to avoid just this scenario.

Think five-hour days is extreme? Do the numbers with a six-hour day. You'll still be late. Really late. However, no matter how many deadlines you blow, management will typically dig their toes into the sand and cling to the myth of the eight-hour coding day. If you want your projects to succeed, be prepared to fight over this. And don't lose.

We glossed over one point when looking at the number of hours that actually get spent coding during the day. I made mention of the estimate being made in hours. This is actually another common and serious mistake that's made in estimating the development effort. When asked for an estimate for any chunk of code, the instinctive response is to offer the estimate in calendar days. This is probably due to the fact that most shops don't spend a lot of time estimating, and it's quick and easy to throw out a time in days, such as the following familiar conversation. "Hey, Joe, how long will it take you to code that user interface?" "Oh, I can have it done in about four days."

Okay, what's wrong with this picture? First of all, you have by now developed a keen eye for such things and doubtless noticed the word *about* in Joe's response. That's scary enough. Additionally, it appears that Joe gave an immediate response to the question. How on Earth could he know with any degree of accuracy that he'd be done in four days without so much as four minutes' worth of research? Finally, how many hours are in a workday? In Joe's case, I can assure you that it will be around twenty.

In the estimation process, calendar days are calculated. They are not raw data. Hours are raw data. If you figure on a six-hour day, then a project that will truly take 24 calendar weeks to complete means you're managing a 720-hour estimate. That seems pretty unwieldy. It's much easier to get your arms around calendar days, and weeks are even easier to conceptualize. How then do we perform an estimate in hours when it feels like the equivalent of building a sand castle one grain of sand at a time? The short answer is that we break tasks down until we can estimate a very small task in a very small number of hours. When we've gone through all of the tasks, we simply add up the hours. Let's have a look now at the overall process for estimating the coding phase of the project.

## Crunching the Numbers

Working on the assumption that you've been able to follow the process thus far of getting firm requirements and completing a design phase of at least adequate duration, you now have what you need to build a realistic estimate. In the end, we may adjust our estimate somewhat to account for any discomfort with the degree of design you were allowed. If you feel the process was extremely short-changed and there will be much on-the-fly design happening, the adjustment will factor this in. We'll discuss this at the end of the estimate.

You will have by now taken care of the partitioning of your system as it was a part of the design phase. From this, individual programmers are assigned their areas of responsibility in the system. The overall estimate for the project will be built in a bottom-up fashion, starting with the detailed view of the individual developers and eventually summarizing the numbers in a manner suitable for management's consumption.

Each programmer will now begin work on his personal estimate. This begins by breaking his work down into progressively smaller chunks. Doing this in a hierarchical fashion, you will eventually reach a level of detail where they're small enough to be identifiable programming tasks.

As you recall, we intentionally kept our design phase at a high- to mid-level view of the system, with the understanding that we would delve down into lower-level details when the estimating was done. We now can perform this low-level design. Our design phase may well have stopped at the level where we said, "Okay, when the user pushes this button, we print the invoice." If you happen to be the programmer tasked with making this printed invoice a reality, you haven't had a chance to think through all the details involved until now. However, you can't really determine how many hours a task will take until you know exactly what it is that you're doing.

In dividing the overall assignment into progressively lower levels of detail, you proceed by continually asking yourself exactly how you will accomplish a particular task. This is the time to think like a programmer. In other words, you need to be thinking specifically about how you will write the code. If you're unfamiliar with a technology that's needed for the work you're doing, take as much time as is realistic to research it and get a feel for what you're up against.

If you'll be depending on routines from other developers on your team (as is often the case), batch up your questions and then get together with the appropriate programmers. You'll want to get an idea from them of the amount of effort that will be required on your part to use their routines. For instance, if you need to get the customer information in the process of printing the invoice, it's likely that another programmer will have written the routines you'll call to access the database. Your question to him will center on how many hoops you'll have to jump through to accomplish this. Will you be able to call one routine to get the data? If not, how much effort and how many calls will be necessary to accomplish this? What parameters are you going to need? The answers to these questions will give you a pretty good feel for how long it will take you to write the code.

Because we don't have the time to do a complete, highly detailed and low-level design in our less than perfect environment, these questions will by necessity be a bit loose, and once again the interpretation skills of the individual programmer will be an important part of the process. Unless you've been given an extremely generous amount of time to do the implementation estimate, the programmers you meet with will not have the fully detailed interfaces prepared and documented for you. They should, however, be able to give you a pretty good idea of how they'll approach things and what's involved for you. That will have to be good enough.

As you're working through the estimates of your assignments, you will also be making use of the document types that you put together in the design phase. As you determine what's needed to implement a given module, you'll use these to sketch it out. In such a manner you will be generating the low-level design documents you need at the same time as you analyze your tasks for the purpose of estimating.

How low do you go when breaking things down into more detail? No individual coding task should ever be larger than four hours, and that extreme is to be avoided. If you're averaging around two hours per coding task, you're probably low enough to have some confidence in how long it will really take to write the code. At this level, you're forced to think through the details at a function level. The larger the chunk, the greater the margin for error when estimating. Even if the number is less than four hours, if you don't feel confident keep breaking it down until it feels realistic. Durations of quarter and half hours are perfectly acceptable. What you'll end up with is a list of individual coding tasks and their associated durations.

Now fire up your favorite spreadsheet program. List each coding task and the number of hours required. Be sure as you're estimating the individual coding portions that you include time for unit testing and a little debugging. Also keep these numbers as real as you can get them. In other words, these numbers won't have any padding. Be conservative, but keep the numbers legit.

Now we want to summarize these numbers. Add up the estimates for all of your coding tasks. If this total is more than forty hours, start breaking your work down into progressively smaller modules with a subtotal for each until none exceed forty hours. Naturally, you'll want to align these divisions to the actual module divisions in your overall assignment. You now have your coding assignments detailed and individually estimated as well as having a list of subtotals that summarize these detailed estimates.

It's a forgone conclusion that, as you code your work and hand it over to whoever is doing the testing, there will be bugs. This means that you'll have to take the time to diagnose the problem and fix it so that your testers can verify the fix and move on. You must leave room for these QA failures in your estimates or you'll just start getting behind when they happen. To account for this, for each subtotal that you've created you will add a line reading "QA Failures" and set the value to a calculation of 10% of the subtotal. You will also hit snags and bumps in the road as you go along that you could never have anticipated. If you ignore this reality, you'll only get behind when it happens. Consequently, for each subtotal you also add a line reading "The Unexpected" and also set this value to 10% of your subtotal.

For each subtotal you now add a "Complete Subtotal" line. This value will be the sum of the subtotal and the two lines you added for QA failures and the unexpected. It's now time to add the bottom line, which summarizes these completed subtotals into one final number, which is the total amount of hours that it will take you to deliver your coding assignment.

## Converting Hours to Delivery Dates

You will actually have two deliverables to pass along. The first will be this summarized set of raw hours. However, a timeline and delivery schedule is more than just numbers. Dependencies must be taken into account as well. For instance, if you're the one doing the invoice printing, you're going to need the data access routines before you can finish. If the other programmer has other tasks to complete before he can get to the ones you need, you may experience a delay.

Additionally, it's not enough to simply calculate how long a project will take based on hours, convert those to days, and subsequently a calendar delivery date before you begin coding. You need to be able to track your progress as it goes along so that you'll know if a problem arises. Naturally, it's our desire to orchestrate our work such that no overtime is required and the project is delivered on schedule. However, even with factoring in the unexpected, we may still fall behind at points. If we realize this quickly, we can apply a brief moment of extra effort to get back on schedule and then continue on with a normal and reasonable workweek. Failure to do this will result in an end-of-project crunch and all the stress, overtime, and nervous little dogs that accompany it.

The way we handle this is to set incremental milestones along the way for each programmer. Along with the estimate figures turned in, each programmer will also define the preferred order of their tasks. I say *preferred* as this may change due to dependencies. In a separate document, the programmer will list the order in which he wishes the tasks to proceed. He will additionally make note of tasks that are dependent upon other circumstances, as well as note tasks that can occur at any point in the process regardless of the preferred order. This information, along with the hourly estimates, is passed along to your team lead or project manager. If team leads are in your structure, they will of course summarize the estimates from all of their developers and report this to the project manager.

At this point, a lot of work falls on the shoulders of the project manager, or whoever happens to be walking point for your project. Even if you're the sole programmer on a project, you should take the time to follow the next steps. Although you may not have any dependencies, the rest of the process applies regardless of the size of the team.

Your first task as project manager is to convert the estimates you've been given from hours to calendar days, based on the five- to six-hour coding days that you've determined are the reality for your environment. Using these days, you'll eventually be building your timeline based on five-day weeks. You must also factor in company holidays, vacations, and any other known days that programmers will not be in the office, such as time offsite for developer training seminars, participation in user training sessions, work as a maintenance programmer on previous versions of products on which they've coded, and so on.

Now that you know how many days that the chunks of work will take, it's time to arrange the individual programmers' tasks according to any existing dependencies. If you don't have a project management software package available to you, see if you can get management to approve one. It's a relatively small expense because you don't need a license for each developer. The project manager is the only one who will be using it. The programmers certainly won't be interested in it and will avoid it like the plague if at all possible. However, when you're trying to order a set of tasks that take dependencies into account, it pays for itself the first day in terms of the time you save.

Naturally, you can order dependencies by hand if you must, although that sort of thing tends to make for cranky project managers, to be sure. Nonetheless, regardless of the tools you have at your disposal, you must now order the efforts of each developer so that, if at all possible, no one is sitting idle waiting on another. If you do find such a stopping point, ask the developer who would be idled if there are any tasks that he can break down further, such that as he's waiting on someone else before he continues with his current task he can switch over and perhaps work on the internals of another task that have no dependencies. If this is possible, these switchover tasks are then broken out and subtotaled separately.

Having ordered the efforts of the individual developers, the project manager then defines a series of milestones for each programmer. A milestone is a date by which a specific task is due. Having these milestones is how you keep track of your efforts and know if you're falling behind. Just as you kept your granularity small on the hourly estimates, keep the milestones small as well. In addition to minimizing the vulnerability of any one portion of your schedule, it has an additional benefit: having many small milestones allows you to rack up multiple successes. At any point in the process that management cares to check in, you're able to report that not only is everything right on schedule, you've already hit 42 of your projected milestones. Remember, every single success enhances your credibility with those further up the food chain. If you want to change the way they do things, you have to be able to prove that your ideas actually work. Having multiple milestones in a project gives you just this opportunity. As such, your milestones should not be longer than two weeks at a time. Smaller is better.

Based on the module dependencies, you now lay out these incremental milestones that will, when combined, represent the overall timeline for your project. Project management software will allow you to plug in holidays and weekends and automatically derive the dates for you based on the number of hours in your day. In our case, that will be between five and six. It's not until this point that you can truly fine-tune the dependencies. Although you were able to take an initial swing at it prior to this point, you're now dealing with actual calendar dates and can see exactly when one programmer is to finish his deliverable and when the next programmer needs it. As such, there may be a bit of tweaking and reordering at this stage of the game. After any ordering issues have been ironed out, you'll be able to determine your actual specific milestones with their associated dates for each of your developers.

You now know how many hours small, granular coding tasks will take. Based on a realistic coding day and the consideration of holidays and other time off, you also know how many calendar days each task will take. You've ordered the efforts of your developers such that there is no idle time due to dependencies, and you've given them their list of milestones. They now know what tasks they are to perform and the order in which they should proceed. They also know what their deliverables are and when they are due. You now have everything you need to keep a very close eye on the project. Based on the programmer milestones, you now summarize these to slightly higher milestones appropriate for management. For larger projects, milestones in months are fine for middle and upper management. However, list each individual programmer milestone that will occur as a line item under each major milestone. This gives you plenty of ammunition when they question your progress as you're able to not only tell them that a major deliverable is on track but exactly which lower-level milestones you're currently implementing. Being able to report in this degree of detail is the sort of thing that increases management's confidence in you. A good field commander must know the status and position of his troops at all times. A good high-level commander must be able to depend on his field commanders for this.

## Don't Forget the Final Details

We have now estimated and organized our implementation effort, but we're not quite ready to turn in the paperwork. Before you can give management a date when they can consider the software ready to ship, you need to take into account several other steps that happen after the implementation is complete. First, using the techniques we just outlined, identify the programmers who will participate in writing the installation programs and scripts or who deal with any other related installation or integration efforts. They'll usually be junior programmers, not because of the skills involved but rather because all of the senior programmers will have mysteriously vacated the premises when it comes time to make these assignments. Add these estimates to your timeline as a separate milestone, breaking them down into smaller milestones if needed.

The next step is a bit less specific: you must estimate the duration of the testing and debugging cycles of the release candidate. This will have to be done based on a combination of experience with past releases and the amount of time that you think management will stand for before they insist that you release the product. In truth, testing is almost always curtailed long before it should be, and this explains the poor state of most commercial software currently on the market. Nonetheless, we're trying to deal with reality here, so the numbers that you come up with on this are again a cross between practical experience and collective bargaining. This phase will also be listed in the timeline as separate milestones.

If you can swing it, your project should have a well-defined beta testing phase as we've previously discussed. The time considerations for this are much as they are for the release candidate testing phase. Take what you can get and put another milestone in the project timeline.

At this point, you have the timeline complete in terms of when the product can be shipped, and you want to label the product release date in big bold letters on the timeline. However, it does not fully represent when the development team will be available for the next assignment. If you don't include this in your timeline, you risk getting sucked into the next adventure before you've brought this one to complete closure, which will surely bite you in the maintenance phase. Actually, it will bite you somewhere else but I'm trying to be polite.

After everyone has had a good night's sleep or two, you want to convene the entire development group including testers, technical writers, programmers, installers, trainers, and anyone else who had a hand in making it a reality. First and foremost, never underestimate the value of morale. If you're in charge, you're looking at a room full of people who just put in a significant effort, kicked fanny, and took names. This is the time to let them know how much you appreciate all that they've done and to tell them in no uncertain terms just how great you think they are to have done so.

Little plastic plaques and awards are considered a shallow and insulting joke by most corporate workers, but, oddly enough, middle and upper management never seem to pick up on this. Maybe they just live in their own little world and don't bother to pay attention to what matters to the troops who do the real work. If at all possible, the best way to reward people for excellent work is with money, or anything else that has real and tangible value such as extra vacation time (that you actually let them use), holiday packages in resort hotels, or any other real, live perk that they can enjoy. Unfortunately, in many companies the project manager just doesn't have that authority or influence over management.

This doesn't mean that there's nothing you can do to maintain the morale that has already given you one success. Although money is the reason we go to work each day, it's an extremely understated and overlooked fact in the business world that people will practically kill themselves putting out excellent work for nothing more than recognition and sincere public appreciation from the people they work for.

I know that this is what the little plastic plaques are supposed to be about, but for some reason it just doesn't sell to the rank-and-file production workers. Maybe it's all the corporate speak and buzzwords that make it seem phony, but there never seems to be any true sincerity behind it. Rather, it comes across as an empty ritual. Praise and recognition work to motivate and gratify people only when it feels personal.

Consequently, if you're a project manager and you can't get any real benefits or rewards for your people, at a minimum you can tell them face to face, in front of their peers, about the things you saw them do that really made a difference. Trivial as it may seem, you can also get the point across by taking some money out of your own pocket to do things as simple as taking them all out to lunch. If you explain to them that you're not able to get them the tangible perks you think they deserve but show them that nonetheless you want to do something for them on your own, you'll find that an extremely loyal group of people are backing you on your next project. If you can do this throughout the course of the project, occasionally ordering the pizza when they're working late, inviting them over to your house for a weekend cookout and all-day boogie to help keep spirits up, or any other little things to show them that you truly appreciate what they do for you, you'll find that there's absolutely nothing they can't find a way to accomplish. Esprit de corps is an extremely powerful thing.

## Wrapping up the Project

This may seem a bit of a digression while we're discussing estimates, but the next milestone we want in our timeline is that of the project's post mortem phase. While the phrase technically translates as *after death*, it's generally used to describe the assessment phase after a project is complete. In our case, it will be the evaluation of what we went through to succeed. This is where your people have a meeting or two and discuss the things that went wrong and how they can be avoided the next time, along with the inspirations that team members have come up with for additional ways to improve the process. This is a crucial phase not only for the purpose of the aforementioned morale but also in terms of fine-tuning your overall development process. After several projects and their subsequent evaluation phases, you'll start getting a really streamlined approach to delivering software in your company's environment. Of course, the time for the post mortem phase will be another time element for which you'll have to negotiate.

The next thing you want to do is put together accurate technical documentation that reflects the reality of your codebase. Your design documents, complete with coffee rings, red ink, and torn pages, will be of some use to you here as a starting point. However, each programmer must take the time to go through his code and from these two create a new set of documents that tells it like it is. Before you slough your way through this, bear in mind that this is the documentation that the maintenance programmer will be trusting when he's trying to fix your bugs at two o'clock in the morning. Unless you've found a way to take the inventory control program offline, I'd suggest you do a good job on this. Besides, you never know. You might *be* the maintenance programmer.

The amount of time you get for post-implementation technical documentation is again a matter of bargaining. Take the amount of time that you think will fly with management, multiply it by 1.5 for bargaining purposes, and list it on the timeline as yet another milestone.

Many of the steps after the actual implementation are ones for which there is no procedure for determining the time. Instead, being aspects that must be negotiated, they might change. Keep this in mind as you turn in your now complete timeline to management and be prepared to tweak the appropriate areas if needed. However, hold firm on your implementation estimates because they're crucial to your ability to deliver on time. Pick your battles if you must. It's much more important to have them sign off on the implementation estimates than it is to gain an extra week for technical documentation. It's nice to get both, but have your priorities in order if you have to fight for one and give a little on the other.

## What If Things Didn't Go by the Book?

The possibility exists that you weren't given the time to do the requirements or design phases. How does that affect the implementation estimates? Naturally, if your requirements are fuzzy, you're going to get into trouble when they change the rules on you in the middle of the game. There's just not much that you can do about that. As for design, if you can at least get a little time to do the implementation estimate, you can compensate somewhat. We've used this phase as a covert way of finishing the design by performing the low-level design as we're in the estimation phase. In a similar fashion, if you're in an extreme bind, you can take your best shot at high- and mid-level design at this point as well. In an extremely abbreviated fashion, you simply gather together at the beginning of the estimating phase and hit the whiteboard, sketching out the major high- and mid-level modules. In extremely poor environments, you may have only a matter of hours to do this, but even this amount of effort gives you a chance to think your way through the system. You then partition the modules out and assign them to the programmers, who perform the implementation estimates and lower-level design just described as much as is possible in the time allowed.

If you find yourself in such a situation, I hope you've got some seasoned developers on your team because much depends on the individual abilities of the programmers. No matter what your situation, however, it is better to take a shot at high-level design and low-level estimating than to do nothing. It may not put you in a position to succeed, but it may at least temper the scale of the disaster on the horizon. In other words, do the best you can with what you have to work with, but have a plan and follow it. A little organization goes a long way.

Once again, there's also the very real possibility that you may turn in your timeline only to have management balk and say that the release date is unacceptable. If your management is completely unreasonable, no books or procedures on the market can help you. Given their position on the food chain, if they insist on your doing something stupid, you must either perform the stupid task or update your résumé. That is the reality with which we all must live. However, you can do some things to increase your bargaining power for the next project.

For example, document the exchanges that you had with management, the dates that you had them, your recommended dates, and the dates they forced upon you instead, along with any other such scenarios where you tried to provide a realistic process and were overridden. Keep these documents at home, not the office. Don't even think about making the statement that information on your work computer should be private. You don't own the computer. The company does. If you want something kept private, keep it at home.

When the project crashes and burns at the end, as you know it will, the records you've kept regarding the progress, the problems you encountered, and the decisions made by management are supportive evidence that you can use to bolster your position on the next project. When you once again fight to put an ordered procedure in place for the development process, you will be reminded that your last project was late, or perhaps even a disaster. Assuming you're prepared to fight until you get control of the process, you now have the highly detailed evidence you need to give them both barrels. Diplomatically, of course. It will be particularly useful if you can show that all of your tasks did in fact take the amount of time that you estimated. This leads to the obvious conclusion that, if your original timeline was honored, you would have delivered on time. If the delivery date was unacceptable to management, the options were either to reduce functionality or give you additional resources, not ignore the realities of how long the work was going to take. No one likes to have this sort of thing thrown in their faces, to be sure. Nonetheless, unless you're content to work on disaster after disaster, you're going to have to stand up and fight for a realistic development process if you're going to institute any degree of change.

In the end, it's all about power. Your power to create change for the better will be based on your ability to document your successes and identify the processes that ensured your failures. The more times that you can prove that your methods work and lead to the successful deployment of software projects, the more power you'll gain for the future. One of the most critical elements of this is your ability to accurately project the duration of your efforts. Learn to estimate software development accurately, and you'll gain the credibility that you need over time to let control of the process come back to the programmers, where it belongs.

A large part of your project being considered a success is not only your ability to hit the deadlines but having a solid and dependable system when it hits the streets. No one cares if you delivered on time if your system is as stable as a house of cards. Consequently, one of the key elements for delivering high-quality software is the quality assurance process, which is curiously absent in all but a few development shops. That's where we're headed next.

# CHAPTER 8

# Fighting for Quality Assurance

Right up there with the fate of all those single socks whose mate goes missing, one of the great mysteries of the universe is how an industry that produces something as complex as computer software can exist with the almost complete absence of highly trained, skilled, professional testers. Actually, I have some theories concerning the secret life of socks without partners that typically involve late nights at a noisy singles bar drinking fabric-softener shooters and dancing to old fifties rock tunes. Isn't that where the sock hop really got its name? You may think that that's a bit fanciful, but it can't hope to compare with the notion of programmers spending months or even years writing hundreds of thousands of lines of code only to have management ship the product with less time spent on testing than it takes for a stray sock to get a date on Saturday night. It's so bizarre it just can't be real. However, for those of us who have spent many a late night in frantic debugging sessions trying to do damage control on such hastily shipped programs, it's a reality that is far too convincing.

How is it that the concept of quality control can be so completely alien to the very industry that needs it the most? Can you imagine the fiscal and navigational chaos that would ensue if automobiles were sold with the same casual attitude that accompanies a software release? Even a casual inspection by the manufacturer would reveal whether wheels were completely bolted on or if the throttle had a tendency to stick somewhere between the posted speed limit and Mach 1. Attorneys would have a field day if automotive manufacturers delivered cars with brakes that worked, well, most of the time. Yet, in the software industry these examples pale in comparison to the state in which programs are commonly delivered to paying customers.

## How Do We Get Away with Buggy Releases?

One of the reasons that our profession is so incredibly sloppy in its standards is a very simple one. Why do companies ship buggy software? Because they can. This is due to a couple of fundamental differences between the manufacture of software and the manufacture of hard goods that you can touch and feel. First of all, if a manufacturer delivered 10,000 cars that each had a dozen fundamental flaws, the cost of returning them to the factory, taking them apart, scrapping the defective parts, putting them back together again, and delivering them once more to the dealerships would be astronomical. Just one such fiasco could very easily put a company out of business. Even if they survived the financial losses, consumer confidence would plummet. Who in their right mind would want to buy a car that might crash into a telephone pole due to faulty steering and undependable brakes? An automotive manufacturer that actually released finished products that are comparable in quality to the typical software release would be out of business within a week.

Software, however, is quite a bit different in this regard. There's very little cost involved in putting out a patch for a bug discovered in a released product, particularly because the maintenance programmer who worked around the clock for three days straight to fix it is on salary. No wonder they're a little cranky. Because of this, we don't have the same financial accountability faced by those who work in factories. The primary cost of software is labor. If you don't pay for overtime, then (from a business perspective) there's no real incentive to avoid it. Consequently, it's easier to just ship the product early to beat your competitors to market and worry about the bugs later. This is done so often that it's probably taught in colleges to the people getting their MBAs. From a very simple profit-and-loss perspective, there are no advantages to spending months on testing, not to mention the additional payroll incurred by having to staff quality assurance professionals. The ease with which users can now download patches from an Internet Web site just makes matters worse. It seems to validate management's decision to skip the rigorous testing that's so crucial to other industries.

Another reason we get away with this has to do with conditioning the consumer. We, as an industry, have been shipping poor-quality software for so many years now that the general public has become convinced that all software will just naturally have bugs. They view it as an inescapable reality that cannot be changed. If you told them that it was possible to deliver software that was 100% stable and bulletproof—an application that never, ever crashed or misbehaved—they'd probably eye you cautiously and ask just how much fabric softener you'd been drinking.

Those who manage software companies believe that they have absolutely no incentive to convince their customers otherwise. Indeed, it seems like they have it made. Why in the world would they want to change the status quo when they have their customers so snowed that they would never dream of holding a software company's feet to the fire as they would an automobile manufacturer's? You can talk to management about excellence, quality, art, moral obligations, and other idealistic things until you're blue in the face. But, if you're not speaking in terms of profit and loss, you've lost your audience in the first sentence. This is the business world. It exists to make money.

When you factor in the general public's insatiable desire for new software, it's easy to see that, between their hunger for the latest gadget and their conditioned acceptance of buggy products, businesses are effectively shielded from the consequences of poor quality control. In short, our management short-changes the testing process because it seems profitable to do so.

Because of this, testing is not taken seriously as a discipline in our industry. What little spot checking that does occur on our systems before we ship them is usually done by whatever general office personnel happen to be available at the moment, and that's only if no other department is screaming for the resources. Consequently, in a classic example of supply and demand, you'll find yourself hard pressed to hire a top-notch quality assurance team. Although some have chosen software testing as their trade and have the skills and training to back it up, there just aren't very many of them around when you compare their numbers to the hordes of programmers kicking out code every day. That doesn't help matters. I have personally spent months and months trying to hire a single senior-level tester without success, and this is in a city with a huge pool of software professionals available. That makes you look pretty stupid after you've just fought tooth and nail with management to get approval for the position. However, the difference in quality that even one good tester can make negates that in very short order.

## Justifying a Quality Assurance Effort

It would seem thus far that, no matter how much sense it might make in terms of quality software, from a business perspective I haven't made much of a case for hiring testers. However, like many things, it seems this way if you look at only a small part of the overall picture. It is undoubtedly true that on the front end the expense of software QA is a net loss when you can get your customers to download bug fixes at no cost to your company. However, that doesn't take into account the bane of software profits everywhere: technical support.

With absolutely no disrespect intended towards tech support professionals (some of these guys make maintenance programmers look positively tame in comparison), support is universally considered an expense by management. As such, it is kept to the absolute bare minimum staff that can be maintained without having your customers show up on your doorstep with pitchforks and torches. That might explain why some of these folks are a bit on the excitable side.

However, what's often overlooked is that the amount of money that must be spent on technical support to keep your office lobby from looking like a village mob scene from an old Frankenstein movie is in direct proportion to the quality of the release. The buggier the release, the more effort you have to expend to convince your paying customers that giving you their money really wasn't a bad idea, no matter how it may seem. If you short-change your support effort, the usually forgiving public will eventually write your company off as an establishment that markets absolute garbage. Let me tell you, folks, given the slack that the paying public gives the software industry, if they get to that point you can kiss your revenues goodbye. Sales will plummet, and the only thing left of your profits will be that shiny red sports car that the CEO somehow managed to buy when no one was looking. Put out enough bad releases and eventually your reputation and your income suffers. That's a net loss that could be prevented by taking quality assurance as seriously as you do any other aspect of the development process.

Another expense caused by bad releases is the end result of programmers working night and day trying to patch up buggy versions. Even if they're being paid salary and given no financial perks whatsoever for the additional hours, the time they spend fixing problems that never should have gone out the door in the first place is time that they can't spend on your next product. While your competitors pour all their resources into getting their next version to market before you do, your programmers are busy putting out fire with gasoline. Of course, you can solve that problem by simply hiring more programmers so that some do maintenance and others work on new development. Now you're spending money and chewing into profits. Either way it's gonna cost you. The latter is just more obvious. Eventually, your best and brightest developers will tire of the treadmill and opt to leave for greener pastures. Losing talent is more expensive than either of the two previous scenarios. All of it is more expensive than hiring professional testers.

Although management is ultimately responsible for the decisions that are made, programmers are not blameless in this area. The plain and simple truth of it is that programmers do not fight hard enough to change these things. They'd rather be coding. And they will be, just as soon as those bug reports start coming in from the field. As in every other area of the development process that we've touched on thus far, it may be an uphill battle, but with persistent effort management can be persuaded to try a quality assurance process. It will be harder for you to track absolute results in this area when you want to demonstrate to those up the food chain that the QA process has more than paid for itself. Still, everyone loves a winner. When your releases start going out the door on time, bug reports slow to a trickle, and the overall feedback from your customers is positive, management will eventually notice. Marketing will notice as well, for your sales will doubtless increase with the quality of your product.

## What's a Tester?

If you can convince management of these things, at least enough to get their attention, the next thing you'll typically have to do in your fight for testing resources is to explain exactly what a QA person actually does. You'll find that, although they think they know what a tester's job description is, it will be a far cry from reality.

The first and most fundamental aspect of a quality assurance professional is a person who, strangely enough, spends their entire workday involved in nothing but duties related to software testing. This will certainly seem unusual to management, who typically considers the receptionist a tester after pulling her off of the telephone for two hours. A full-time tester is just that—a full-time trained professional. Hijacking anyone who can at least click a mouse is not going to yield the highest quality results.

A professional tester is also a person who studies the art and science of software QA with the same degree of devotion and interest that a programmer applies to learning the latest coding technology. They are constantly thinking of new ways to improve the process and keep up with the latest approaches and methodologies, just as we do in our world.

What output does a tester produce? The cornerstone of any testing process is the test plan, a detailed approach to putting your software through the wringer in a very thorough and methodical manner. Test plans are an organized and structured collection of test cases. An individual test case is the procedure for verifying one small and specific piece of functionality.

For instance, if you've written a word processor, one test case would involve invoking the file-save mechanism and making sure that the work is, in fact, saved to disk. However, it's not as simple as scribbling on a piece of paper a reminder to save the file. Most GUI applications feature multiple ways to accomplish the same task. You might save the file by invoking a selection from the main menu, or you might also select a button on a toolbar. Additionally, there will probably be a keyboard shortcut as well as multiple places where you might be able to choose the function from a context-sensitive menu. The test case for saving a file would offer step-by-step instructions for each of these discreet operations. Furthermore, you can't really say that you've successfully saved a file until you've read it back in and confirmed that the contents don't now look like hieroglyphics from some ancient language. Consequently, each test case will also have explicit instructions for verifying that the desired result did in fact take place. The combination of performing the detailed actions and validating the results constitutes the complete execution of one test case.

As you can no doubt imagine, writing such detailed test cases for the entire software system is a full-time job in and of itself. Of course, that's rather the point. There's no way that the developers or any part-time resource is going to be able to build a test plan of this quality and comprehensiveness. Typically, the tester will create these documents in the company's standard word processor, and they should be stored in version control in a separate project dedicated to QA. Along with the detailed steps to perform, these documents (when done well) also have a checkbox next to each case so that whoever is running the test can keep track of their progress. A signature line with a date is also common so that the QA manager, or project manager if the former doesn't exist, can keep track of what tests were performed and by whom. A database can also be used to track the information, but it's frequently handier to have paper and pen nearby when executing the test cases because running a database app might interfere with the test. Never underestimate the value of low tech.

Automated testing tools are also available for most major platforms. These are powerful programs that offer the ability to record the user's actions for subsequent playback, thus speeding up and automating specific tasks. It is common for such programs to save these operations in the form of a script, typically using its own proprietary language or API. This will then allow the tester to edit the scripts and customize the operations further. Along with automated program execution, these systems have various methods of capturing screenshots for comparison to a previously saved reference, comparing file contents and other such things. This allows them to generate reports at the end of a test run so that you can fire off an overnight regression test and check the results in the morning. As with so many other computer-automated tasks, you can perform a tremendously complex series of tests overnight or in the space of an hour or two that would normally have taken manual testers a week to run. As you've no doubt already guessed, a professional quality assurance person is someone who learns to manipulate such automation systems with the same degree of skill and productivity that a programmer demonstrates with a compiler.

Earlier, I mentioned both art and science in relation to testing. Just as programming is neither art nor science alone, but rather a creative but still scientific combination of the two, so too is testing. We've just touched on some of the more technical aspects. To these the veteran tester adds the concept of free-play testing. Actually, that's probably the only kind that most apps have seen. In free play, the tester simply uses the software, noting any deficiencies encountered while doing so. It's not as simple as it may seem, however, because when a bug is found the tester must write up a bug report. A crucial requirement of any bug report is a list of detailed steps to reproduce the problem. This is easy when using a test case because it's already documented. However, in the case of free-play testing, many times a tester must spend hours trying to find a consistent method of reproducing an obscure and intermittent bug. They must then be able to communicate what they did with the same step-by-step precision required in writing a test case so that the programmer can first reproduce and then fix the deficiency. This is an acquired skill.

Beyond simply using the application in a manner that's likely to be similar to that of end users in the real world, the seasoned tester also adds another approach to the free-play phase in which they actively and cleverly try to break the application and intentionally cause problems. This is often a rather intuitive approach that combines years of testing experience with an intimate knowledge of the application under test. You just wouldn't believe some of the stuff these guys pull. When they come to you with some rather fanciful scenarios, you must chant to yourself, "better here than in the field."

I once had a tester perform a particularly nonsensical sequence of keystrokes that culminated in the application crashing in a very vivid and memorable fashion. After offering the obligatory profanity, I told her that her example was ridiculous and that I strongly suspected that she came up with this sequence by randomly banging on the keyboard. Who, I asked, would ever perform such a highly speculative sequence of events? Her response came swiftly and with conviction: the user might.

She then admitted, with pride, that she *had* in fact been randomly banging on the keyboard and then subsequently figured out exactly how to reproduce it. Without question, she was a testing goddess. The bottom line is that no application should ever crash, no matter what the user does. If it's a bogus action and will cause harm, the programmer should simply not allow it. That's how you write a solid app. It takes seasoned, veteran testers like this to help you make your system bulletproof. You won't get there without help. Of course, this may also explain those mornings where I could swear that I saw tiny canine footprints on my keyboard. In their quest for quality software, testers can make some strange alliances.

After getting a quick look at the life and times of a professional software tester, you can see why you need people who dedicate their professional career to garnering these skills. Any programmer knows all too well how complex even the simplest of applications can be. The thought of trying to methodically test every possible code path just makes me twitch. Truly achieving this goal may be possible only on paper, but the closer you can get to it the more confidence you can have in your program. It is the tester's goal in life to do just that, and it requires every bit as much skill, experience, and training as does coding.

## Building Your Team

Now that you know what professional testers do, all you have to do is get management to hire some, right? Good luck. To those in positions of power, testers are perceived as nothing more than minimum-wage workers who sit in front of a computer and use the program. Like so many other things in the corporate world, if you insist on trying to change that all at once, you're doomed to failure. Instead, the road to success is an incremental one.

In the beginning, management will probably not commit the money to hiring trained professionals, even if you've managed to at least partially convince them of how important it is to the overall development effort. You'll have better luck building a quality assurance team by sneaking it in the back door. Just make sure they don't leave the door ajar when they come in. The watchman's partner has been known to tiptoe into the company cafeteria for a late-night snack or two given the chance. Your design documents are typically the preferred desert.

How do we surreptitiously build a team of testers when management won't authorize the expenditures? We train our own. In the beginning, use any warm body you can get. As you gain momentum, you'll eventually have the credibility to start hiring professionals, but you must first show some results to justify your request for funding. It's fairly common for management to dig up a person here and there to help with the testing, particularly in the end stages of the project. What we'll do is start asking for those people early on in the process. Although the testers should really start writing test cases based on the requirements and design docs as soon as they're available, that's going to be a hard sell on your first attempt. Wait until you've got some form of user interface up and running on your program. As soon as you do, start lobbying for resources. Take anyone even moderately trainable that you can get, for however many hours that they'll agree to commit. Beggars can't be choosers.

Once you have some fingers on the keyboard, it's going to be up to you to train them. As if you didn't have enough to do already, right? Of course, to train a tester you must understand the process yourself, but we've covered much of the basics already. Just as it's not been my intention to teach experienced programmers how to write code in this little treatise, neither will I make any attempt to represent myself as a testing guru. If you're not familiar with the fundamentals, some decent books are available. There isn't the volume of reading material available that there is on programming, but with dedicated effort you can find some worthwhile references.

However, getting started with a skeleton testing effort is often just an exercise in the obvious. Well, perhaps it's obvious, but the second part of that is actually *doing* it. Therefore, we start by putting together some simple test cases that cover basic and obvious functionality. Continuing with our word processor example, you might write quick test cases for opening a file, saving it, and printing it. After walking through these with your borrowed resources, you suggest that they continue with the effort by simply working through the main menu one item at a time. In other words, for most programs the main menu is the entry point for the most fundamental operations in the system. Starting with the first menu entry, have them write a test case for each option that a user can access by this menu. If they're given enough time to do more, move on to the toolbars and buttons. Next, give them a list of the keyboard shortcuts and context menus. While they're doing this, your team is continuing with the coding. Of course, as they're performing the actions themselves in order to write up the test cases, they'll encounter the occasional bug. As this happens, they'll document the incident in the prescribed manner and continue on with writing the test cases.

# Training Your Testers

I mentioned an incremental approach because it may be too much to expect in the beginning that you'll get test cases for all scenarios. That's why you start with the main menu. If you can get even that much done, it's a huge step in the right direction, and those test cases don't go away. At any point in the future, you can always build on them when you get the opportunity to add more. If you feel that you'll start getting some resistance after the first level of test cases, have the testers switch over to running them, or perhaps move on to free play. Management views the work of testers in much the same way as that of programmers. If they're not actively testing the application, they're not really testing.

It's important that you not only start training your testers but also maintain the support and enthusiasm of management. Without this, you have nothing. Make sure as you're training the testers that you also keep notes of exactly how you're training them. Keep your training documents as organized as you would your design docs so that you can use them for the next person that management throws your way. Okay, perhaps you won't write your training documents on cocktail napkins, but I'm sure you get the idea. You're building a process here, so document it well.

One of the most fundamental things you'll need to teach your testers is how to write up a bug report. It will help tremendously if you can provide them with a database form or a printed document that will step them through all of the required fields, providing a list of acceptable choices wherever possible. The easier that you can make it for them, the better chance you have of their actually doing it. Most of the fields, such as the criticality of the error (incorrect functionality, cosmetic, full-blown system crash, and so on), version of the code, and so forth will be easy for them to understand and work with. The most difficult but important part of the bug report is the steps to reproduce the bug. As any developer knows, the bug report is next to useless without this. This procedure requires attention to detail, and you'll have to teach them how to think in steps. Part of this success will come when they understand that they can't assume any knowledge on the part of the person reading the report. This means that they must spell out in mind-numbing detail exactly what you must do to create the bug, such as the following series of steps.

1. Start the application.

2. From the main menu, select File.

3. From the File menu, select Open.

4. From the File Open dialog, select the file BugReport1.txt.

5. Press the Page Down key exactly three times.

6. Press the Enter key to start a new paragraph.

7. Type the phrase "This is never gonna work."

8. From the main menu, select File.

9. From the File menu, select Save.

10. Observe that the application has crashed, displaying a diagnostic dialog box.

Our example has several points to note. First, we started the application. It seems obvious and pointless because you can't perform the subsequent actions if the app isn't running. Ah, but what if the bug happens only when you start the application fresh? Furthermore, if you don't start fresh, who knows how the previously performed actions may affect the state, perhaps masking the bug altogether? Also, in our example the bug really occurs as soon as you attempt to save a modified document. However, the more specific the bug report, the better chance you have that people can reproduce it. By explicitly specifying that the user should press the Page Down key three times, start a new paragraph, and enter a specific bit of text, you know that you can reproduce the bug each and every time. This is not important to only the developer because, when the bug is fixed, a tester will have to run these steps to verify the fix and close the incident. Particularly because you're training your own QA team, you can never assume the level of technical expertise that the tester who closes the incident will have. The other thing to note is that there is a specific file, BugReport1.txt, that is used to reproduce the problem. Attaching or otherwise making available specific data files is always a very useful step in reproducing bugs, as often the data in the file gives clues to the problem.

Even if the list of steps seems obvious to you, I can assure you that this level of detail will not be obvious to the newly trained tester. Instead, left to their own devices, your bug report will look like the following.

1. Program crashed while saving a file.

That's all you'll get, and it's not their fault. Testing is a specific discipline in the software development business. It's unreasonable for you to expect that anyone without experience or training will possess these skills. That's why you have to help them. It's also worth remembering, once again, that you're dealing with people. Testing is repetitive, tedious work that's about as exciting as doing your tax returns. It's also going to be new ground for your testers. People are always less comfortable in situations in which they know they don't possess the appropriate skills. Your encouragement, enthusiasm for their efforts, and sincere appreciation will go a long way.

## Make Them Feel Like a Part of the Team

Above and beyond the fact that it's just a good way to treat folks, you also need allies to support your efforts to build a testing team. If you greet each new bug that the testers find with unreserved enthusiasm and make it a point to tell the world what a huge difference in the project their great work is making, you'll find a significant change in their attitudes. Where they once may have been dragged grudgingly into doing your testing, they now feel like a valued and important part of the software development team. Indeed they are. Make sure that whenever the rest of the team gets together for lunch that your testers are invited as well. When you call an all-hands meeting, their presence should be requested, even if management won't always give them the time to attend. Any emails sent to the team at large should include the testers. In short, even if your testers can spend only four hours a week on your project, treat them with as much value and respect as your full-time members.

If you do this, you'll find that they will begin to take ownership of the testing process. They will become emotionally involved in the project, and its success will be as important to them as it is for you. Now, in addition to your own lobbying efforts, you'll find that your testers will themselves start lobbying for more time on the project. Some will even put in a little overtime if they can't get the time free during the normal course of the workweek. If you make them a part of your team in every regard, you'll find that more and more they'll push to get testing time until, in some cases, they get a permanent reassignment. At this point, you truly do have the beginnings of a dedicated testing department. It all starts from small, incremental steps and making your part-time testers feel as important as the rest of the team. Never have a reindeer game without them.

Above all, no matter who you have to strong-arm, when you gather your team for a celebration or company-wide recognition after your successful release, make sure that all of your testers are sitting with you, equal in stature and praise to every other member of the team. If one of them can't make it, reschedule. "All for one and one for all" is not just a corny line out of a book. Esprit de corps is more powerful than any management course you could ever attend. When you make each person on your team feel like the full weight of the group is behind them, they will move heaven and earth to help your project succeed.

The more that management sees this, and the more your software quality improves (as it certainly will), the more time they're going to allow these people to spend on the project. Between your lobbying and that of your testers, you will continually chip away at the stone until you can get them assigned permanently to your team. Also make sure that you keep careful notes of the ever-increasing quality of your software with each passing release. Any information you can gather—the decreasing number of tech support calls and user complaints, the fact that any bugs encountered are of a less severe nature, and so on—is ammunition that you can use as you continue your efforts to build a quality assurance process that becomes the de facto standard in your company.

Ultimately, if you're successful, you should have a testing group that mirrors your programmer group. In other words, you want one tester for each developer. If you have team leads, you'll want an equal number of test leads. If your project is large enough to be broken into subgroups based on functionality, you'll want to mirror that in your testing group as well.

This may seem like the southern colloquialism of the fox guarding the henhouse, but you'll want all of your testing resources to be under your project manager. Just as it's important for them to feel like a part of the team, you also want to avoid the "us versus them" mentality that can sometimes arise between standalone QA groups and the programmers whose work they test. If your testing group gets large enough to warrant it, however, you'll want to appoint a testing manager to oversee the group. This manager will report directly to the project manager, although the project manager may interact directly with testers in the same way that he interacts with programmers.

Once things get rolling, it's a good idea to give the testers a little room to grow. You now have a testing department in large part due to the enthusiasm and efforts of your previously part-time resources. They were fired up enough about the project to help you make your dream of a full-time testing staff become a reality. Allow them the elbowroom to take that enthusiasm and pursue the skills, procedures, techniques, and structures of the testing profession. They worked their way from the ground up, just as many of us have done as programmers. If they start having ideas of their own about how to improve the testing process, let them roll with it. It's their career now, and this is really what you wanted all along. Everybody wins, especially your customers and your company.

## Establishing the QA Process

Whether you've managed to build a full-time testing staff or you're still working with a few people who can give you only a couple of hours a week, you'll want to incorporate a few things into your overall testing procedures. First, go out and buy a big stone tablet, suitable for hanging over the main door of the programming department. Then, chisel on it in big bold letters a statement that no releases, whether beta, public, or patch, shall leave the room without going through a regression test of whatever test cases you've been able to put together. You'd be surprised how much this alone will improve the quality of your releases. Of course, a large stone block above the main doorway may have additional uses if your management walks in and declares that the product will in fact be shipped without testing.

As in so many other cases, the easier you can make a process to be followed, the better your chances of success. You now have well-organized test cases and a staff of at least part-time people who know how to run them and document any deficiencies. Demonstrating to management that you're well prepared to run this test before you ship and that it's a simple and straightforward process makes it easier for them to say yes. Furthermore, should you catch any blatant and potentially embarrassing bugs in this prerelease regression test, fix the bug and advertise loudly that this would have been a customer disaster had it not been for the testing process. This gives you more credibility for your testing procedures and more horsepower the next time you need to ask for something, such as more time for your testing resources.

In addition to the full regression tests in which you run every single test case that you have, some additional tests should be on your list as well (if you can get the time to do them). If your system can be set to operate on automatic pilot, tests that run overnight or over the weekend are great for smoking out cumulative errors. If your app always requires user interaction, pester management until they approve the purchase of a testing automation program. Even if you buy nothing more than a single license of the cheapest product going, your ability to run overnight tests will pay for the software the first week.

Not content to just run the program until it drops, a good testing effort will also try to push it until it squeaks. Whether it's a database app, a word processor, or a Web browser-based system, all programs consume system resources such as memory, processor cycles, and disk space. How snippy does your app get when these things are in short supply? Do your really know how your program will react if your computer runs completely out of disk space? What happens when it can't allocate memory? What if other programs are chewing up the processor and it can't get much done? These scenarios and many like them should be a part of your stress testing. Buy or write simple applications that consume these resources, and see how your application reacts. You'll be surprised at the bugs this sort of thing will flush out, sometimes in rather unexpected places.

Hardware failures, particularly when your system interacts with external dedicated hardware, are another avenue to test. This may not always be practical or relevant to your system. It's hard to suddenly invoke a video card failure. However, if your program depends on anything physical in the outside world, make sure you test the behavior if that outside resource suddenly vanishes or misbehaves. In the real world, hardware fails from time to time. That's not the fault of your software, but that also won't be remembered if your program crashes and corrupts data as a result.

Speaking of hardware, having an appropriately stocked testing lab is another luxury that you should work for. Having computers running all the various versions of the target operating systems is incredibly valuable. If there are any networking aspects to your project, you need a nontrivial network on which to test it. You'll also find that some printers react better to your output than others, and of course the list goes on.

When you're scrounging for hardware resources, you're in a tough neighborhood. In Corporate America, that's one of the first things that everyone fights for. The best way to get your foot in the door without too much competition is to first determine the most obsolete hardware that your system can tolerate. Armed with this list, begin your scavenging by trying to get possession of old hardware that meets these requirements. Often, the old stuff works just fine for testing, but of course nobody wants old stuff on their desk and so you stand a good chance of getting it for your testing lab. As your lab grows, it'll eventually reach a point where it's recognizable as a dedicated testing resource of a reasonably serious nature. As you start documenting more and more bugs that never made it to the field because the hardware in your lab caught it first, you'll begin to gain some power to requisition additional hardware that you couldn't scrounge. The more you can prove that your testing efforts are bringing real value to the party, the more resources you'll be able to commandeer.

You should also have, in addition to your regression test, a baseline critical path test, a series of test cases that exercise the most fundamental and critical aspects of your system. These are the things that absolutely must not fail. Make this test as short as it can possibly be and still maintain its effectiveness. This is your backup plan for any occasion when management declares a release over the loud protests of you and your testers. Under no circumstances should your system leave the building without this test, even if you have to sneak in at midnight to run it. It will save you from many embarrassing encounters.

It's not going to be easy putting together a professional testing department if you don't already have one. You're going to have to use every political trick in the book to get your hands on the resources, both people and hardware, that you'll need for your product to be adequately tested. You'll probably want to pull your hair out in the beginning stages as you try to take people who are not software professionals and teach them the basics of QA. However, if you'll stick to your guns and make it a priority to build this team, the rewards will far outweigh the aggravation. It doesn't matter if you're a project manager or just a front-line coder. You have to put the full weight of your personal involvement behind the overall effort to make a dedicated, full-time testing team a reality. It will forever change the quality of the software you deliver. It might even allow you to get a good night's sleep from time to time. Such things will make you the envy of your peers when you gather at your favorite programmers' cappuccino bar. Just make sure that you invite the testers, too.

# CHAPTER 9

# Keeping the Project Under Control

So far, we've concentrated on the different tasks that must be addressed in preparation for the actual coding. Some of these have been a matter of setting up procedures, and others constitute a large body of work to be performed in and of itself. Although it's imperative to establish a solid organizational structure for your approach to software development, keeping a close eye on the day-to-day details of the process is equally important. Even if you've done everything right, it's still possible to miss the deadline if you lose control of the project in midstream.

Most people consider the oversight of daily operations of the development process to be the domain of the project manager. In reality, many details are inherent to the creation of any significant piece of software, and every member of the team should attend to them. Just as a fireplace is built by stacking one brick upon the next, so too are programs created by the individual efforts of each member of the team. If everyone works with a common mindset and thinks not just of their particular tasks but of the group effort as a whole, much of the process becomes self-maintaining.

With any luck at all, this won't be the last development effort you work on. All of the steps we've taken thus far to keep the deadlines achievable and in sight require skills that will improve with each subsequent project. Because so much of the focus of our efforts is based on time, it's only natural that we'd want to know how our projections match up to reality. To know for certain, we're going to have to do some bookkeeping.

## Keeping Track of Your Time

If you don't have dedicated software to manage this sort of thing, a simple database will do the job nicely. At the beginning of the project, whenever tasks are delegated to team members, they're added to a list in this database. Additionally, you add a field for the individual performing the work and populate that list with the names of all team members. To this list of fields, you add three more: one for the date, one for the start time, and one for the stop time. Also add a comment field, but don't make it required. You can add more information, of course, but keep it simple. What you're building is a data entry system for your team members. Remember, the more of a pain it is to use, the better chance that it won't be, no matter how much you beat your chest.

During the course of each day, your team members will work on one or more tasks. With just a little bit of discipline, it's easy to fire up the data entry form, pick your name, pick the task, and enter the date and start time. Later, when you switch tasks, you edit that record with the stop time and add a new record with the start time of your new task. Yeah, yeah, I know; it seems like a hassle. And it is, in the beginning. However, you quickly get used to it, and in reality it takes less than thirty seconds to make an entry. If it takes any longer than that, you might want to brush up on your typing skills.

But where's the payoff for the individual programmer? Isn't this just a tool for the project manager? True, it does serve him as well, but each time you have a new task assignment it gets put into the database, right? This includes each and every line item that you estimated in your detailed implementation figures, which means that you now have small tasks to perform, a record of how long you thought it would take, and ultimately from this database you'll have the numbers of how long it really did take. When you complete each task, if you finished significantly sooner or later than you anticipated, make sure you enter some explanation for it in the comment field.

For the one to five minutes that fooling with this database will consume in your day, you get a wealth of useful information that will make you much more effective in estimating your next effort. We do so many tasks in a week and touch upon so many technical issues that it's literally impossible for us to truly remember what took how long and why. Without this key information, we have no chance of improving our estimating skills. Without adequate estimation skills, there's no way we can propose a realistic deadline, and we are forever doomed to occupy our cubicles late at night every week as we try to hit a deadline that we underestimated. However, if you maintain the simple discipline that it takes to make these entries, you'll have extremely precise information with which you can raise your estimating skills to new heights. We already know how to code. That's the easy stuff. Estimating is hard, and this is how you get better.

Not only does this information improve your ability to project effort, it keeps a running status of all aspects of your project. When you know to the minute exactly how long any single part of your project took, you're going to be speaking with tremendous authority the next time you talk to management about schedules. Furthermore, you'll have database reports and spreadsheets to document your trail and back you up. Management responds to that sort of thing. When you're offering reports and spreadsheet printouts, you're speaking the language that they understand, and it boosts your credibility significantly.

One last note on this topic: enter your times right then and there, as you start or stop them. The temptation is great to figure you'll just summarize it all at the end of the day, or at the end of the week. You won't get precision that way, and precision is the entire point of this exercise. If you take shortcuts here, you're cheating only yourself.

## Managing Your Team

If you find yourself in the position of project manager or team lead, you'll be responsible for the efforts of others as well. This adds to your workload on a daily basis, of course. For the most part, though, it's been my experience that, if you treat programmers like grownups and just let them do their job, you'll get the most from them. As a class of creature, we don't respond well to micromanagement. If you do find that there's someone on your team who isn't pulling his share of the load, either through lack of ability or laziness, that should probably invoke the question of whether or not that person should be there in the first place.

In general, though, I find that the position of team lead or project manager is more concerned with supporting the programmers than trying to manage or motivate them. They're already motivated, and for the most part the only management they need is the sort of organizational stuff that we've been talking about all along. When it gets down to getting the work done, the first and most fundamental job of a manager or team lead is to provide air cover. Your highest priority is to shield your programmers from the nonsense and bureaucracy of middle and upper management, keeping them off of your programmers so that they can get some work done. This means that you take the heat from management, you deal with the insipid requests from marketing, you shuffle all the paper that needs to be shuffled, and keep your programmers out of meetings that don't truly require their presence.

Additionally, depending on the level of effort your team is putting in, it's up to you to keep spirits high. Morale is more important than most businesses ever realize. If keeping morale up means bringing in the occasional pizza, then do it. If you can come up with any perks that are actually meaningful to your team, then hand them out. Every opportunity you have to reinforce the fact that you feel your team is the absolute best of the best, jump on it. When at all possible, pass the credit for successes along to your team and take the flak for the problems yourself. When your people see that you're covering them even when you get grief for their mistakes, you'll find an ever-growing loyalty among your team. This is where treating programmers like adults and letting them do their job starts to pay off. Eventually, you'll find that loyalty and esprit de corps have risen to a point where people do whatever it takes to put out a fire without ever being told. They simply do it because they're good, and they believe in the team. This may all sound a little corny to you, but it's worth reiterating that at the end of the day you're dealing with real, live human beings, and people have feelings. It doesn't matter if you have a hundred people in your department or you're just the technical lead on a two-person team. Take care of your people, and they'll take care of you and your project.

## Improving Your Coding Discipline

Another aspect of keeping the project on track has to do with maintaining an organized approach to your coding efforts. Standards and procedures are nothing new to programmers in the corporate world. Whether or not they're actually adhered to is another matter entirely, of course. Probably the single most recognizable standard to those of us who spend our days in front of a compiler is the coding standard. Because programming is as much of an art as it is a science, we take it a bit personally when constraints are placed on how we write our code. However, when you get right down to it, there's only one proper way to write your code: the way that everyone else in your shop does.

You can do a great many things to enhance the readability of your code, but the most important consideration overall is consistency. Any programmer should be able to bring up any file in the system and be in familiar territory. If it's a struggle to wade through different and ever-changing methods of indentation, commenting, variable naming conventions, and so forth, you're going to find your maintenance programmer shopping the Internet for good deals on bulk ammunition. Comprehension will suffer, and it just generally takes longer to do whatever you had in mind. Naturally, any programmer worth his pocket protector should be able to read the code and figure it out. However, deadlines are all about time, and anything that slows you down adds up and contributes to the potential for missed deadlines, even if it's a seemingly small thing. It's all incremental.

A number of good books about coding style and practices are available, and it's not my intent to duplicate that information here. Additionally, some of these issues will be, to a certain degree, language dependent. If you're a Basic programmer, you couldn't possibly care less where a C++ programmer puts his braces. I've actually heard the occasional Basic programmer make some rather specific suggestions about where they should put the braces, but I suppose that's another story. In any event, just as it is between these two, so is it for all of the languages. Each has specific nuances that won't be relevant to others. Nonetheless, a number of common threads run through the programming experience regardless of your choice of weapons.

Beyond the simple formatting issues regarding how the code should look, another of your primary considerations when cranking up the editor should be the debugging experience. I've known many programmers over the years who simply wrote code, and then eventually spent some time debugging it. I've watched as they struggled with their debuggers, not always having the information that they needed in the context of the problem they were tracking. Often, too, debugging is an intrusive experience and interferes with the normal execution of the program you're testing. This can mask the problem entirely or demonstrate different symptoms than those that are seen when the program is run normally. This can often be fairly misleading, and can waste many hours while barking up the wrong tree. You can do a number of things when you code that will make life much easier for you when problems arise. And they always do. The most important step is to simply think about how you will debug an application from the moment you start coding it. It would probably be a good idea to avoid barking as well. That sort of thing could be taken the wrong way by Security.

Although this book is aimed at programmers of all disciplines, the majority of my personal experience has been in writing C and C++ code for Microsoft platforms, starting with early incarnations of DOS and working through all of the versions of Windows from 3.1 on. I've encountered a few things along the way that seem useful no matter what flavor of program you're building. The first was a concept that was given to me as a mandate from one of my managers. The sentence started, "You're not going to like this, but…." He was right. He was talking about a variable naming convention known as Hungarian notation, which is familiar to most Windows programmers.

The idea is a simple one: you use a well-defined prefix on all variables that instantly identifies exactly what type of variable it is. To the uninitiated, it seems to add a lot of visual garbage to the code, and I fought it tooth and nail in the beginning. Well, it isn't fair to say that I fought it because not using it wasn't an option, but I grumbled long and loud about what a pain it was. It didn't take long, however, for me to get used to it. Once I did, I was amazed at how it improved my debugging experiences. When you hit a breakpoint and immediately recognize exactly what the variables are as well as their scope (another facet of Hungarian notation), it's much more of a timesaver than you might initially expect. Although this naming convention is popular for Windows developers, it doesn't really matter what convention you use. The important thing is that you use one that makes sense for the language and development environment in which you work and that the entire team applies it consistently. It will take a little getting used to, but if you're so set in your ways that you can't adapt to a change here and there then you're probably not going to survive for long in this business anyway. The increased productivity will be worth it in the long run, and productivity is a major issue for those of us on a deadline.

Along these lines, anything else you can put in your code with debugging in mind will save you countless hours in the debugging sessions that are sure to come. One of the first things I tend to do on a new assignment is put together some diagnostic routines before I write the first line of system code. It's important to minimize the overhead that these diagnostics require because the idea is to use them liberally in your code on a daily basis.

As an example, it's a familiar struggle for the C++ developer to deal with good pointers gone bad. Among my tricks are macros that not only test for null pointers but also confirm that they point to valid memory blocks and are indeed a pointer to the type of class that I think they are. What do they do if these conditions are not met? Bark loudly. Never mind how nervous that makes the night watchman.

My environment offers the use of assertions, and I suspect that the majority of programming languages have similar features. An assertion is effectively a Boolean test that does nothing when true and offers a diagnostic message when false. This message displays the filename of the source code and the exact line number where the mishap occurred. In other words, it says in big, bold language that something is screwed up and it tells you exactly where. As you might imagine, this is extremely helpful information. I suspect that most programmers are familiar with this sort of technique. Consequently, if I get a bogus pointer, I make sure that the world knows about it immediately, at least in a debug build, via a popup message box. Unfortunately, the stock assertion routines offered are only useful in a debug build, which brings us to another point.

When you're peppering your code with diagnostics, you need to think in terms of both the debug and release environments. Not all languages or compilers make a physical distinction between the two types of builds, but the logical problem is always present. You may write code that's designed to offer a lot of troubleshooting information when you're debugging but remove it or comment it out before shipping the final product. Then, at two o'clock in the morning, your product crashes in the field and you sit on the phone, bleary eyed, trying to determine exactly what went wrong. Of course, because the diagnostics were present only when you were coding and debugging, your program in the field is conspicuously silent about whatever made it unhappy. This makes for a much more difficult debugging experience, made all the worse by the frantic pressures that always accompany problems that occur in a production system. This is when you need the full complement of debugging and diagnostic tools, and it's typically when you have the least.

While I'm drawing on my personal experience as a Windows/C++ developer, these ideas are not tied to this platform in even the slightest manner. I take a little teasing from my fellow developers about having exceptionally whiney code, and I'm guilty as charged. In my bag of tricks, I make sure that I have routines that will give me information both in the field and in the debugger. When the program goes south, the assertions that I previously mentioned are nonexistent in release builds. Consequently, I roll my own routines that give me popup messages in a debug environment and the exact same information written to disk in both debug and release environments. This means that when I'm rousted from bed in the middle of the night, I immediately ask the person on the other end of the line to bring up the error log and read me the contents. This doesn't fix the problem, but it sure speeds up the process. I then stumble into the office and fire up the debugger knowing exactly where the crash occurred. If you have more than twenty minutes of programming experience behind you, you know how valuable this is. However, it didn't happen by default. It happened because I thought of debugging before I started building the system and put together some tools to help me when I got there.

## Thinking Ahead to Debugging

Although it's a good idea to build a library of such diagnostic routines, sometimes it's helpful to write another app or two to help with the debugging as well. Does your system require nonstop execution of routines? If so, you may want to consider a trace utility that allows you to put diagnostic lines in your program but have them displayed via interprocess communication in your trace utility. This means a real-time display of what's going on in your code without disturbing the execution of the program. For all of you Windows programmers out there, yes, I know that there's some trace features built into the compiler, but sometimes you need more information than that. And it certainly doesn't save this information to disk. In other words, no matter what your development environment offers, it may not be enough. But there's no reason to accept that as a limitation.

Other examples of diagnostic utilities include tools to view data file contents and snooping utilities to show what's happening on serial ports, network connections, or even interprocess or thread communications. In general, the idea is simple: think ahead to what you'll be encountering as your system progresses and build a suite of tools and routines to help you deal with the inevitable debugging adventures. You're a programmer. If you need a tool that's too specific to be available on the open market, there's no reason that you can't cook it up yourself. That's one of the advantages of our trade. A carpenter doesn't have the manufacturing capabilities needed to create a specialized type of hammer that he may need (although I've certainly seen the creative use of other tools to compensate for this). However, for the professional developer, we can create our own hammer anytime we like. It's not as much fun as beating on the monitor with a blunt instrument, of course, but then we don't want to spoil its appearance before it goes out that fifth-floor window.

Many aspects of how you write your code can contribute to the ease of debugging, and some are less obvious than others. For instance, in my little world, I can legally write a method in a single line, curly braces and all. This is a style that many C++ developers utilize particularly for such routines that set or get the value of a variable. It looks very neat and clean. Unfortunately, when stepping through in my particular debugger, I cannot inspect the value of the variable. If, however, I reformat the code into three lines with the curly braces each occupying a line of their own, the debugger behaves differently and I can in fact inspect the variable. Leaving aside any comments I might have about this little feature of my debugger, the point is that, in this case, even the visual aspects of how the code is formatted have a very real implication on debugging. As such, I now have removed the practice of single-line routines from my coding, even if it ain't pretty.

This is as close as we've come to talking about writing code thus far, as we've been focusing primarily on procedural issues in the preceding chapters. However, a procedure lurks here just beneath the surface. In the beginning of the project, you should include time to look into and write whatever diagnostic routines and tools that you'll need. Furthermore, all of the coding standards and related issues should be defined up front and then adhered to by all. Although it's not uncommon for coding standards to be considered in a shop, you might not have had a group discussion about the preferred use and frequency of diagnostic routines, or which routines and what functionality would even be useful. Take the time to do this, and make debugging a priority when you're writing your code. You'll end up with more lines of code than you otherwise would have had, but the payoff at debugging time will far outweigh the time it takes to add the diagnostics up front. The sanity you save will be your own.

## Incorporating Version Control

Another procedure that should be standard in every shop is the use of a version control system for source code. It's one of those things that seems as obvious as mentioning that you have to have a development environment before you can start coding, but I've actually known good developers who were either completely unfamiliar with the concept or for whatever reason didn't have a system available to them. If you're new to version control systems, the short explanation is that it's a system that lets you store multiple versions of the same source code file in a central repository. This means that you can fetch a particular revision of this file at any later time. These systems are typically augmented with a number of features, and the ability to slap a label on a particular revision is a fundamental feature.

One obvious use of labels is stamping the codebase for your current release product. In this way, when version 2.13 has a problem in the field but you're already coding version 3.0, you can fetch the entire 2.13 codebase and debug it. However, labels are cheap. Any time you make a change to your codebase that you might want to come back to, slap a label on it. For instance, if you're about to rewrite a portion of your code to use a different architecture, you'll want to first label the existing one that actually works. So, if the new architecture doesn't work out, you can drop back to where you were and either try something new or keep what works.

Most professional shops already have a version control system in place because the benefits are too extreme to ignore. However, if management has not authorized the money for you to have such a tool, grab your pitchforks, light the torches, and gather every developer in the entire company at the offending manager's doorway. Get the maintenance programmers to guard the exits, and don't let him out until he signs the check. No tool short of the development environment itself is more crucial to an ongoing software development effort. And do be careful with those torches.

## Improving Productivity

While we're on the topic of productivity, it's important to keep human nature in mind no matter what procedures you're putting into place. The unshakable reality is that, if it's not easy, it simply won't happen, even if you pull rank (assuming that you have any). The more of a pain or distraction a particular procedure is, the better the chance that team members will just conveniently forget that they were supposed to do it. Without a doubt, some rules that should be followed generate additional work we'd rather not deal with. Discipline certainly has a place in the professional software development environment. Nonetheless, if you can find ways of automating or simplifying a cumbersome task, you've got a much better chance of success.

For instance, if you want information entered in a database and the form requires twenty fields to be entered, how many of these can you default to the most commonly used values? If your team uses status reports, are they easy to fill out? Are they paper or electronic? If the latter, do you have document templates set up to minimize the amount of typing required? If you train yourself to think along these lines, you'll be much more effective in getting what you need from the rest of your team without the fear of torches at your own doorstep. It's a good idea to periodically get together with everyone and find out what works and what doesn't. Never be afraid to tailor your approach as you go along. Remember, results are what matter.

Another thing you can do to improve your productivity has to do with your personal coding environment. Whether you're using a development environment that's built in with the language or you have a dedicated programmer's editor in which you do your coding, chances are good that you've only scratched the surface of the power available. When we're pressed for time, it's common to do something manually because it would take longer to set up an automated process than it would to just do it. However, you should always question whether you'll ever need to perform this particular task again. If the answer is yes, especially if it will be a frequent occurrence, it's worth taking a break and finding out what your environment can do to streamline the task.

This isn't a new idea to those who already use a full-featured editor. However, the editors that are shipped with many database or language environments are often much less powerful or flexible than a program whose sole purpose is editing source code. I realize that sometimes the reasons for not having a hot rod editor are financial, but often it's simply because programmers don't push for this critical tool. We also tend to get comfortable with the editing environment that we've learned and don't want to have to learn a whole new set of keystrokes. I've moved through a few different editors over the years, but for the last decade I've been able to use one of the standard key mappings from a popular editor of days gone by that most everyone still supports. Even so, there were a couple of times that I had to learn a completely new way of typing to get more power. It was a distraction to be sure, but in the end it was most certainly worth it.

I've often told the story of a particular project manager I worked for who was adept at dealing with the political insanities of the company that employed us. I was using a rather clunky set of tools and had lobbied along with my fellow developers for a more popular and significantly more powerful development environment. After a difficult political struggle, I got the word from him one morning that we were authorized to use the desired tools. (We already had the software but had been forbidden to use it in the name of departmental standards.)

We were at the very beginning of the application, and I didn't want to give my boss's manager any chance to change his mind, so I kicked out around 10,000 lines of code over the course of the week. This was what I needed to do to get the system visibly up and running, and doing so made it harder for management to pull the plug and send us back to the chisels and stone tablets that we were using previously.

I later heard some interesting comments about my efforts that were made from those on a team who were politically opposed to the tool transition (and our very existence, for that matter, due to turf wars). The first was that there was no way that I could have written that amount of code on my own, implying that I must have had other developers helping me. The second comment was that I was no hotshot programmer; my tools just did all the work for me.

Frankly, I have no idea if 10,000 lines of code in a week is a lot or not. I have no metrics for comparison. Apparently, however, it was a lot by these programmers' standards. There was no way I could have written all that on my own? They were, of course, correct. I didn't have help from other programmers, though. My tools generated a lot of this code for me. That, of course, validated their second thought. I'm certainly no hotshot programmer; I'm just smart enough to use power tools. I found it entertaining that their comments validated the very effort they were opposing just weeks prior and they didn't even realize it.

Whether it's standardized comments for file and function headers, templates of code for classes or routines, on-the-fly macros, powerful multifile search-and-replace mechanisms, or any of a host of other features, there is almost no end to the work that you can automate with a good editor. Those who work in a UNIX environment are familiar with a particular editor that is almost always available no matter which flavor of the operating system you're running. It generates extreme feelings among programmers: they either love it or hate it. Probably because I didn't grow up on UNIX boxes, I fall into the latter category. However, I would rather use that editor any day of the week than work with one from a standard development environment. I may have some personal issues with the user interface, but it is without question extremely powerful, and power is the point.

No matter which dedicated editor you choose, what used to take five minutes of typing will now be done in two keystrokes. You don't think this adds up over the life of your project? Remember, if you're struggling with unreasonable deadlines, then every single minute of productivity that you lose will add up. In the end it can cost you the delivery date. If you don't have a hot rod editor, get one. Which brand to use is a religious issue among programmers, but I'll tell you right now that it doesn't really matter. They're all competitive and any of them will shave literally weeks off of your project. There is a learning curve, but the payoff is huge. Of course, if you're in a shop that won't allow you to get one then the only other option you have is to squeeze every last ounce of performance out of what you have. I strongly suspect that most programmers don't use even half of the power that they have available. No matter how you get there, if you wish to be productive and enjoy your coding experience more, it is imperative that you soup up your editing environment. Just don't forget the seat belts.

## Knowing When to Walk Away

We're conditioned both by our passion for our work and the pressures of our career to work hard and work often. Burning the midnight oil is a common experience for the professional developer, and one of the reflexive solutions to any problem is to simply work more hours. Although at times this is just what has to be done, at other times it's the absolute worst mistake that you can make. Programming requires sharp focus, perception, attention to detail, and hopefully eyes that are in the open, not half-closed, state. A friend of mine used to routinely say that he didn't work until two o'clock in the morning because you didn't *want* the code that he wrote at two in the morning. There's tremendous truth to that. Sometimes the very best thing you can do to meet your deadline is to learn when to walk away. This seems counterintuitive—walking away when there's work to be done—but it's a trick that can actually enhance productivity.

This isn't an abstract philosophy. It's simple math. You've been struggling with a problem and working enough hours to get a little crispy. It's the end of the business day on Wednesday, and your deadline is Friday morning. Things aren't going well. You're worried that you won't resolve the issues before the deadline, and so you pull an all-nighter to make it happen. Your dedication to your job is not in question; your common sense, however, could use some work. You do indeed go without sleep Wednesday night and continue working on through Thursday. The code you wrote in the all-night affair isn't working, and each attempt to remedy the situation just results in one more layer of hacks and confusion. It's now Thursday evening and you're panicked. You find a conference room and sleep for two hours and then head back to your cube determined to go all night and have the code ready for Friday morning. You're bleary eyed and unfocused, your memory is impaired, and you're having difficulty even concentrating or thinking clearly. You have absolutely no chance of delivering a solid codebase Friday morning, and yet you've worked your tail off and gave it everything you had. It's true, you worked hard. You just weren't very smart.

Let's rewind to Wednesday and try this again. This time, realizing that you're already pretty cooked and that your efforts to solve the problem are not gaining you much ground, you decide to do something highly unconventional. You inform all concerned that you're going home to get a good night's sleep and warn them that you're close personal friends with the maintenance programmer should anyone think of disturbing you. You take the phone off the hook and sleep soundly. Early Thursday morning you're once again looking at your code, only this time your head is clear and your focus sharp. You've also had a little time away from the problem. Now, with a fresh perspective and a more balanced state, you clearly see the flaws in your approach and either make a surgical strike or perhaps even throw it all away and start from scratch with a better plan. Either way, by noon, your coding is complete and you're deep into unit testing only to find that there just aren't that many problems. You check in your code, go home at the end of the business day Thursday, and on Friday morning deliver your work on time and in a stable state. You worked much fewer hours and delivered much better quality, all because you knew when to walk away.

Does this example seem a bit contrived? I can assure you both from personal experience and that of my friends that this is a very real story, in both scenarios. It's all too easy to get caught up in frantic desperation, thinking that you'll make "just one more pass" at the problem until it's 4:30 in the morning and you're crispier than the day-old French fries on your desk. To realize when you've hit a point of diminishing returns and call it a day takes both discipline and the courage to explain to management that you are in fact doing the most productive thing that you can to hit the deadline. More is not always more. Sometimes, as musicians are known to say, less is more. It doesn't seem to make a lot of sense when you say it, but then what in this business does make sense?

# Optimizing Your Meetings

Another thing that's a continual drain on the productivity of any software development effort is the dreaded meeting. Depending on the size of company and its level of bureaucracy, you can end up spending half your life in meetings, most of which don't accomplish anything more than setting the date for the next meeting and determining who's going to buy the donuts. Even so, many aspects of our work require a gathering of two or more people. Communication is very important in our business. However, just because you have a meeting doesn't necessarily mean that you're communicating effectively. If it's a given, then, that meetings are a requirement in the course of writing a program, why not take the same approach to them as you would software development? You optimize your code. Why not optimize your meetings?

Much of the pain and suffering that we encounter regarding meetings is due not so much to the fact that we must attend them as to how poorly they are typically run. Gatherings are held with poorly defined or unrealistic objectives, people are often unprepared, and many just seem to ramble on without end. It's little wonder then that most programmers would rather admit to an attack Chihuahua that they abuse monitors than they would attend a meeting.

Like most things, though, the problem can in fact be remedied if we first break things down into building blocks that are small enough to address effectively. With that in mind, what are the bricks of which a well-ordered meeting is constructed? The following list describes the key components:

- A leader

- Someone to take notes

- Participants

- A list of specific issues

- Optional supporting documentation

- One or more specific goals to achieve

Let's talk about the components first. The person who leads a meeting is typically, but not always, the person who calls it. For instance, if someone in upper management wants a status report on your project with feedback from the developers involved, he may call the meeting but delegate leadership to the project manager. The role of the leader is to keep the meeting on track and avoid the long, rambling, and useless gatherings that we've all attended. The leader opens each topic for discussion and grants each person the permission to speak. This is not so much an opportunity for a power trip as it is a job working as a traffic cop. If each person waits until being recognized by the leader before speaking, much of the confusion that results when people try to talk over each other is eliminated. Even if you have a small and informal gathering, observing this will get you out of the meeting much quicker because less time will be wasted. The leader also has the authority to table an issue and move on to the next topic, particularly when it's apparent that you're beating a dead horse. When it's obvious that there's no further benefit to be gained by additional discussion on a given topic—whether there's insufficient information, all the bases have been covered, or a couple of people will simply never agree—it's time to pull the plug and move on.

By controlling the flow of the meeting, keeping people from rambling and straying off topic, and pruning any unproductive tangents as quickly as they sprout, the leader of a meeting is capable of keeping it lean, to the point, and effective. The person who takes notes has the responsibility of documenting all that takes place in the meeting. When you have a room full of people trying to scribble on paper, understand the points of others, and in general keep their minds on the topics at hand, keeping notes is sporadic and inconsistent among the participants. By dedicating one person to the process whose job it is to note all details in the proceeding, everyone else is freed up to concentrate more on the matter at hand. When the meeting is concluded, this person then summarizes the outcome of the meeting and either emails or distributes a document to all concerned. This gives the added benefit of everyone having a consistent view of what really took place.

The participants of the meeting are those who have been invited to attend because they have either something to offer or something to gain. If a person doesn't fall into at least one of these two categories, they shouldn't be there. Often, the person who stirs up the most trouble or rambles on and chews up the most time is the one who didn't need to be there in the first place. Because they have nothing to offer or gain, they can only entertain themselves by distracting others. It is the responsibility of the leader, either directly or through delegation, to choose participants wisely.

The leader also brings to the meeting a list of specific issues that this group will discuss. The smaller and more concise this list of issues, the better chance you have of getting something accomplished. This list may have been generated by one or more people other than the leader, but in the meeting it is the leader who walks through these topics and opens them for discussion.

Prior to the meeting, optional supporting documentation may also be distributed. It's important to make sure that you pass this out to the participants enough days before the meeting so they can actually read and absorb the information, taking into account how busy their days usually are. If you hand out information that no one has seen before at the beginning of your meeting, one of two things will happen. Either they'll ignore what you're saying because they're busy reading the documents, or they won't read them at all. Either way, they're missing information and that won't help the cause.

Listed last is something that should probably be considered first. What are the specific goals that you hope to achieve by holding this meeting? I'm speaking here of short-term goals, in other words something that can be seen as the direct output of the meeting. If you don't have an objective clearly in mind, don't call the meeting. You may indeed have a larger goal, such as delivering a complex piece of software. However, you're not going to address something at that level in a single meeting. If, on the other hand, you wanted to make a decision regarding the specific user interface to be utilized on a specific piece of functionality, that's small and well defined enough to be attainable. In short, know why you're meeting in the first place, but, most importantly, know what you need to accomplish.

Often, you'll hear of people heading off to attend or hold meetings. When you ask what the meeting is for, they'll reply that they're gathering to discuss a particular topic. That's not a sufficient definition for a meeting. I could call a meeting to discuss the phases of the moon. However, when it was all said and done, I might know a little more about why Chihuahuas howl in the wee small hours of the night, but I wouldn't have accomplished a darned thing. If I instead held a meeting to discuss the fact that the maintenance programmer grew long hair and fangs during the full moon and opened the floor to possible safety precautions that could be taken to avoid any unfortunate incidents, there would be a constructive point to the meeting.

This leads us naturally to the output of a meeting. Now that we have an idea of what we'll find in the conference room, what do we hope to achieve once we get there? A meeting can generate one or more of the following deliverables:

- A report of the conclusions

- Action items

- Future meetings

The first result of a meeting can be the documentation of the proceedings by the person who took the notes. I used the words *can be* instead of *is* because it's not necessary to distribute this unless there's a point. That's the thing to keep drilling into everyone's head when it comes to meetings: what's the point? If an action does not serve the desired goals, ditch it.

Action items are effectively a list of actions that need to be taken as a result of the meeting. This usually takes the form of individuals being assigned tasks to perform. Along those lines, let me offer a word of warning to those of you who are new to the corporate world: don't miss meetings. Who do you suppose gets tasked with the stuff nobody wants to do? In any event, action items are a logical and expected output. Even if the purpose of the meeting is to decide between Plan A and Plan B, in the end someone's probably going to get assigned the job of carrying out said plan.

The third bit of output from a meeting can be future meetings. This isn't as bureaucratic as it seems. To understand why, let's touch on another critical topic of effective meetings: the duration. I'd love to have the following sign hung in brilliant neon above the doors of every conference room in the world: *No meeting should ever, under any circumstances, last more than two hours.* It's the leader's job to make sure that this is so. Furthermore, two hours is an undesirable extreme. One hour is better. Much, much better. People start fidgeting after an hour and you lose their attention. This is why the output of meetings can be more meetings. It's actually more efficient to table a topic for a future gathering that would be dedicated exclusively to it than to try and address it in one marathon session.

If you're looking for decisions on three separate topics, you may come to a quick consensus on the first. The second, however, may bog down. Frequently, this is a sign that more research needs to be done before a decision can be made. Rather than chew up everyone's time trying to hash this out, the leader simply tables this topic and declares that a future meeting will be held to resolve the issue after sufficient research has been done. The group is then free to pursue the third topic, which they quickly do. You're in and out in an hour, and you've accomplished two of the three goals. Subsequent research is performed, and in a follow-up meeting the elusive second topic is nailed down in fifteen minutes now that people have had a chance to better prepare.

The first meeting could have gone on for six hours while everyone offered their opinions, prejudices, and arguments on the second topic. In the end, you still would have had to hold the second meeting because there was simply insufficient preparation to resolve the issue. Instead, it wrapped up within the one-hour limit, and the subsequent work involved in the follow-up meeting took only another quarter of an hour. Those are much better numbers. It's all about making the most efficient use of the most critical resource in the programming industry: your time. Focus is also much better when you have shorter meetings that are aimed at very specific issues. Often, two concise meetings are much more efficient than one long rambling meeting in which you try to solve all the problems of the world at once.

Complete books have been written solely on the topic of holding effective meetings, but these key points can make a world of difference in the duration and productivity of your gatherings. Of course, we didn't discuss who has to buy the donuts. Traditionally, it's the person who calls the meeting. That's the other way that we discourage frequent and pointless meetings.

# Wrapping It Up

When all the coding and debugging is done, when the last QA person has signed off on the last bug, and when development has truly come to closure such that even the night watchman's dog can sleep without one eye open, it's time to hand management the keys and call it a wrap. That's not, however, the end of the story for this release. Now is the time to run the reports from the time database and compare them to the original estimates. It's also the time to gather the troops for the best pizza in town and a frank and friendly discussion of what went right, what went wrong, what came up that was unexpected, and how you can improve the process in general for the next project.

If it's been a tough project and everyone's a little cooked, you might want to give it a week and let everyone decompress. The goal is a positive and constructive interchange aimed at reaffirming what was good and improving what was lacking. It's not an opportunity for finger pointing, recriminations, or any negative attitudes. That's why you should defer it if your people need a break. Tired people are pessimistic people. Nonetheless, when your troops are rested, go over every single step of the process from the initial requirements down to the last bit of testing and installing. You'll want to keep records of all this so that you can see your progress and improve from project to project. Depending upon the political climate of your company, you'll either put it in version control or keep it at home. In any event, you learn from history, so keep your records and make the improvements to your process that are needed.

This is also the time that you take for technical documentation, that less-than-glamorous task of looking at the code and documenting what is as opposed to what you thought it would be in the beginning. Remember, this documentation is not for anyone's consumption but your own. There's no need to generate a 5,000-page document, but you should detail the codebase sufficiently or it'll just be trouble when there's maintenance to perform. Of all the tasks in the development cycle, this is typically the least favorite. Just remember, you're doing this for the poor sucker that has to fix a bug at two o'clock in the morning, and you might even end up being that poor sucker. Document defensively.

No two software development shops are the same: some are huge organizations that are much more susceptible to bureaucracy and corporate politics, and others are small and understaffed, and more likely to take shortcuts than waste time in pointless meetings. You will also find yourself in different positions as your career progresses. Much of this advice applies to every level. Even the parts that don't seem relevant to you today because you're only coding may suddenly become important when you find yourself unexpectedly drafted into a team lead or project management position. Hey, you don't think these guys volunteered for those positions, do you? A project manager is often nothing more than a programmer who didn't know when to duck. In any event, keeping a firm grasp on your project as it progresses is as much an attribute of preparation as it is of managing details along the way. When both are done properly, you'll find that the road is much smoother and that the stress level is greatly diminished. That certainly makes it easier to digest your pizza.

# CHAPTER 10

# Managing Your Management

I've often speculated about the origins of those who find a career in the middle and upper strata of software development management. In fact, I suppose if I had any business sense I could have made a fortune long ago by selling my ideas to Hollywood script writers who specialize in science fiction, for in all of my ruminations there is a single, overriding question: what planet are these guys from?

Without a doubt, there is traditionally a huge conceptual gulf between the rank-and-file programmers and those who manage them. The Suits never really seem to grasp the fundamental issues that drive the software development process. Instead, they proceed as if they believe that a computer keyboard is the modern equivalent of a magic wand, a device capable of all forms of sorcery if the wizard chooses to wave it. For what it's worth, I've waved more than a few keyboards at management over the years. For some reason, security seems to take a dim view of this. Perhaps it's the way that I wave it.

Managers fare little better in their attempts to understand programmers. We speak a strange, technical language that seems to have no relationship to profits, expenses, or long-term business strategies. They're never quite sure exactly what it is that we're talking about and are often frustrated by our lack of enthusiasm for the truly important things in life as they see it. And then there are the short tempers and those darned flying monitors. It's little wonder that management treats us as wild animals that lack the ability to communicate.

Truly, a more dissimilar coupling of people I've never seen. It's like two wet cats thrown into a burlap bag, and the fur will continue to fly until we figure out a way to deal with them. The first step in this process is to understand and accept that those who roam the halls in the guise of management have a completely different perspective than do the techies. This makes perfect sense because they're trained in business, not software development. Just as you wouldn't expect a plumber to have a master's degree in philosophy, it's impractical to expect a businessman with an MBA to be extremely technical. Although I've known some pretty philosophical plumbers in my day, when there's water pouring all over my kitchen floor I'm much more concerned about his skills with a pipe wrench. In a similar fashion, if it weren't for the financial and business skills of management, we'd all be writing extremely cool programs at night while flipping burgers during the day. It's their business skills that bring in the money, some of which goes towards payroll. And that's a trend that we'd all like to see continue.

Still, realizing this does little to help us in our predicaments. Left to their own devices, management consistently makes a shambles out of almost every software development project that they touch. To have any hopes of delivering quality software on a reasonable schedule, we must wrest control of the development process from their hands. That's a tall order when you consider our position in the food chain. We work for management and not the other way around, and so we lack the authority necessary to dictate the changes that a controlled approach to development requires. This means that, for programmers to take the wheel, management must voluntarily give it up. Although history shows that those in power are typically reluctant to relinquish it, there are ways of accomplishing our aims nonetheless.

## Improving Communications

Working on a time-honored principal of human nature, to get what we want we simply need to show management what's in it for them. Although it's typically a source of frustration, in this case it's to our advantage that decisions in the corporate world are not made based on merit but rather on what advances the career of the decision maker. We can use this to our advantage. If the individuals in management can be shown that their current model of development is costing them money and prominence in the marketplace and that our approach will both boost profits and further the corporate goal of market dominance, they will be much more motivated to listen. That's because the manager who makes the company more successful has a better shot at improving his personal career path.

In short, to gain control of the development process, we must first motivate and educate those who have the authority to make changes. The time to do this, however, is before the project begins. Once the status quo kicks in, it's hard to alter, which means that we'll be facing yet another project with ill-defined requirements and arbitrary deadlines. Although not impossible, it's very hard to correct this problem in midstream because the time has passed for much of the groundwork that is needed for an orderly approach to the project.

Certain fundamental issues must be addressed for us to establish and maintain control over the development process. First, requirements gathering, design, and estimating must be accomplished in a compressed time frame and still remain effective. In the beginning, we won't be given the amount of time we'd like, but we must still prove that our approach works. If we don't, we won't be given the flexibility to do things our way in the future.

Additionally, throughout the project, developers must be responsive to the actual needs of the company. It's not enough to simply immerse ourselves in technical bliss. We must make it a priority to address the business issues that our software was commissioned to improve. That's more a matter of a perspective than it is a list of specific actions to take, but it's worth mentioning. As programmers, we tend to get caught up in the technical side of things and completely lose sight of (or just plain don't care about) the underlying business issues. And yet, for the company to prosper, the business issues are truly all that matter. It's hard to accept that the solar system does not revolve around our code, but if we're to be successful we must not lose sight of the fact that the business issues are, in fact, the ultimate priority.

Lastly, to get our points across to management and garner the respect that we'll need in order to induce change, we must speak their language, learn to make presentations to which they can relate, and in general bolster our credibility. If we can accomplish this, we'll be dealing with management on their own terms. We're never going to turn them into techies or make the programming issues that are so dear to our hearts their highest priority. Instead, if we really wish to institute change, then we must fight from the inside. This means slipping behind enemy lines and blending in with the scenery. It's not always fun, it's not always safe, and it's almost never easy. However, if programmers in every company in the business world can change the way that software is developed, we will not only improve the quality of our own professional lives but also the overall quality of software in general. To me, that makes it all worthwhile.

The programming community is an international one, and I've had the good fortune to work with people from all over the world. Born and raised in America, I speak English. Of course, one of my friends from England once corrected me, saying that I don't speak English, I speak American. Be that as it may, having never had a need to speak any other languages, it's the only one I know. Those who travel here from other countries speak many languages, English among them. Were they to speak to me in French, German, Italian, Spanish, or any other language, they'd simply get blank looks from me because I wouldn't understand what they were saying. However, because they were intelligent and motivated enough to learn my language as well as their own, they are able to converse with all of the English-speaking people in my company. That means that they are able to achieve their own objectives in the business world, much of which involves getting a job kicking out cool code.

It's absolutely no different in the business world. Programmers employ a form of geek speak, and business people speak their own peculiar language. Attempting to communicate with a manager using a programmer's language and point of view is futile. You'll get the same blank looks that my more educated friends get from me and for the very same reason. If you don't speak a common language, you won't have effective communications.

One of the first steps in learning the lingo is to change your perspective. Believe it or not, the world does not revolve around programmers, and other priorities and points of view exist in the business world. We need to become comfortable with this reality. Consequently, it helps if you can start thinking like a business person. It's not beyond your capabilities. It's just something that most programmers don't want to do. This doesn't mean that you now have to start spouting empty buzzwords or adopt a more bureaucratic approach to your work. It simply means taking a look at how they think and understanding what motivates them. Although this varies a bit from person to person, some things are true in general of our pinstriped friends.

In the business world, you'll find that management is a culture that values statistics and reports from business newspapers, industry analysts, and so on. This means that you can benefit in your communications by gathering similar statistics of your own when there's a point you wish to make. Of course, the nice thing about statistics is that you can find numbers to support virtually any theory or position. Even so, you'll find that management respects statistics nonetheless. When starting with an agenda that you wish to promote, hit the bookstores, trade magazines, and newspapers to find corroborating numbers that support your view. Rightly or wrongly, printed publications are given more respect and credibility than an Internet Web site, so research accordingly. Armed with this information, prepare a presentation in a format that they take seriously and give it to them in their language and from their perspective. You'll be surprised at the difference in their reactions. Where you may previously have encountered a rather dismissive attitude from management, you'll now find that they're actually listening to you. That doesn't guarantee that they'll agree, but there's no way that a proposal can succeed if they aren't interested or paying attention. It's the first step in achieving your goals.

Another method of conveying what you wish them to hear is to adopt their manner of speaking. As distasteful as I personally find the shallow nature of corporate speak, if you learn the catch phrases, buzzwords, and metaphors that management uses and communicate in a similar manner when speaking with them, you will again have their attention. Think of it as learning a foreign language that you'll need when traveling to a strange and distant land, for the domain of management is about as alien to programmers as the landscape of the moon. Learning their language is actually rather easy, by the way. If you were smart enough to grasp a programming language, comprehending the verbiage of the Suits is a piece of cake. It simply takes attention and effort. Just make sure you revert to normal speech when around your fellow programmers, or you'll never hear the end of it.

Another method of speaking their language is what I previously referred to as changing your perspective. You have to talk about the things that are important to them, not to you. Well, actually you have to talk about what's important to you, but put it in terms of what's important to them. As an example of this, let's look at dissipating the idea that managing software development by shooting from the hip is really quicker than the ordered and structured approach that we're promoting here. Truly, management considers our procedures to be nothing more than lost time. This is why they shoot from the hip to begin with, because they think it's the quickest and most cost effective way to get software out the door. As long as they go on believing this, they'll have no reason to change.

## Instituting Change

Programmers could probably write an entire operating system in the time that's lost on a typical project because of rewrites due to scope creep and sliding requirements. The amount of time lost from integration issues and architectural rewrites stemming from an incomplete design phase is typically more than all of our procedures would take combined. However, designing and coding from the hip can be done. Companies do it every day. Software projects are always late and buggy, too. Coincidence? Not likely. Even so, because of the perception that coding is the only work that moves the software project forward, all else is considered a waste of time that delays the ultimate release of the program. The fact that we know otherwise has no impact because they don't understand the technical side of things.

Now let's look at how we would change the way they think using their point of view. They believe that shooting from the hip delivers software quickly and is more cost effective. First of all, we need a common definition of what delivered software really is. Management would probably agree that a software project is not really complete as long as you're still spending money on it. When a hurried program makes its way out the door, there is inevitably a cycle of bugs being found in the field, with the programmers fixing them and patches being made available to the users. This takes both time and money, as programmers don't work for free. Additionally, technical support costs increase dramatically due to the higher call volume that these bugs cause. As changes are made, documentation may also be updated to reflect the new state of the software. Tech writers don't work for free, either. This particular bit of money spent on support and documentation would not have been spent if the project was stable before it shipped. Therefore, in dollars and cents, not following our proposed procedures directly drives up the cost of the final delivered product. Due to unstructured rewrites and the massive debugging adventures involved, it also takes longer to write something poorly and fix a gazillion problems than it does to spend a little time in preparation up front and do it right the first time. That's more money out the window.

If you make an emotional argument based on the amount of sleep you're losing or the number of times you've had to rewrite the code, it will fall on deaf ears. However, if you do a little research, find some reference materials that support your arguments, and then show them how delivery time is actually longer and in particular how costs are dramatically increased with the current way of doing things, they'll listen to what you have to say. That's because you've presented it in a language that they understand, used meaningful reference materials, crunched some numbers, and showed them a bottom-line impact on the profitability of the company. Furthermore, if you're clever, you've also alluded to the fact that, when the manager you're dealing with institutes these changes and saves the company a ton of money, he'll also be an obvious choice for promotion. You have spoken his language and addressed what's in it for him personally. You have a very real chance of prevailing. If you approach all of your proposals to management in a similar fashion, you have the opportunity to truly change the way in which your shop develops software. Who knows, your fellow programmers may even pitch in and buy you a gold-plated pocket protector.

We've been focusing thus far on middle and upper management. However, for many programmers, the person that they need to convince is either another programmer on their team (such as a technical lead) or a project manager. These types of people have a different set of motivations than do the upper levels of management. Both programmers and project managers will relate more easily to the ability to get the next cool project that they want, or the opportunity to move to a position they desire. This could be a chance to use a new technology they want to work with or moving up to a position of team lead, system architect, or project manager. It's also convenient that you won't have to learn a new language to speak to this group, as they're techies. Project managers might be the exception to this, however, if you work in a large enough company in which project managers take on the guise of half programmer, half Suit.

Now that we're all speaking the same language, what else do we need to sell management on if we're to improve the state of software development in our individual companies? First, they must understand the dependencies of the development process. This is a pretty straightforward procedure that requires little explanation to most programmers:

- Design must not proceed without final and detailed requirements.

- Implementation must not proceed without complete design.

- Final QA must not proceed without implementation.

- Deployment must not proceed without final QA.

It is imperative that one phase be completed before beginning the next. They must be made to understand that real progress is being made even if they don't see programmers coding. If, during the design phase, functionality is added or changed, you must revert back to the requirements phase and make the appropriate modifications before continuing. The same goes for every step in the process. It's important for management to realize that, if you spend the proper time in requirements and design, the coding and delivery of milestones proceed much more quickly and with fewer roadblocks. Again, you can convey tangible, business-oriented results to make this point, because time is money.

Management must also be shown just exactly how important accurate and detailed estimating is if the deadlines are to be successfully met and therefore reliable. A good estimate takes time, and therefore time for estimating itself must be factored into the schedule. Detailed estimates also produce milestones of small granularity. This is better for project management as well as upper management because it allows both to keep a close eye on the progress of the project and keep it on track. For all the time that detailed estimating takes, doing it right yields estimates that are dependable. This reliability greatly reduces the risk of a project running late. Risk management is also an important concept to those in the upper reaches of the food chain. Dependable timelines are also better for marketing because they'll help avoid the embarrassment and additional expenses that result from advertising a product, missing the delivery schedule, advertising the next release date, missing it again, and so on.

Many people don't want to do a thorough job of estimating because they don't really want to hear that the project will take a long time. They must understand that, if the amount of time is unacceptable, it is far better to know it up front and cancel the project than it is to find out the hard way after committing the company's money, manpower, and position in the marketplace. An easy way to make this something that the individual manager cares about is to point out the obvious. If the project turns out to be a disaster, who do they think is going to get the blame? The person who has the authority to say no to a detailed estimation process is the very same person who will be burned at the stake when the project fails. If you can make them understand this, they'll have a new personal motivation for hearing what you say. The ultimate reality is unchangeable. It takes as long as it takes. No amount of denial will change that.

## Bolstering Your Position

If you're proposing a new or different way of doing things in your department, you're going to need some justification. People are quick to point out that they've always done things a certain way and the world hasn't come to an end. Therefore, if you want them to take the risk of changing the status quo (and that's perceived as a huge risk in Corporate America), you'd better be able to justify your proposal. This shouldn't be much of a problem because you doubtless have plenty of ammunition. All of the previous projects that were late or became some form of a disaster can be used to provide examples of the consequences of an improper approach. This is part of your proof and their motivation. At the risk of pointing out the obvious, if you can't find examples of these disasters, then it seems to me that your company's doing just fine and you don't need to change the way you're doing things. Any details that you can point to from failed projects (such as figures, statistics, demoted managers, significant layoffs, plummeting stock prices, bad press, poor sales, a parking lot littered with shattered monitors, and so on) will provide a motivation that they can readily appreciate. Fear can be a great motivator. Of course, if you can map it to dollars and cents it's going to help a great deal with middle and upper management. Additionally, if you can map it to promotions, more power, and an upward career path, that helps with everyone from the project manager on up. This sort of preparation will prove quite valuable to you in demonstrating why things should change.

Eventually, with persistence, you will get the opportunity to put all of this into practice. Once you do, it's critical to make sure that your project is considered a success. Regardless of where you get your foot in the door, you absolutely, positively must be perceived as a success if you wish to continue doing things your way. Note that I didn't say that your project should succeed but rather that it should be *perceived* as a success. It doesn't matter if you're right if no one else recognizes this fact.

To make sure that the world acknowledges your achievements, you must keep track of all the low-level timeline details we've discussed previously and be ready to kick out a report on a moment's notice that will show all of your successes thus far. That's why we keep the granularity small. The more milestones you have, the better chance you have of hitting most of them. Furthermore, reporting that you hit nineteen of twenty milestones is much better than showing that you hit one of one. The latter could be a fluke, while the former establishes a clear pattern of success.

Additionally, it's important that you subtly ensure that the whole world knows you're on track, on time, and under budget. I say *subtly* because if you're constantly in everyone's face about it you'll eventually irritate people to the point that they'll want to see you fail just to take you down a notch or two. They may even actively work against you because of this. One way of going about this is to gather as many cheerleaders as you can get. It always looks better when other people tout your achievements rather than doing it yourself and appearing egocentric. You'll find support in a lot of places if you look hard enough, such as other programming groups who'd like to have the same freedom, managers who are impressed with your success and look good because of it, and political hangers-on who just want to be associated with a winner because they're social climbers. Who cares what their motivations are? It all adds up to a good support base, and it's all good advertising. You'll need it from time to time, no matter how well things are going.

Of course, to be considered a success, you have to get the chance to prove that you're right. Look for every opportunity that you can find in the beginning to work on small, isolated startup projects. Management will be much more likely to take a chance on a small risk rather than a large one. If you need to gain more credibility and you have no track record, propose that you be allowed to prove your concepts on one of these small projects because it's obviously a low risk to management. Be sure to point out that, even though a success on this pilot program may not change the world, the implications for the rest of the company could be quite large. As always, be sure to also mention that the manager who first fields the concepts that ultimately lead to overall benefits for the company will surely be given a boost on the career path. What if no small projects are handy? Create one. Programmers are always good at coming up with an idea for a useful program.

You need to consider one additional thing when trying to convince management that the current approach to developing software needs improvement. What do you do if none of this sways them and they insist on continuing with chaotic development approaches that consistently create disasters and stress? Update your résumé. Life's too short to work for clowns.

## Frontal Assaults (For Those Who Respond to Reason)

The business world is no different than any other aspect of humanity. Just as some people are obstinate by nature, there are those who are open to direct persuasion and for whom convincing arguments are sufficient motivation for change. We've talked about the retraining that management requires and a little bit about how we should proceed. Now let's take a look at some of the direct approaches to achieving this goal.

In general, business people can relate to airtight, well-prepared presentations. Conveniently, so can project managers and programmers. The most important aspect of making a direct proposal for change is to use the right presentation for the given audience. Find out by observation and investigation exactly what language they speak and what forms of presentations they take seriously. For high-level Suits, this may mean formal meetings and polished reports with lots of pie charts, graphics, and summarized corroborating statistics. For project managers or middle management who take more of a hands-on approach, a more technical perspective backed up by detailed reference materials, real-world examples, and unambiguous information will be more appropriate.

If you have occasion to attend meetings that the people you wish to present to either hold or attend themselves, you have the perfect opportunity to gauge this. Pay attention to what they respond to, what they seem to immediately dismiss, and—most importantly—how they present things themselves. What do they use for supporting materials? Videos, slideshows, printed documents? If they use printed materials, how fancy is the formatting? Do they lean towards dense, information-intensive pages or very sparse presentations that are heavy on graphics and light on verbiage? In short, do your homework and find out as much as possible what pushes your manager's buttons. It's important to have solid facts, but, as anyone who watches television can tell you, advertising is typically more about presentation that content. Television advertising is extremely expensive. If they spend that much money and yet concentrate on how they're saying things more than what they're saying, there's a reason. It works.

I once worked for a consulting company that dealt with many banks. I'd been asked to put together an assessment of a particular client's codebase in preparation for a project we were proposing. Being a programmer, the result that I handed in was one very dense page of highly detailed points. The manager who requested it looked it over, approved of the contents, and then told me to get together with another manager who would show me how to turn one page into twenty. The result was a very highly polished, bound presentation sporting a fancy cover, with rich graphics taking up most of each page and perhaps a line or two of explanatory text at the bottom, all laid out in a neat, sequential manner. I remember at the time scoffing at such fluff. However, in this case my management was much smarter than I. They knew the language that the bankers responded to and they spoke it well. We got the project.

When it comes to making proposals, *where* is just as important as *what*. If you don't hold an official meeting in a conference room and conduct it just as they do their meetings, many managers won't take you seriously. If you want to be successful with these guys, all you really need to do is observe and mimic their behavior. Informal gatherings in cubicles or hallways may suffice for programmers or project managers. Just make sure that your arguments are still well thought out and bulletproof. The single most important aspect of making a successful proposal in the corporate world is simply to adapt to your target's environment and mannerisms.

Once you have their attention and they're taking what you say seriously, you must still make a winning presentation if you want them to accept your plan. A few ground rules need to be observed here. From the very first moment that you approach them about your ideas, always be sure to focus on what's in it for them. Otherwise, why should they care?

Often, what you propose may be a change to the way that they personally have decided to do things. It's absolutely critical to keep their ego in mind with every word that you speak. People frequently make emotional decisions. Stepping on someone's ego is the quickest way in the world to trigger this, and I can assure you that you won't like the decision. Consequently, take great care to avoid criticizing their plan. Point out the portions of their approach that you intend to keep and be sure to highlight the things that you think are great about them. When suggesting something that would replace or contradict their current way of doing things, approach it by pointing out that their current plan has many good things going for it and that what you're suggesting is just something to make a good plan even better. Never, ever offer a perspective that they can take as personal criticism. You'll be dead the minute you do.

Overall, your proposal must not only be presented well, it must offer them lower risk and higher benefits. Specifically, it must do so from their perspective, not yours. By speaking their language, using common phrases, acronyms, points of reference, and tailoring your way of presenting your argument to the style to which they are accustomed, you have a very good shot at walking away a winner on every point. If you can manage to phrase things in such a manner that they also walk out feeling like a winner on every point, you can be assured of continued support and enthusiasm on their part as you proceed. Everyone loves a win-win scenario. What you propose may not, in fact, be such a situation, but that doesn't matter. All that matters is that they perceive it as such.

## Stealth Tactics (When Reason Is Not Enough)

Life would be much more simple and people much easier to deal with if everyone made their decisions based on logic. Unfortunately, we're dealing with human beings, and they just don't work that way. Very often in your career, you're going to find yourself in a situation in which logic, common sense, and clearly presented arguments will still lose, time after time. All the pie charts in the world aren't going to help on such occasions. However, the people who give up are the people who never win. If we can't make it in through the front door, we'll simply sneak in through a window. Just keep an eye out for tiny dogs wearing combat fatigues. Those little teeth can really get your attention.

I've heard it said that there is often more power in being a king maker than in being a king. If your position is such that you just don't have the power to institute change, then what you need to do is alter the perspective and actions of someone who does. There are two types of people in this regard. First are those who actually do have the power to make changes. In this case, your efforts can get them to make the changes for you. The second type of person is someone who is effectively almost as powerless as you are, but who has access to those with more clout. If you can get this person on board, you can still promote change. It's a little like playing pool. Sometimes one ball hits another, which then hits another, and so on before you achieve the desired effect. Who cares, as long as the right ball goes into the right hole?

One method of influencing another person in your company is to become an ally. I'm not suggesting a campaign of brown-nosing, as I have difficulty dealing with the types of people who suck up to others. Rather, as mercenary as it may sound, what I propose is that you learn to manipulate others to do your bidding. In a perfect world we wouldn't have to do such things, but Corporate America is a far cry from perfect. Business is war, and I like to win.

By becoming a trusted lieutenant and confidant of the person who can help you make changes, you'll be in a position to continually whisper things in their ear that others would not have the opportunity to suggest. To gain this kind of access, however, you have to become a valued commodity. The first thing you need to do is get a clear picture of their personal agenda in the company. Everyone has an agenda, including you. You simply need to find out what this person wants to achieve. That's typically not too difficult because people often advertise such things openly.

With a knowledge of what they want to accomplish, you then look for ways to offer support. Becoming a source of hard-to-get information is one tactic. You may also offer strategies and solutions for their problems, but if you do it's important to position yourself in a supporting role and allow them to take credit for anything you might do on their behalf. Look ahead and meet their needs even before they realize they had them. Demonstrate loyalty, and let them see that you're watching their back. In such ways are allies made.

As they continually see you supporting their position and backing them up in any way that you can, they'll come to count you as one of their own, regardless of the departments in which each of you works. One note on this approach is to make sure that you offer all of this help with an attitude of strength and self-respect. Regardless of the fact that I personally don't care for groveling, subservient creatures, it's strategically important to avoid being perceived as someone who's just sucking up. If that's what they think, they won't have any respect for you, and you will consequently have no power to influence their decisions or actions. Instead, you must be seen as a person who is strong, sharp, and capable and who is offering your help only because the two of you share a common vision. They must feel fortunate to have such a capable ally. It's okay to position yourself behind them; their ego may require it anyway. Just make sure that you have their respect.

Mentoring is another way of doing this, particularly if the person you're dealing with is new to their position or just young in general. If such is the case, you will have experience in areas where they're weak. Often, they will have already paid the price a couple of times for their weaknesses. If you casually and quietly show them the ropes, you can gain both their respect and support. This is often very easy to do. When you see them about to do something that you know will result in their getting nailed, let them know what's lurking just around the corner and how to avoid it. They may be skeptical the first time you do this, so make sure you're right, particularly about the repercussions that they're about to experience. When things go just exactly as you said they would, you'll immediately have their undivided attention.

Once you're in this position, look out for them as you would your own family and share with them every trick you know. Don't worry about reaching a point where you have no more to show them. By the time you've reached that plateau, you will have gained an ally and a friend. As always, remember the chain of command and watch their ego. Equally important, never allow others to see you helping or take credit in any way. The idea is to strengthen their image, not your own.

The next method of gaining access is something you can learn from marketing. Many transactions in the business world happen not at formal meetings with three-piece suits lined up all in a row, but rather over cocktails. Socializing can be an extremely powerful tactic when done properly. Whether it's playing golf, dodging handballs, going out for drinks, or any other form of contact with them outside the workplace that forms a bond, it establishes you as someone in the inner circle. As such, you have access, which is what we're after here.

When socializing, it's important that you never talk business unless they bring it up. If you do, you'll find out quickly that you're no longer invited to any of the really good reindeer games. Rather, be a good listener. As you hang out with them, they'll start grumbling about the office problems all on their own. Take mental notes of the difficulties they're having. In addition to being a social friend, you're also arming yourself with the information that you need to make yourself more valuable. If you know what problems they're encountering, then you know where you can try to make a difference and bring them aid and support.

Another means to an end is that of gaining consensus and support from others who can influence management for you. This is very dangerous stuff and is only for the most extreme of situations because getting people to gang up on management can easily be construed as mutiny. Most commanders take a dim view of such things. You'll typically either win big or lose big. Make sure that you can afford it before you attempt this approach. No matter what you do, care should be taken to avoid being seen as insubordinate. That's just the polite term they use in the business world for *mutiny*, but that single word is also all that needs to show up on an employee review to end said employment.

Whether you instigate a little friendly persuasion or an all-out revolution will depend on the gravity of the situation, how much support you can truly count on, and in general which way the wind blows in the company. If things are going so badly that you need to instigate a mass uprising, you should probably have your résumé updated anyway because there are only three possible outcomes. The first potential outcome is that you'll succeed, in which case you just forget about the resume. The other two possibilities, however, are that either it doesn't make a difference (in which case you should put that résumé to good use and move on to new opportunities) or it will be seen as a mass revolt. In that case, life will get bad in a real hurry. However, if things are so bad that you're thinking about looking for another job anyway, you have much less to lose by taking one last shot. Just remember that a good reference is among the things you risk.

## Credibility, the Key to Success

Credibility is not something you come into the business world with. No matter how many college degrees you have and regardless of how impressive your résumé, the only way you're ever going to get a solid standing and the respect that you deserve in your company is by demonstrating time and again that you can deliver on your promises. To middle and upper management, everything else is just talk. This may seem like a no-win scenario when we've observed that many companies choose deadlines that guarantee that their developers will fail. On a large scale, this is true. However, credibility is something that tends to be cumulative. Consequently, many small successes are often more effective than one large one. You often have to artificially create your own scenarios for success to rack up the points. However, the first rule of maintaining your credibility is to deliver the goods. If you're successful, they'll take you more seriously with each new venture.

There are, however, more aspects to building credibility than simply doing what you said you would do. Keep personal notes of all your successes, the times that your recommendations were right, and all of the benefits that either the company or the management you deal with received. Keep these notes at home. I've mentioned this before, and I do so again here only because you are never guaranteed privacy in the business world. Consequently, it's the safest way to keep confidential information to yourself. Also keep notes of every software-related disaster that you've observed, on any team, with as much detail as possible on why it happened and what would have prevented it. Make meticulous notes regarding who the responsible parties were as well. This is to make sure that you never mention them directly. It's not only good manners, it avoids creating adversaries unnecessarily. Style counts.

There will be times when these notes will come in handy when you need to reaffirm or defend your credibility. If you need to defend your position in a particular power struggle, it's hard to work from memory. At such times, what you really need is precise and specific information that you can convey without fear of contradiction. Get into a habit of jotting things down in a notebook when you get home from work. If you're more ambitious, punch it into a database on your home computer so that you can do specific searches later. Either way, make your notes at home, not at the office. If you're seen doing it at work, you simply make yourself vulnerable to attack by others. Doing it at home at the end of the day, while the events are still fresh in your mind, is both perfectly safe and more accurate.

Another aspect of credibility is simple physical perception. From a political point of view, it's best to look, act, and dress like the herd. Honestly, I've never been very good at this, and I'm more likely to show up in blue jeans and a black leather jacket than I am slacks and a golf shirt. Frankly, I would have done better in many circumstances had I conformed more. However, that said, it's okay to establish your own individuality (within acceptable company boundaries) provided that you're recognized as someone who always comes through. In fact, at times you can play it to your advantage. Some people love me, some don't, but few ever forget me. This comes in handy sometimes.

Of course, coming back to a recurring theme, you must never forget that you're dealing with people. In the business world, a huge number of decisions are made not on the black-and-white issues of profit and loss but rather due to emotions, personal inclinations, and bonds with other people. Kindness, consideration, and just being a nice guy in general are always in your favor. It may be necessary to defend yourself from time to time, but never show your teeth if you can avoid it. People remember that sort of thing. In fact, avoid antagonizing people whenever possible. You'll do enough of it as it is, and there's no advantage in creating animosity if you don't have to.

Additionally, never underestimate the power of charisma. You don't have to be a movie star; they just have to like you and trust you. People will do all sorts of unreasonable things if they like you. You can even get them to do reasonable things. Of course, always watch their egos. People will also do unreasonable things if you hurt their feelings.

Part of credibility is being a trustworthy person. Therefore, make sure that, if people follow your recommendations based on personal affinity or trust, you never let them down. Furthermore, if things go south because of your ideas, step up to the plate and take the consequences yourself. Doing so will contribute to their perception of your integrity, as well it should. From a tactical point of view, though, the blame would have landed on you anyway. You may as well get some mileage out of it.

In general, reliable delivery dates can come from only the developers. Management, however, has somehow gotten the impression that they're in charge. This means that, if we're to have any chance whatsoever of changing things for the better, we have to retrain our managers. To do this, developers must gain not just their trust but also the opportunities to prove that we have a better way. Accomplishing this requires effective communications, credibility, and more than a little behind-the-scenes maneuvering. It's not what you signed on for when you took your job as a programmer, but the choices are clear: learn to manage your management or continue to cope with the disasters that their inept techniques cause. Although it's not the sort of thing that most of us care to spend our time doing, in the end the improvements we make in our development process, not to mention our ability to get a decent night's sleep, make it all worthwhile.

# CHAPTER 11

# Corporate Self-Defense

It's a common dream to live in a world in which everyone is always treated fairly, with respect and equality. If you ever find such a place, be sure to save me a seat. I'll bring the doughnuts. Although it's a tall order for humanity in general, in Corporate America it's not even on the horizon. No matter how good the intentions or benevolent the company, when you have a building full of people vying for money and control, somebody's gonna get hurt. If you're not careful, it'll be you. It's been said that in the animal kingdom it's either get dinner or be dinner. Thankfully, we don't have to go to such extremes in the business world. Nonetheless, if you don't know how to exercise a little self-defense, you're going to have a very unpleasant stay. But at least it will be short.

Exactly what kind of defenses are we talking about here? Barbed wire and machine gun nests? Although I've had days when that was indeed tempting, there's no need to break out the weaponry or start renting a bunch of overdubbed martial arts movies. The self-defense we need in this case has little to do with bodily harm. Besides, we have attack Chihuahuas for that job. The threat in the business world is not that you'll find yourself dodging bullets (at least if you give the maintenance programmer a wide berth). More likely, you'll be dodging bad assignments. Those who have chosen a career in buildings crammed with cubicles soon find that it's a dog-eat-dog world in which nothing is sacred, although I'd recommend against using that phrase around the security shack. Turn your back for just a moment, and they'll steal your project, your programmers, and even your stapler. Make no mistake: the very first targets are the ones who look like easy prey.

Does all of this sound overly dramatic to you? If so, you either lead a charmed life or you simply haven't spent enough time in the business world yet. The software development business, whether you're working on a commercial product or internal software, is a collection of highly competitive people, each with their own agenda. Some pursue this agenda in an aggressive and cut-throat manner, and others take a more civilized approach. Many struggle in the area between, grasping and fumbling, sometimes winning and sometimes losing but usually making a mess of things in the process. It's true that many go about their business in a reasonable and considerate manner, but it only takes one or two of the other sort to put a premature end to an otherwise good day.

## What Do You Have to Lose?

But exactly what sort of dangers does a professional programmer have to guard against? Let's talk about some of the bad things that happen to good programmers. Just to have an extreme to start with, consider the loss of your job. Projects come and go, and the size of a company's development department is often in a state of flux. When times are good, human resources is hiring anyone who can breathe and type three words a minute. Six months later, however, a couple of major projects get canceled and suddenly it's a game of musical chairs as people scramble to avoid being laid off. Who do you think ends up keeping their job: the most talented and qualified? Sometimes. But not always. Invariably, when times get tough, the people who thrive and survive are the ones who can maneuver, even if they're drooling idiots when they sit down in front of a compiler. Perhaps you've known such people.

This can get a bit ugly, fostering situations in which one person goes out of his way to make others look bad to management so that they're the ones who get cut from the herd. Many times such unscrupulous people succeed, and good programmers unjustly lose their jobs. Why? Because they didn't know how to defend themselves or—worse still—somehow felt that they didn't have to participate in a struggle that was beneath them. Occasionally this will be a blatant event, but it happens much more often than you think, and in subtle but effective ways. The end result is always the same: those who do not defend themselves are the first to go.

At other times, your employment status may not be in jeopardy. However, you could lose many other things. We get up each morning and rush to work because we're excited about what we do for a living. Most programmers are always looking for new technologies to play with and typically have a pet project or two going on for entertainment purposes if nothing else. The types of assignments we get are a very fundamental part of our job satisfaction. If there's some hot, sexy new technology that you're just dying to get your hands on but someone else is better at playing the game, you may well find yourself relegated to doing post mortem technical documentation while the more politically adept programmer props his feet up and has one coding adventure after another. It may not be fair if you're senior or more qualified, but it's the way it is. Again, if you don't learn a little hand-to-hand combat, you'll start losing battles that you care about.

Ever notice how some programmers seem to have all the luck? They're the ones with the 75-inch monitors, a connection to the Internet via direct satellite hookup, a couple of super computers tucked under their desk, and all of this in an actual office with a door. How is it that these guys end up with all the cool toys? Are they really *that* good? Well, they're certainly good at saying the right things to the right people. That's why they get the best toys. And wait a minute, isn't that *my* stapler on his desk?

I could go on for days but by now you probably have a pretty good picture of what I'm talking about and can see it in terms of the company where you work. In Corporate America, there are takers and the taken. Now, just for the record, I'm not advocating that we should all become grasping, cold-hearted, back-stabbing meanies. I personally believe in treating people with kindness and respect, the same as I'd want for myself, and I believe that to a degree this will bring its own rewards. In the context of the workaday world, people like doing things for nice folks. Given the choice, that's how I prefer to spend my days. Unfortunately, not everyone shares the same attitude about this sort of thing, and I occasionally find myself in a situation in which I either must take action or be the victim of someone else's questionable morals. The world can be a dark and scary place. I shoot back.

I once worked on a team where one of the analysts was fairly outspoken and worked very hard to try to bring a quality product to the users. He truly cared about their needs and lobbied hard for anything that promoted better quality or functionality. In contrast, some of the programmers who felt that the user requests would be too much trouble would literally lie to them about why something just couldn't be done. As you can imagine, the sparks flew on more than one occasion.

Then one day the middle manager to whom our project manager reported was transferred. The new guy who took his place was the immediate target of pressures and arm twisting from the programmers who felt that the analyst was, well, inconvenient. As it happens, the analyst was also a friend of the project manager. Unfortunately, the other programmers had a number of friends and allies in middle and upper management and they turned the heat up on my project manager's boss to have the analyst fired. Having about as much backbone as a lot of the middle managers I've known, this guy caved. I actually heard him tell my project manager to make a decision about the analyst. The middle manager acknowledged the fact that, because my boss was the project manager, it was of course his decision one way or the other. However, he followed up by saying that if my boss didn't make the right decision he'd make it for him. And so, my project manager had the unenviable task of firing someone who was both a friend and had done nothing wrong beyond being politically inconvenient. And so, he was fired. Why? Pure politics. The corporate world is full of such tales. You don't want to be one of them.

## Picking Your Battles

The art of self-defense is a complex one with many facets. One thing that might be learned from our previous example is that there are many battles that can be fought every single day. However, fighting them all isn't always a good idea. There are no actions without consequences. Part of staying alive in the sometimes dangerous political environment of the business world is knowing when to fight, when to run, and when to just keep your mouth shut. The enemy rarely shoots just for the fun of it. That wastes ammunition. They shoot when they have a target, and the more noise you make, the better target you are.

Programmers are fiery and temperamental artists. When you're talking about software and how to write it, it's something we take personally. Consequently, it's easy to get all worked up about something and find yourself in the middle of a big blowout because you feel strongly about an issue. Whether it's a matter of design, how something should be coded, or even which brand of soft drinks that should be stocked in the kitchen, you may be tempted to argue and fight passionately with everything you have. In fact, the issues are truly that important at times. However, they aren't always critical. Any time you fight for something, you stand to win or lose. If you lose, it could really cost you. The first question you should ask yourself is a simple one: is it worth it? If it's not, let it go. Save your bullets not for the skirmish, but for the invasion.

It isn't always obvious what you stand to lose in any given confrontation. Those who practice judo make very effective use of a simple characteristic of human nature. When you push against someone, they instinctively push back. Say the judo instructor wants to throw you in a southerly direction. He will first push you north. You will, of course, resist and push in the opposite direction with all your might, at which point the instructor smiles and simply helps you throw yourself south. Hope you learned how to tumble. Those carpeted hallways are never as soft as they look.

In a similar fashion, when you take a stand on an issue and push hard for things to be done your way, others will instinctively push against you as hard as they can. Under normal circumstances, these very same people might not have been inclined to work against you at all. However, this is the way people react when they're threatened. In the end, you may lose much more than you thought possible simply because of a strong backlash. In effect, you created that backlash yourself.

Another problem with fighting every fight that comes your way is reputation. Eventually, people tire of one who is always confrontational and will look for ways to neutralize or eliminate him. In the case of the analyst, this is exactly what happened. If he'd fought fewer battles, he wouldn't have garnered such intense animosity that an entire department conspired to get rid of him. This doesn't mean that he was wrong when he stood up for an issue, but in the end it just didn't matter. Not only does it bite to lose your job, once you're fired you can't accomplish anything else that you were trying to achieve there. Management takes a dim view of ex-employees showing up for design meetings. Security isn't real big on the matter, either. It interferes with the doughnut breaks.

Consequently, before you stand up in your next meeting and arm yourself with a few whiteboard erasers, stop and consider the importance of the issue at hand in the grand scheme of things. Start by looking at the basics. Does a change in the project affect the amount of hours you have to work, the amount of money you make, the quality of your day-to-day life on the job, or your overall value on the job market? This is our livelihood, and these are the real issues. If you're about to push for something that will undoubtedly make a big stink, you need to ask these questions. If none of them come up in the affirmative, then sit down and be quiet. And put those erasers back where you found them.

Sometimes, however, the issues are truly important. If so, how major is the matter at hand? Is it something worth changing jobs over? If so, make sure that you're prepared to do so before engaging in the fight. This means that you need to have already quietly updated your résumé. You should also have taken a good look at the job market and your personal finances. How long will it take you to find another job? Do you have offers already? If not, how long can you go without income before you have to start ordering your pizzas without extra pepperoni? These are the practical considerations that you need to have in mind when you're ready to go to the mat over something.

If you're not willing to quit your job over the matter, how good are your chances of winning the fight? If it gets tough and you lose, is it something that could cost you your job? If so, you need to weigh the risks against the benefits. Again, is it worth it? However, even if your chances for success are good, how many people will you alienate in the process? There's almost always some hard feelings after a major battle. If you make people angry in the process of getting your way, are they significant enough to cause you trouble later on? Remember, just because you win a decision in a meeting doesn't mean that your adversaries disappear. They still work at the same company, and people hold grudges. Depending on how ugly the confrontation got, you may have created some enemies that will be working against you for some time to come, just out of spite. No, that's not very professional, but people are people. To expect them to be otherwise makes about as much sense as starving a lion for a week and then sticking your head into his mouth.

Be aware of the fact that with every battle you fight you may create your own adversaries. Some will be powerful and some will not. Even if you alienate only the peasants, though, be sparing in your battles. If you slam dunk enough people, it's eventually going to make you look bad, and that will catch up to you. Image notwithstanding, though, even those with little power in the company can still nail you. It's like that town square full of angry villagers with the pitchforks and torches. Individually they may not be very powerful, but as a group it's a scary thing to see.

If your chances of winning are low and it's also not worth quitting your job over, there's only one path to take: get over it. If you feel particularly strong about the matter, perhaps it would be a good time to take some of your vacation days and come back when you have a better attitude. Conceding a point doesn't count if you sulk about it. That just irritates people. Remember the pitchforks.

In general, the best approach is to not only choose carefully the issues that you think are worth fighting for but also to be prudent in your approach. Although there are times for overwhelming firepower, in general you'll ruffle fewer feathers if you use no more force than is absolutely necessary to get your point across convincingly. In short, be a gentleman about it. When you do win, do so graciously and don't rub it in. People aren't always happy when things don't go their way, but they can shake it off pretty quickly if the winner is nice about it. Again, style counts. The people you argue with today may be your allies tomorrow.

## Avoid Being a Target

What we've discussed thus far is in fact a way to avoid having your peers use you for target practice. Choosing to not fight every battle that comes along is simply one way of maintaining a low profile. The obvious advantage, of course, is that the less of a profile you present, the less they have to shoot at. There are other things that you can do as well to keep those red concentric circles off of your posterior.

One very good rule to live by is to never put anything in writing that you wouldn't want broadcast worldwide on the evening news. Email is particularly dangerous. It's true that, if I snail mail a letter to someone, they can give it to a friend or read it aloud at the next bridge party, but that takes effort. Furthermore, there's only one letter, so, unless they feel like making photocopies, they lose the original if they give it to someone. Not so with email. With the simple click of a mouse, what you thought you told someone in confidence is suddenly broadcast to everyone on the company mailing list. Of course, it's rarely done to that extreme, but you'd probably be surprised and more than a little uncomfortable if you knew how often your email was silently forwarded to someone else. The truth of the matter is that you simply don't know where it's going to end up. Few things are as embarrassing as an email surfacing publicly in which you're insulting someone in your very own words.

As a techie, however, you already know that this is just the simple and straightforward part of it. Email is nothing more than fancy text files that get passed around from computer to computer until they land at their intended destination. Anyone with an administrative password and an agenda of their own can read every email in the entire company. I've actually had people tell me on sensitive matters to email them at their home address rather than the office because they've actually witnessed this sort of thing. Absolutely nothing you send in an email is private. If you need it to be so, take a walk and have a conversation. Otherwise you're just making yourself vulnerable.

Furthermore, if you think that you might change your mind about an issue at some point in the future, don't put it in writing at all. Whether it's a word processor document, a scribbled note, an email message, or any other such thing, once you put it in writing it's in a physical form that you cannot completely control. This may sound a little cloak-and-dagger to you, but I'm sure that there have been times when you needed to discuss sensitive topics at work and the breaking of that confidence would have had unpleasant consequences. It's simply a matter of avoiding potential trouble. The fewer holes you have in your defenses, the fewer attacks that will get through.

You may be reading all of this and thinking to yourself that you simply don't have any political skills to begin with. This may be true. Not everyone possesses the instincts necessary to play the game effectively, and there are no guarantees even to those who do. However, you do have a good set of eyes and some perceptive abilities. If you don't have political skills, do your best to keep a low profile around the potential troublemakers who do. They're easy to spot. You could probably make a list of all the ones in your company right now. Furthermore, align yourself with as many people as you can who have more maneuvering abilities than you do, assuming that they have some common sense as well. The combination of not sticking your head up for someone to shoot at and running with a pack that's capable of defending themselves will reduce your vulnerabilities tremendously.

As I discovered many years ago, choosing to not participate doesn't get you out of the game. It only makes you a target that doesn't shoot back. Whether you have no talent for politics or you simply don't think that you should have to deal with these things, if you don't find ways of keeping yourself safe that work for you and practice them continually you're going to find yourself continually under fire. I freely acknowledge that if you get hired as a programmer you shouldn't have to do anything but focus on programming. However, the reality is that you're in the game whether you like it or not. How you fare is up to you. Personally, I hate losing.

## Assessing the Lay of the Land

One of the simplest and most effective techniques that you can employ to keep your tookus out of a sling is to just pay attention. Be aware of the political landscape at every level you can, from your small corner of the world to as far up the food chain as you can see. Ask yourself the following questions.

- Who has the power?

- Who are the followers?

- Who is loyal?

- Who is opportunistic?

- Who has integrity?

- Who is out for themselves regardless of the cost to others?

- Who is fighting the good fight?

- Who is causing problems?

- Who's winning?

- Who's losing?

- What's changing?

The answers to these simple queries will tell you much about where you should be and whom you should avoid. One of the best self-defense techniques I've ever heard of was a man who said that he could smell trouble three weeks away but be out of town before it got here. If you can identify who the aggressive and manipulative players are, then you'll see trouble before it gets to you. Equally important, just like meerkats on the prairie, you should poke your head up every now and then so that you always know which way the wind is blowing. Management comes and goes, and projects come and go. The way things are done today may not be the way they'll be done tomorrow. Maybe that's a good thing, and maybe it's not. In any event, if you pay attention to the overall trends of how your company is run, you'll be in a position to either capitalize on change when it happens or have the foresight to put your résumé on the streets long before anyone else figures out that their job is a disaster waiting to happen. This doesn't require political savvy. You just have to pay attention.

## Escape and Evade

Periodically, you'll find yourself cornered by someone pressing you to endorse their position or to take some action on their behalf. This can be a real problem if it's someone who's higher up the food chain than you are, particularly if what they're selling is something you wish to avoid. On the one hand, you could be pressured into committing to a task or an opinion that will cause you problems. Refusing, however, could create an adversary who may try to find ways to take it out on you later. The best thing you can do in these situations is find a way to be someplace else.

You can actually accomplish this in a number of ways that require very little assertiveness on your part. Essentially, you simply look for the first opportunity to politely excuse yourself. Apologize for having to cut them short and then explain (as you start walking away) that you have to go to the restroom and it simply won't wait. This isn't a terribly elegant solution, but it's an effective one. Social etiquette demands that they not impede your journey. Then make sure you go directly to the facilities. If they follow you, find a stall and close the door. Eventually they'll get tired of waiting and go away.

Of course, you can substitute other scenarios. You can claim that you have to get to a meeting right away, that you are expecting a phone call, have to return one, are late for a lunch appointment, et cetera. However, whatever excuse you offer, make sure it's something that can't wait. And make certain they never see that it's otherwise. No one likes having the wool pulled over their eyes.

## If You Must Attack

It's often said that the best defense is a good offense, but I disagree. Although a good offense can certainly be an effective tactic, I believe that the best defense is simply being somewhere else when the bullets fly. If you're not there, you don't get hurt. That being said, there are certainly times, whether it's a routine design meeting or a struggle to keep your project from being canceled, when you must go on the offensive to protect your position. If you're going to take a swing at someone else's position, there are a number of things you can do to increase your chances for success while minimizing your risks.

First and foremost, know your strengths and your weaknesses. If an issue must be pushed, but you're not assertive by nature, arrange for a coworker who is more persuasive than you to do the fighting, with you working in a supportive role. This doesn't mean that you just put the work off on them. You can plan, you can prepare, you can detail the arguments, write the documents, prepare the slide shows, brainstorm with your partner, and so forth. You just let them do the talking because they're better at it. A good partnership with each person utilizing the best of what they bring to the party makes for a formidable presentation. Conversely, if you talk a good line but are a little weak on preparation and detail, find an ally who can help you in this area. In general, be frank and honest with yourself about where your talents and deficiencies lie. If you can do that, you'll know how to shore up your defenses and you'll be way ahead of the game.

Knowing what to expect out of people is also important. If your expectations are unrealistic, you'll get acquainted with reality at the most inconvenient moment. One good example of this has to do with the herd instinct. Never assume that someone will come to your rescue in a meeting. They never do. Be prepared to stand on your own.

In a similar fashion, never assume that silence or the nodding of heads at a meeting means that everyone agrees with you. Often they will say yes only to strike behind your back the next day. Don't let this take you by surprise. To a certain degree, you'll have to learn to trust your gut instincts. Any time that something seems too easy to be true, it is. If you expected significant resistance to an idea but encounter only nodding heads and tacit agreement, you can bet that something's up. Work on that assumption and you'll be much less likely to get blindsided.

Also never assume that the people who said they would support you in a meeting actually will. Be prepared and have a plan ready should they all just remain silent and stare at their shoes when it's time to back you up. It's amazing how fascinating shoes can be. If you find yourself on the losing end of a heated debate and you know that several other people in the room share the same convictions as you, don't be surprised to find them avoiding eye contact with you. They may have been behind you one hundred percent before the meeting and they may indeed grumble with you about the outcome afterwards, but, if you expect them to stick out their own necks in the meeting when you're taking heavy fire, you're in for an unpleasant surprise. When you get right down to it, people are typically much more concerned about saving their own skin. However, if you're prepared for this going in, you'll have thought of some alternate strategies to fall back on if things don't go your way. That's what's important.

No matter how technically correct you are, if you don't evaluate the political dynamics of what you're about to propose, you could stir up a hornet's nest that you never saw. For example, you may point out a flaw in the way orders are processed in a meeting that has your boss and his superior in attendance. Although you did so to propose a solution, your boss's manager interprets it as a major mistake on the part of your project manager and proceeds to slice and dice him in front of the entire meeting. Little wonder, then, that the next day you find that, instead of working on that cool little database project you had in mind, you find yourself relegated to scraping gum off the bottoms of chairs. And you thought your boss had no sense of humor.

Remember, there are no actions without consequences. Whatever ideas you propose, whatever issues or problems you raise, make sure that you have first evaluated every possible political ramification that you can. Who is in attendance? Do they have an agenda with which this would conflict? Are any egos at stake? Will there be competition for who gets control of the idea? Does this make anyone look bad? These are just a few of the questions that you should train yourself to ask instinctively before you set upon a course of action. It may seem a bit paralyzing to you at first, but you'll be surprised at how quickly this becomes instinctive. It's worth noting that, in the wild, the critters with the best instincts are typically the ones who survive, even if it's just playing possum.

It's also worth evaluating the consequences of both winning and losing. Although it's easy to work your way through the various disaster scenarios that accompany losing, it's just as important to think through the chain of events that winning will set into motion. In addition to concern for the egos of others, keep the domino effect in mind. For instance, you may have proposed that reporting would be much easier if someone would write a print library to handle all of the commonly used formatting issues. This would allow the person writing the report to simply make a few function calls and be done. Because you're the one tasked with writing the reports, this will no doubt seem like a very good idea. Everyone else in the room argues against it. However, after a persuasive presentation and to your utter delight, your project manager agrees with you. In fact, because you have such a good grasp of the matter, he assigns the task of writing the print library to you. Of course, your deadlines for the reports don't change. But you won, right? It's impossible to foresee every possible outcome. However, it's even less possible if you don't try.

Regardless of what you're proposing, always do your research on the opposing points of view. Find your opponent's strengths, weaknesses, who will support him and who won't, how much weight that support has, and so on. If you've thought things through thoroughly, you're in an excellent position to rebut any arguments that he is likely to make in the meeting. However, this doesn't just apply to the strengths and weaknesses of his argument. Do your best to discern the temperament of the opposition as well. What are their hot buttons? Are they emotional? As such, if you can get them to react emotionally, will it throw them off balance or make their position look weaker? Are they stronger in abstract concepts? Then hit hard on the details. Are they better at details than grasping the conceptual? Then emphasize the big picture. Everyone has weaknesses. Learning where they are tells you exactly where to hit.

Another thing to keep in mind is your own credibility with those who matter. It doesn't make a bit of difference that your idea is completely bulletproof. If your credibility is not sufficient in the eyes of those who make the decisions, you're going to be dismissed with little attention given to your issues. That can also put you in an embarrassing or precarious situation. Don't start something that you'll later regret. If you don't have the horsepower, don't have the meeting. Instead, take some time and build an alliance with those who do. When you finally do make your presentation, allow the focus to drift away from you and onto the people who can get the job done. It may not be as good for the ego, but it'll be much more effective in terms of achieving your aims.

Just as you looked for weaknesses in your opposition, give the same attention to your own. Be prepared with defenses to any perceived weaknesses. Think of how you would attack the argument if you were on the other side, and then close that window. If there truly is a real vulnerability in your position, you can choose to abandon the proposal or try to make it fly regardless. If you do plan to go ahead, make sure you have an answer of some sort prepared and then quickly try to change the subject after you use it. Sometimes you'll get away with it.

Never underestimate the value of overwhelming firepower. If you can win by just minor rebuttals or dazzling a little, that's all good and fine. However, if it's a battle you simply cannot afford to lose, it's best to just come out with both guns blazing. If you're well prepared to shoot down every single opposing view in your opening volley, the room will simply rustle nervously and take a step or two back, and you'll save a lot of time from arguments that just won't happen.

## Improving Your Skills

You'd be quick to buy a book on the latest coding technique. However, very few people spend anywhere near the same amount of time or effort sharpening their self-defense skills. A wealth of literature is available in every bookstore covering negotiation, proposals, politics, and the many paths to achieving success in business. Don't dismiss the book just because the guy's wearing a three-piece suit or isn't speaking specifically about programming. You're a programmer, true, but you're a programmer who lives in Corporate America. It only makes sense, then, to read books that relate to the business environment. In fact, some of them may be less obvious than others. Many people the world over understand the adage that business is war. Consequently, you'll find that they study some of the classic books on warfare and military strategy and apply those concepts to the daily struggles faced by people in the business world.

All of this nontechnical stuff may seem like a waste of time when you'd rather be coding, but if you pay attention to these details you'll find that your days are disrupted much less by the maneuverings of others. When your defenses are strong and none dare attack you, that's when you can sit back undisturbed and enjoy moments of pure coding bliss.

# CHAPTER 12

# Controlling
# Your Destiny

Unlike those who pursue more traditional vocations, there are probably as many self-taught programmers in the world as there are those with college degrees. It's one of the rare careers in which ability is often more important than pedigree. (Don't mention that to our faithful watchdog, however. He's rather proud of his.) Nonetheless, although attorneys and accountants would have a hard time finding a job without the appropriate certificates, many of us started our professional lives as little more than enthusiastic hobbyists. Only later did the notion strike us that we could actually get paid for this stuff, and college may or may not have followed that realization. Consequently, the time eventually comes when developers, whether degreed or bootstrapped, set off in search of gainful employment using the skills that have become their passion.

For many, that exciting first job search was a rather unstructured affair with little thought given to anything beyond getting a paycheck for writing code. It often involved simply grabbing the newspaper and applying for every opportunity for which your skills were even a remote match. When asked what we were looking for by our friends, the answer was simple: a job. Nothing more, nothing less.

However, as most of us now know only too well, working as a professional software developer involves a tremendous number of variables. A programming job can range from Utopia to Hades, and sometimes both in the same day. Even though a lot of folks out there went to school, had a long-term career plan, and were in general quite organized and forward thinking, many of us didn't have the slightest idea what we were getting ourselves into. For that matter, the guys with the career plan probably didn't either, but at least they had some goals.

Like most anything in life, it's hard to achieve your dreams if you don't know what they are. Quick, grab a piece of paper and write down all the details of the perfect job. As you look over your shoulder, you probably won't be too surprised to find that some of the newer guys have written down only a couple of things before stopping. The ones back in the corner frantically wearing out their pencils are the seasoned old dogs who have been in the business long enough to have a better idea of what they want. For the most part, they learned the hard way. Take a peek at their lists and you'll likely find that the majority of lines involve things they'd like to *avoid* in the perfect job. A few years in Corporate America does that to you.

Although most of you already have a job at present, we've all been doing this long enough to know that the tides of technology turn quickly. The job that's here today may be gone tomorrow. Even more likely, the job that's fun today may well turn into something about as exciting as working in a dog biscuit factory. Although that may be enticing to some of the staff here, in general it's sufficient to say that in our line of work looking for a job is often just a part of the job.

It's hard to construct a building without a good blueprint, and landing the perfect programming gig is no different. You won't get the job of your dreams unless you know what it is. So, without further ado, let's take a look at some of our options in the wonderful world of software development.

When considering exactly how you want to spend your days as a certified, working-class programmer, the first step is deciding what style of employment best suits you. There are always variations on the theme, but you generally can get three types of jobs as a developer. You can either work for a company as an employee, don the armor of a mercenary and work as a contractor, or hang out a shingle and be your own boss. No one path is better than the others, and each approach has its pluses and minuses. It all comes down to personal preference. Let's break it down and take a closer look at each career path.

## The Company Man

Working as an employee is probably the most familiar approach to the majority of us, and choosing this road has a number of positive aspects. Salaried employees get paychecks that come on a regular basis for a predictable amount. Having spent many years doing more entrepreneurial things, I can't tell you how exciting it can be to know every month just exactly how much money you're going to make. It does wonders for the budgetary planning and keeps the antacid bills low as well.

In addition to the stability of income, being a company man has additional financial advantages. First among these are the tax benefits. For openers, an employer will withhold your taxes for you so that you don't have to worry about how you're going to come up with the money at the end of the year. You may think that this is no big deal because we're all obviously smart enough to save some money for taxes each month instead of spending it, but having all that extra cash available can be a mighty temptation. If you've ever had any extended adventures with the Internal Revenue Service, you'll be more motivated than most to avoid any such encounters in the future. Even though we're certainly capable of managing our own tax money, having it out of sight and out of mind is a definite benefit.

That's not the only tax benefit, however. Without getting into all the fine details of the federal tax code, when you work as an employee, there are additional taxes that you don't have to pay because your company does it for you, typically in the area of additional social security and unemployment taxes. This isn't out of the kindness of their heart, of course. It's federal law. Still, the person who benefits is you, for at the end of the year it's money you didn't have to pay out of your own pocket.

Additional financial benefits are available to employees in the form of paid or copaid medical insurance, sick days, vacation days, stock options, and a good many other options that businesses offer to entice the better-quality programmers to set up camp at their place. Regular jobs have a number of non-cash benefits as well, and these can range from company cars and continuing education programs to seemingly little things like reserved parking and an office with a door.

Beyond compensation, life as a full-time employee has a number of intangible benefits. The first and most often cited is job security. Of course, anyone who has been working for more than a couple of months can tell you that, to a large degree, job security in the technology business is an illusion. Full-time employees are not immune to layoffs when times are hard or projects get cancelled. However, in a company that hires contractors and permanent employees alike, the contractors are typically the first to go. Many companies will also go to a fair degree of trouble to take care of their employees and make job cuts the very last option. So, even though nothing in this business is guaranteed, employees do have a more secure position than others in the industry.

Another thing that many people prefer about working for the same company for many years is, well, working for the same company for many years. Not everyone is comfortable with interviewing or looking for a job. People who work as contractors accept frequent job changes as a part of their lifestyle. However, that's not for everyone, and, if you're someone who enjoys keeping a little consistency in your life, there are definite advantages to life as an employee.

For the ambitious, there's also the opportunity to advance your career and move up through the ranks. Although most programmers prefer to write code and just be left alone, some enjoy working in management. Staying at the same company for any significant amount of time also gives you the chance to consider different avenues altogether. Some who code actually enjoy testing, and some find that they prefer firing up a word processor and writing technical manuals. You didn't hear this from me, but some even gravitate towards marketing. All in all, life as a company man offers many options and advantages.

It's not a complete bed of roses, however. For some, exposure to company politics—a requirement for climbing up the food chain—is an extremely unpleasant prospect. If you have a long-term job with a company, then you have a career path to protect. That can take a bit of maintenance from time to time, depending on the level of corporate insanity prevalent in your place of business.

Money is another area in which the employee typically doesn't come out ahead. Those who work as hourly contractors make a significantly greater wage, assuming they work all through the year. Although contractors don't get all of the benefits and perks of an employee, the full-time employee is the lowest on the overall pay scale in terms of annual bank deposits.

However, probably the biggest disadvantage to being a salaried employee is the fact that, by definition, you're not paid by the hour. The predictability of paychecks is certainly a consideration, but employees are all too often exposed to significant amounts of unpaid overtime. This is true of salaried employees everywhere, but overtime is legendary in the deadline-driven world of the professional programmer. Furthermore, because they don't have to pay you anything extra for your time, many companies are all too eager to abuse this aspect of the arrangement. A sweatshop by any other name is still an unpleasant experience.

Like any other aspect of the business world then, working as a salaried employee has both positive and negative aspects. Just as it's true in programming, choosing a career path is an exercise in tradeoffs, and no one size fits all. So, to have as many options to choose from as we can, let's look at our next contestant, the hired gun.

## The Mercenary

Another thing that sets the software development business apart from other professional pursuits is the hiring of temporary workers. Although programming is certainly not the only aspect of the business world that hires in this manner, you're less likely to find hired guns in a biscuit factory. One of the first things that sets the contract programmer apart from the employee is the fact that he is paid by the hour, typically at a rate much higher than what the employees make. In a sane and controlled development environment (I've read about them in the trade magazines so I'm sure they must exist somewhere), they work forty hours a week like everyone else and are paid accordingly. However, when the overtime hits the fan, the contractor is paid for every hour that he works. If it's crunch time and everyone on the team is putting in eighty hours a week, the contractor has the additional motivation of knowing that it will be a good month financially.

Of course, working hourly cuts both ways. Contractors are not paid for time off due to illness, nor do they get holiday or vacation pay. If you have to take your dog to the vet, it'll cost you much more than the price of those little doggie antibiotics. You'll lose a day's pay as well, and that adds up in a hurry. Fortunately for all concerned, the night watchman is on salary. Actually, so is his trusty attack Chihuahua. You didn't think he got those camouflage collars for free now, did you?

There's also another thing to consider when thinking about living out of a briefcase. In some companies, contractors are decidedly treated like second-class citizens. They're herded two and three at a time into cubicles scarcely big enough for one and given the old hardware that no one else wanted. Don't even ask about the chances of getting a stapler. I once worked for a large financially oriented corporation as a mercenary. One day I went to the supply person to request a stapler. I was informed that staplers were capital expenditures and consequently something to which contractors were not entitled. To this day I'm still not entirely sure what that means, other than the fact that I had to become adept at slipping in and out of cubicles to surreptitiously fasten a couple of sheets of paper together before meetings.

In addition to the overall company culture and how they treat contractors, be prepared for a fair degree of resentment by the regulars. Anyone who's been around for a while has a good idea of the hourly rates that contractors make. Some employees are highly offended that they dedicate their lives to the company and yet some outsider comes in, writes the same code, and gets paid quite a bit more. Having worked as both an employee and a contractor, I can see both sides of that sentiment. Although it's true that at the end of the day both may produce the same work and one is paid more, at the end of the year one may have a job and the other may not. Reward often comes to those willing to accept the risks. I must also say that I've never had much patience for that kind of attitude because each person is free to make their own career decisions. The disgruntled employee could probably be working next week as a contractor for the same money as the person he's offended by, but some people would rather whine than take action. If it weren't the contractors, they'd just find something else to be unhappy about.

Having said this, I must say in fairness that the overwhelming majority of contracts I've worked were in environments where I was just another guy on the team. We all went to lunch together, we all worked the overtime together, and we all participated equally in the design meetings. The only distinction between the employees and me was on payday, a matter I tend to keep to myself no matter how I'm working. Well, the other distinction is that they're still working there, and I'm not. Sometimes that's a good thing; sometimes it's a bad thing. Overall, I've had both good and bad experiences as a contractor in about the same proportion as my experiences as an employee. A gig is a gig.

Of course, for some contractors, the fact that they don't have a career path to maintain at a given company is an advantage in and of itself. When all the petty power struggles kick in, the contractor just goes out to lunch. There's no need to grapple over promotions or keep up with the latest company gossip. They're only there to get the job done, and that can be liberating. This is not to say that the life of a mercenary is one completely devoid of politics and corporate maneuvering. Far from it. It's just that all the nonsense one deals with as a contractor (and there's plenty to go around) has to do with the actual project itself, not the bobbing and weaving that some indulge in to get that juicy promotion.

Although it's my firm conviction that anyone who's unwilling to pull the occasional all-nighter at deadline time should get out of the business fast, I also enjoy one of the other benefits of being a merc: if a company has to pay you for every hour that you work, they tend to think twice about demanding a lot of overtime.

I'm still passionate about programming, but I also have other things going on in my life. I have no desire to participate in a software death march on a regular basis. There are too many other things in life to do. No one lies on their deathbed and wishes that they'd spent more time at the office. I don't know who originally said that, but I sure do try to live by it. In fairness, I'll freely admit that I've sometimes made it a point to get my job done and be out of the office in eight hours so that I could then go home and code all night on some other pet project. That doesn't matter. The point is that I need time for the other activities in my life. Consequently, minimizing overtime, even though I could get paid for it, is a benefit to me.

Another nice thing about living the life of a gypsy programmer is the chance to work in a lot of different shops with a lot of different technologies. On top of that, you continually meet new programmers. Most of the cool stuff I've learned over the years has been due to hanging out with some really gifted developers. Of course, that's also where I learned how to dodge whiteboard erasers. There are tradeoffs for everything.

Contractors, of course, don't have even the illusion of job security. If you read the contracts you sign (and I hope you do), you'll notice that the rules are fairly simple: you must give two weeks notice, and the client can fire you with no notice whatsoever. I haven't encountered such an extreme in my mercenary life, but it's part of the game and you have to be prepared for it. This means that you also have to be comfortable with looking for a job and doing the interview dance. Some handle this better than others.

A final wrinkle in the life of the itinerant programmer centers on exactly how they get paid. There are a couple of different approaches. By far the most common involves working as an hourly employee of a recruiting company. This doesn't mean that you work for the same company each time, only that for the duration of your stay with the current client you're listed on their payroll as an employee. This means that your taxes are withheld just as any other employee's would be and that the company pays the same portions of the self-employment tax as it would for a permanent employee. This keeps your life nice and simple and again helps avoid those unsightly tax bills at the end of the year.

However, as a contractor, many companies will also let you work as an independent company. It may require that you incorporate, but in general the idea is that you then get your entire hourly rate paid directly to you. Your tax deductions and every other aspect of running your company are your own affair. Some people have enough tax deductions and expenses overall, along with the requisite business skills, to make this a preferable situation. I've also seen people get in deep with the tax man at year's end because they lacked the financial discipline needed to save money for taxes and make the quarterly payments. That's someplace you just don't want to be.

Regardless of which way you get paid, working for a recruiting company has another reality. The hourly rate that the client gets billed is not the hourly rate that you get paid. The recruiting company gets a cut. It's easy to spot the rookie contractors. These are the guys who find out for the first time just what the margin is that their recruiting firm is making and go ballistic. You'll hear them go on to no end with tremendous righteous indignation about how they're doing all the work while the recruiter gets paid for every hour doing nothing more than sitting back and drinking coffee. I very often want to make a fairly pointed reply to such tirades but discretion typically gets the better of me. Here's how it really works.

First and foremost, yes, your recruiter gets a piece of the action. If you're not happy with the hourly rate that you bargained for when you took the job, then you shouldn't have taken it to begin with. No one forced you, and the offer of money was yours to negotiate, accept, or refuse. Personally, I bargain hard. However, when I take a job, it's because I'm happy with what I'm getting paid. I don't accept it otherwise. If I find out later that someone else makes more than me, or that the recruiter got a particularly big chunk of the money, who cares? I was happy with what I had before I got that information. I'm still happy.

The second point has to do with what the recruiting company does to "earn" their share, seeing how we do all the coding. I could go out and shake the trees myself when I'm looking for work, but I've run businesses before in my life and I know just exactly how much work marketing can be. No thanks. I live in a major city with a lot of recruiters. I just pick up the phone and let them beat their brains out trying to find a good fit for me. Above and beyond the amount of effort involved in doing that, recruiting companies provide me with a couple of very tangible financial benefits. First, the amount of money the company pays in taxes for me, as does any company in an employer-employee relationship, is significant. If I went into business for myself, that would be money out of my pocket. In simple terms, that works out to a nontrivial number of dollars per hour, and it comes out of their cut, not mine.

Additionally, they handle billing and collections. As I mentioned, I've run businesses before and consequently know the joys of trying to hammer money out of a deadbeat customer who's 120 days late on an invoice. It's a real stress inducer, particularly when you're counting on that money to pay your own pressing bills. The recruiting company protects me from that. I get paid every couple of weeks no matter what happens between the recruiter and the client. In fact, I was once on contract working for a fairly big company and through my relationship with some of the recruiting staff learned that the client was over six months late on paying a little over $500,000. And yet, I got paid every payday, direct deposit, with no fuss and no worries.

In my opinion, these companies provide a very real service to me, and I strongly believe that they earn and deserve the profits that they make on my hourly rate. On a more practical note, what if they didn't make a profit? Who would be there for me the next time I needed a job? They would be long out of business by then.

If you work as a contractor, make sure that you have a realistic and practical attitude about how the money gets split and who does what. Not only does it make you look like a stark raving amateur to go on a rant about what your recruiter makes off of you, it also doesn't endear them to you in the slightest. I treat my recruiters with gratitude and respect, and some have even become friends over the years. Consequently, they always return my calls, and, when we go out to a business lunch, they buy. They also know by now that I eat the most expensive steak in the house (you get a reputation for this sort of thing, you know) and are happy to specify that the chef cook it just the way I like. Treat the people who take care of you as you would your friends and they'll always be happy to hear from you.

## The Entrepreneur

Although a lot of us enjoy getting up each day and going to work in an office where someone else is minding the farm while we code, for some the thrill of the chase is irresistible. Sometimes it starts as a software idea that turns into a marketable product. Other times it's just the adventure of being your own boss. No matter how it happens, some choose to break out of the mold and start their own company.

Running your own business can certainly be exciting. So can plugging a pair of needle-nosed pliers into a live electrical outlet. This is not the path for the faint of heart. There's much more to running a software company than coding. Depending on whether you get the capital to do a big-time startup or kick it off from your kitchen table, you'll find yourself performing a wide variety of nontechnical duties, from accounting and management to marketing and even a little janitorial duty. I'll leave the interviews for hiring your own attack Chihuahua to the imagination.

One of the lures of starting a company that makes all the work seem worthwhile is the chance to make it big. Some of the major software corporations in our country seem powerful enough to be a government unto themselves, not to mention the gobs and gobs of money they make. That sure can seem appealing. For the few and the motivated, these dreams truly are attainable. It's also great fun for the ego to tell your friends at the local programmer's bar that you're the president of XYZ Software and Assorted Clever Gadgets, Incorporated. If you can't have a little fun with your job, then what's the point?

Building a company is also a creative endeavor that isn't dissimilar to writing a song or painting a masterpiece. You're building something new, something from your own imagination, something that never existed before you brought your vision to reality. There's a lot of gratification in that alone.

Of course, what most budding young entrepreneurs dream of is a company that runs itself while the boss plays golf. In reality, the boss's workweek *starts* at forty hours. You're the first to arrive and by far the last to leave. One of the requirements for a sane life and a healthy company is the discipline to know when to *not* work. If you can't develop the strength of will to call it quits for the day and leave it at the office, you'll burn out in a heartbeat. You also may find that whatever family and friends you had when you started thin out considerably once you spend day and night working. Balance is an important art for the new entrepreneur to learn.

Of course, with all the freedom and potential comes a fair amount of expense and risk as well. If you don't have any experience or training in some of the basic aspects of business, the very best thing you can do for yourself is to find a partner you can trust who is a professional Suit. Know your strengths and weaknesses, and don't let your shortcomings become your company's as well.

Even if you do it all correctly, the business world is an uncertain one, and there's no guarantee of a weekly paycheck. Make sure you can survive for a year without income from the company. One of the reasons that there's such a high mortality rate for new businesses is that many people overlook this and expect to have the money rolling in from day one. Sometimes it happens that way. Often it doesn't. As an entrepreneur, a conservative financial outlook is your best friend. Live to fight another day.

Running a business also involves a host of legal issues. Talk to some people you respect and trust, get some recommendations, and hire a good lawyer and accountant. Unless you have an accounting or law degree (and a whole lot of time on your hands), hire professionals to handle these critical tasks for you. That's a hard choice to make for a small startup company, particularly if kitchen tables are involved, but in the long run it'll cost you much less this way.

If you do decide that you've come up with the superior mousetrap and want to show it to the world, I say go for it. Give it heart, body, and soul. Then go home at 5:00 and spend time with your family. Remember, nobody every wishes they spent more time at the office.

Having reviewed all of the obvious choices for making a living as a professional developer, the next thing to look at is actually landing the job. Assuming that you'll be working either as a contractor or an employee, you need to keep a number of considerations in mind when it's time to seek those greener pastures.

## Landing the Job

You're a good programmer or you wouldn't be out making a living at it in the first place. However, although technical skills matter, you're not the only one who has them. If you want to nail the interview and get precisely the job you're looking for, you're going to have to know how to make yourself stand out from the herd.

Probably the first and most obvious thing that comes to mind when thinking along these lines is your résumé. Tons of resources are available to teach you how to string together an effective set of words to help you succeed. However, a couple of aspects of the résumé may not be obvious at all and are, in my mind, just as important.

Let's hit some of the obvious stuff first just to get it out of the way. It's a common tendency for people to go nuts with the description of their technical skills when writing the résumé. It is without a doubt a sales tool, but if you go overboard you're going to crash and burn in the interview. The résumé has one and only one task: getting you in the door for an interview. Beyond that, it can quickly turn into a liability if you stretch the truth too much. If you have a moderate amount of skill with a language, tell it like it is. Give priority to how you say it rather than embellishing the facts. The people who interview you aren't stupid. Well, most of them aren't, anyway. Nonetheless, if you make a statement on paper, be prepared to back it up. If you don't, you'll lose more than just the points on that particular question. Your credibility will suffer, and that's a show-stopper.

Neatness and formatting count as well. If you've learned nothing else from all the hours that you've spent in front of the television, it should be that visuals sell first, long before the information kicks in. Make sure that your résumé looks like a professional document. I know this sounds like something everyone already knows, but I've known really good programmers who blew it because they had the somewhat arrogant attitude that technical information was the only thing that really mattered. Their résumés looked like something hastily kicked out by a 1920s typewriter. Dumb, dumb, dumb. People *do* judge a book by its cover.

Now we get down to the fun stuff. I'm assuming that your skills are more than equal to the task. If they're not, go home and study. Because you no doubt already have a job as we speak, it's a safe bet to assume that you're up to par technically. However, who are you personally? Remember, you're dealing with people, so people skills are just as important as coding skills, and surprisingly often more so. That should be reflected in your résumé as well. The overwhelming majority of résumés I've seen over the years when hiring programmers could have come from the same cookie-cutter mold. Very professional yes, but also dry as a bone. These types of résumés do little more than recite what the applicant's skill set is and how they applied it on previous jobs. That doesn't help me out much when I have a stack of résumés from equally qualified people on my desk and I'm trying to decide which three to call in for an interview.

I should preface my next set of comments by telling you that I never have really fit into the corporate mold. What works for me might be a disaster for you. That said, I make it a point to put a very large personal stamp on my résumé. It reads like the books and articles I write. I'm a wise guy who's irreverent and not afraid to poke fun at the things that we all know need poking fun at in this business. I've had recruiters turn white as a sheet after reading my résumé and inform me, hands still twitching, that they would have to completely rewrite it. I simply smile and tell them that if they do the deal's off. All of the wise guy stuff in my résumé is my idiot filter. Anyone who's going to freak out because I made a joke in a job description is going to have an absolute panic attack when he meets me personally, so why do I want to interview with him? Life's too short to work for clowns. As an example, following is an actual excerpt from my résumé regarding experience working on a nationwide air traffic control system. I suppose people expect me to be somber and serious about something as important as landing airplanes, but that's not the guy they'd get if they hired me. So, here's a bit of what they get to help them determine whether or not I'm the right one for their team, with some of the technical stuff snipped out:

This system supports controllers in their management of large, heavy flying objects containing people who typically prefer uneventful landings, so the system must run 24/7 with zero failures. ... Design phase of the system utilized UML and only a small number of cocktail napkins, all of which were object oriented.

I can assure you, many managers will read this and immediately toss it into the trash, which is precisely my intent. Interviews are a two-way street. I'm actively weeding out the stuffed shirts that I know I wouldn't enjoy working for. The résumé continues on in this tone throughout. If that's not enough to send any reasonable recruiter running for a therapist, there's always the cartoon at the bottom of my résumé containing an interview between two cavemen and the observation that all the applicant's references are baboons. Yes, I really do put a cartoon at the bottom of my résumé. Above and beyond the sheer fun of watching recruiters twitch, there's another practical aspect to this. Not only have I weeded out the faint of heart, I can assure you that, by the time a hiring manager has gone through one hundred résumés, he'll remember mine. He may love it or he may hate it, but he'll never forget it.

Am I suggesting that you take ridiculous chances and drop any vestige of professionalism in your résumé? Absolutely not. What I've shared about my own is merely a way of making a point. Your résumé should be a reflection of who you are, and it should stand out in a stack of others as memorable. Find a way to get your personality into what you write. If you can think of something else that they'll find memorable, like my example of a cartoon, do it. However, heed these words of caution. I take chances because I know from experience that I can pull it off. Even so, my approach falls flat on its face with many people. I'm sure there have been jobs I would have enjoyed that I never got a shot at because of my flippant approach. If you're going to take some chances, be aware that there will be some cost involved and use your common sense accordingly.

Although I've concentrated on the résumé, these ideas apply to every aspect of your job search. You're going to be dealing with real, live people. Whether it's a recruiter, a hiring manager, the programmers who do the technical interview, or even someone in human resources, you have to make them see that you're something different and something special that they just can't live without. I'm boisterous and upbeat, and I order expensive steaks and put silly drawings on my résumé. That works for me because it's who I am. Give some time and serious thought to who you are. Then make sure that all of your marketing reflects that. You'll be the one they talk about over dinner with their family. Guess what that does for your job prospects?

## Thinking Ahead

Whether you work as a contractor or an employee, few jobs last forever. However, sometimes we'd like for them to. When the project that you're on is looking a bit thin, sometimes the best thing to do is simply create a new one. Programmers are never short on ideas. Put that to good use. Take a moment and think, not like a programmer, but like the owner or manager in your company. What needs do they have that you could address with software? How would your proposed project save them time, reduce expenses, and bring in revenue? With just a little creative effort, you can find yourself moving from someone who's about to lose their job to someone in charge of a new project. You'd be surprised how easy it can be. As we've talked about all along, remember the basics of communicating to the Suits in the language that they understand. If you truly do have a worthwhile idea that brings value to the manager you pitch, you have a very real chance of making it happen. Just remember the other basic rule: people make decisions based on what will further their own career. Keep that in mind. It'll help you make the sale.

Of course, sometimes when the party's over it's just over. It doesn't matter how much money you make each week. If you're out of work for an extended period of time, your average salary doesn't look so good anymore. Consequently, you should always keep one eye on the future and be out the door before the axe falls. If you can see the writing on the wall that your project and those who sail her are soon to be history and you can't navigate into a new project, make sure that you have a job search underway long before there's any real danger of losing your job. If you wait until the last minute, you could end up out of work, so think ahead and plan ahead.

Another thing to consider along those lines is being aware of which technical skills you need to maintain your value in the marketplace. The technical market is always shifting. What's hot today is old news tomorrow. Make sure you keep up with the trends in your particular technical environment so that, if you do have to hit the streets, you'll do so fully armed.

## The Art of the Deal

If you've planned ahead and have good marketing materials, people are going to ask you to work for them. If you're anything like most of the programmers I know, you're going to want some money for your services. Many people make the mistake of assuming that whatever a company offers is written in stone. In the job search, as in every other aspect of life, everything's negotiable. If you don't ask for it, you don't get it.

When looking at an offer, the first thing you should do is to ask yourself some basic questions. How strong is your position? What's important to you? What are you willing to be flexible on? What are the deal breakers? Before you know how hard you can push, you have to have a good feel for these issues. You must also get a sense for what the market will bear and not go overboard. Companies rarely make their best offer first, but there's obviously a limit to what anyone will offer. Going too far beyond that will be a deal breaker. However, if you make reasonable requests, the worst that they can do is say no.

Many people are afraid to ask for anything extra because they're afraid it will blow the deal. Consider this. If simply making a counteroffer causes them to walk away from the table, it was a fishy deal to begin with, and they did you a favor by ending the conversations. No reasonable person is going to be offended because you asked for a little more. And you really don't want to work for unreasonable people.

It's also worth noting that you don't have to be pushy, abrasive, or unpleasant to negotiate. In fact, if you're bargaining in good faith, it's always better to be nice. There's a real difference between being confident and occasionally assertive and being an overbearing jerk. Nobody wants to hire an unpleasant person. Remember, you have to work for these folks when the negotiations are done. Don't make a bad impression before you even start the job.

Make sure before you accept an offer that you're happy with it. If you're not, bargain for more or walk away. It's not fair to them if you start off your new job already disgruntled about what you got. It was your decision, and not theirs, to take the offer when you could have opted to continue the job search. Above all, once you make an agreement, honor it unfailingly in both deed and spirit. People really do remember those who have integrity, and the city you live in is not nearly as large as you think. The benefits may not always be obvious at the moment, but treating people well and living with honor will always come back to you. You'll be in this business a long time.

## One for the Road

Getting paid as a professional software developer involves a great many things, only a few of which involve writing code. Even though we'd love to do nothing more than watch the compiler dance, maintaining a successful, profitable, and gratifying career requires that you master a great many skills that they just don't teach in school.

While it takes a little effort, if you're smart enough to develop software, you're certainly capable of dealing with the additional issues that come from working in Corporate America. Keep your eyes open, learn all the tricks that you can from your peers, and make it a point whenever possible to share with others the things that you've learned about breaking the rules, defying the odds, and successfully delivering quality software in the corporate world. If we all band together and fight from the inside, we can change the system.

# Index

# Apress Titles

| ISBN | PRICE | AUTHOR | TITLE |
|---|---|---|---|
| 1-893115-73-9 | $34.95 | Abbott | Voice Enabling Web Applications: VoiceXML and Beyond |
| 1-893115-01-1 | $39.95 | Appleman | Appleman's Win32 API Puzzle Book and Tutorial for Visual Basic Programmers |
| 1-893115-23-2 | $29.95 | Appleman | How Computer Programming Works |
| 1-893115-97-6 | $39.95 | Appleman | Moving to VB. NET: Strategies, Concepts, and Code |
| 1-893115-09-7 | $29.95 | Baum | Dave Baum's Definitive Guide to LEGO MINDSTORMS |
| 1-893115-84-4 | $29.95 | Baum, Gasperi, Hempel, and Villa | Extreme MINDSTORMS: An Advanced Guide to LEGO MINDSTORMS |
| 1-893115-82-8 | $59.95 | Ben-Gan/Moreau | Advanced Transact-SQL for SQL Server 2000 |
| 1-893115-48-8 | $29.95 | Bischof | The .NET Languages: A Quick Translation Guide |
| 1-893115-67-4 | $49.95 | Borge | Managing Enterprise Systems with the Windows Script Host |
| 1-893115-44-5 | $29.95 | Cook | Robot Building for Beginners |
| 1-893115-99-2 | $39.95 | Cornell/Morrison | Programming VB .NET: A Guide for Experienced Programmers |
| 1-893115-72-0 | $39.95 | Curtin | Developing Trust: Online Privacy and Security |
| 1-59059-008-2 | $29.95 | Duncan | The Career Programmer: Guerilla Tactics for an Imperfect World |
| 1-893115-71-2 | $39.95 | Ferguson | Mobile .NET |
| 1-893115-90-9 | $44.95 | Finsel | The Handbook for Reluctant Database Administrators |
| 1-893115-85-2 | $34.95 | Gilmore | A Programmer's Introduction to PHP 4.0 |
| 1-893115-36-4 | $34.95 | Goodwill | Apache Jakarta-Tomcat |
| 1-893115-17-8 | $59.95 | Gross | A Programmer's Introduction to Windows DNA |
| 1-893115-62-3 | $39.95 | Gunnerson | A Programmer's Introduction to C#, Second Edition |
| 1-893115-10-0 | $34.95 | Holub | Taming Java Threads |
| 1-893115-04-6 | $34.95 | Hyman/Vaddadi | Mike and Phani's Essential C++ Techniques |
| 1-893115-96-8 | $59.95 | Jorelid | J2EE FrontEnd Technologies: A Programmer's Guide to Servlets, JavaServer Pages, and Enterprise JavaBeans |
| 1-893115-50-X | $34.95 | Knudsen | Wireless Java: Developing with Java 2, Micro Edition |

| ISBN | PRICE | AUTHOR | TITLE |
|---|---|---|---|
| 1-893115-79-8 | $49.95 | Kofler | Definitive Guide to Excel VBA |
| 1-893115-57-7 | $39.95 | Kofler | MySQL |
| 1-893115-87-9 | $39.95 | Kurata | Doing Web Development: Client-Side Techniques |
| 1-893115-75-5 | $44.95 | Kurniawan | Internet Programming with VB |
| 1-893115-19-4 | $49.95 | Macdonald | Serious ADO: Universal Data Access with Visual Basic |
| 1-893115-06-2 | $39.95 | Marquis/Smith | A Visual Basic 6.0 Programmer's Toolkit |
| 1-893115-22-4 | $27.95 | McCarter | David McCarter's VB Tips and Techniques |
| 1-893115-76-3 | $49.95 | Morrison | C++ For VB Programmers |
| 1-893115-80-1 | $39.95 | Newmarch | A Programmer's Guide to Jini Technology |
| 1-893115-58-5 | $49.95 | Oellermann | Architecting Web Services |
| 1-893115-81-X | $39.95 | Pike | SQL Server: Common Problems, Tested Solutions |
| 1-893115-20-8 | $34.95 | Rischpater | Wireless Web Development |
| 1-893115-93-3 | $34.95 | Rischpater | Wireless Web Development with PHP and WAP |
| 1-893115-89-5 | $59.95 | Shemitz | Kylix: The Professional Developer's Guide and Reference |
| 1-893115-40-2 | $39.95 | Sill | An Introduction to qmail |
| 1-893115-24-0 | $49.95 | Sinclair | From Access to SQL Server |
| 1-893115-94-1 | $29.95 | Spolsky | User Interface Design for Programmers |
| 1-893115-53-4 | $39.95 | Sweeney | Visual Basic for Testers |
| 1-893115-29-1 | $44.95 | Thomsen | Database Programming with Visual Basic .NET |
| 1-893115-65-8 | $39.95 | Tiffany | Pocket PC Database Development with eMbedded Visual Basic |
| 1-893115-59-3 | $59.95 | Troelsen | C# and the .NET Platform |
| 1-893115-26-7 | $59.95 | Troelsen | Visual Basic .NET and the .NET Platform |
| 1-893115-54-2 | $49.95 | Trueblood/Lovett | Data Mining and Statistical Analysis Using SQL |
| 1-893115-16-X | $49.95 | Vaughn | ADO Examples and Best Practices |
| 1-893115-83-6 | $44.95 | Wells | Code Centric: T-SQL Programming with Stored Procedures and Triggers |
| 1-893115-95-X | $49.95 | Welschenbach | Cryptography in C and C++ |
| 1-893115-05-4 | $39.95 | Williamson | Writing Cross-Browser Dynamic HTML |
| 1-893115-78-X | $49.95 | Zukowski | Definitive Guide to Swing for Java 2, Second Edition |
| 1-893115-92-5 | $49.95 | Zukowski | Java Collections |

Available at bookstores nationwide or from Springer Verlag New York, Inc. at 1-800-777-4643; fax 1-212-533-3503. Contact us for more information at sales@apress.com.

# Apress Titles Publishing SOON!

| ISBN | AUTHOR | TITLE |
| --- | --- | --- |
| 1-893115-39-9 | Chand | A Programmer's Guide to ADO.NET in C# |
| 1-893115-42-9 | Foo/Lee | XML Programming Using the Microsoft XML Parser |
| 1-893115-55-0 | Frenz | Visual Basic for Scientists |
| 1-893115-30-5 | Harkins/Reid | SQL: Access to SQL Server |
| 1-893115-49-6 | Kilburn | Palm Programming in Basic |
| 1-893115-38-0 | Lafler | Power AOL: A Survival Guide |
| 1-893115-28-3 | Challa/Laksberg | Essential Guide to Managed Extensions for C++ |
| 1-893115-46-1 | Lathrop | Linux in Small Business: A Practical User's Guide |
| 1-893115-43-7 | Stephenson | Standard VB: An Enterprise Developer's Reference for VB 6 and VB .NET |
| 1-59059-002-3 | Symmonds | Internationalization and Localization Using Microsoft .NET |
| 1-59059-010-4 | Thomsen | Database Programming with C# |
| 1-59059-011-2 | Troelsen | COM and .NET Interoperability |
| 1-893115-68-2 | Vaughn | ADO.NET and ADO Examples and Best Practices for VB Programmers, Second Edition |
| 1-59059-012-0 | Vaughn/Blackburn | ADO.NET and ADO Examples and Best Practices for C# Programmers |
| 1-893115-98-4 | Zukowski | Learn Java with JBuilder 6 |

Available at bookstores nationwide or from Springer Verlag New York, Inc. at 1-800-777-4643; fax 1-212-533-3503. Contact us for more information at sales@apress.com.

**books for professionals by professionals™**

# About Apress

Apress, located in Berkeley, CA, is an innovative publishing company devoted to meeting the needs of existing and potential programming professionals. Simply put, the "A" in Apress stands for the "Author's Press™." Apress' unique author-centric approach to publishing grew from conversations between Dan Appleman and Gary Cornell, authors of best-selling, highly regarded computer books. In 1998, they set out to create a publishing company that emphasized quality above all else, a company with books that would be considered the best in their market. Dan and Gary's vision has resulted in over 30 widely acclaimed titles by some of the industry's leading software professionals.

# Do You Have What It Takes to Write for Apress?

Apress is rapidly expanding its publishing program. If you can write and refuse to compromise on the quality of your work, if you believe in doing more than rehashing existing documentation, and if you're looking for opportunities and rewards that go far beyond those offered by traditional publishing houses, we want to hear from you!

Consider these innovations that we offer all of our authors:

- **Top royalties with *no* hidden switch statements**
  Authors typically only receive half of their normal royalty rate on foreign sales. In contrast, Apress' royalty rate remains the same for both foreign and domestic sales.

- **A mechanism for authors to obtain equity in Apress**
  Unlike the software industry, where stock options are essential to motivate and retain software professionals, the publishing industry has adhered to an outdated compensation model based on royalties alone. In the spirit of most software companies, Apress reserves a significant portion of its equity for authors.

- **Serious treatment of the technical review process**
  Each Apress book has a technical reviewing team whose remuneration depends in part on the success of the book since they too receive royalties.

Moreover, through a partnership with Springer-Verlag, one of the world's major publishing houses, Apress has significant venture capital behind it. Thus, we have the resources to produce the highest quality books *and* market them aggressively.

If you fit the model of the Apress author who can write a book that gives the "professional what he or she needs to know™," then please contact one of our Editorial Directors, Gary Cornell (gary_cornell@apress.com), Dan Appleman (dan_appleman@apress.com), Karen Watterson (karen_watterson@apress.com) or Jason Gilmore (jason_gilmore@apress.com) for more information.